By the same author

CONFLICT AND CONTROL IN THE CINEMA: A Reader in Film and Society (*editor*)

CHEKHOV:
A STRUCTURALIST
STUDY

John Tulloch

First published 1980 by
THE MACMILLAN PRESS LTD
London and Basingstoke
Associated companies in Delhi
Dublin Hong Kong Johannesburg Lagos
Melbourne New York Singapore Tokyo

Printed in Hong Kong

British Library Cataloguing in Publication Data

Tulloch, John
    Chekhov, a structuralist study
    1. Chekhov, Anton Pavlovich – Criticism
and interpretation
    I. Title
    891.7'2'3   PG3458

    ISBN 0–333–27043–6

Contents

Preface

There have been two earlier drafts of the subject matter of this book. The first was a long Ph.D. thesis examined by the University of Sussex in 1973. The second was a longer version of this book containing two chapters which publishing exigencies have led me to omit. What I have retained is the major thesis of both these manuscripts: the evidence, which I believe to be conclusive, that Chekhov's world view as an environmentalist doctor profoundly determined the thematic structure of his literary works. What I have, regretfully, omitted is a minor thesis addressed to the reader who, while perhaps sympathetic to my main thesis, might still quite fairly ask: 'but why did *this* doctor, this Anton Pavlovich Chekhov, and not any other doctor from his medical group write these works?' In so far as this is a sociological question, it is one about the *interaction* of the individual and his social group, the specific artist and his society. We must, in other words, find answers related to Chekhov's particular biography; and that, as Sartre has pointed out, means asking questions about Chekhov's idiosyncratic family background, the relationship of this 'primary socialisation' to his adult roles as doctor *and* as writer (since, of course, it is not *necessarily* the case that our many adult roles are coherent with each other—it is possible, for most of the time, to keep them discrete).

In one of the chapters now omitted I looked at these problems. First of all I showed that Chekhov's roles as writer and doctor were not in fact discrete, but that his literary aesthetic was profoundly influenced by his positivism, inculcated as a medical student (part of this section, where I consider Chekhov's notion of 'typicality' is included in chapter 4 of this book). His *literary* advice to minor writers like Shcheglov and Sazonova as well as his criticisms of the few writers he had some respect for, such as Tolstoi, Gor'kii and Bourget, derived from his scientific education. Secondly, I showed that, despite his belief that 'loneliness is hard to bear as a creative artist', Chekhov never found a literary reference group comparable in terms of identity-definition to his medical one. Chekhov worried about the problem, 'for whom do I write?', for most of his career, and turned successively to all parts of the writing fraternity for an answer—to journalists (especially Suvorin), to writers (especially Tolstoi), to the theatre (especially the Moscow Arts Theatre), to critics, and to the public. But in each case he finally found them wanting, and always on the grounds of lack of 'objectivity', knowledge, universalism. So Chekhov was always ambivalent in his literary identity while being far more secure in his medical role, a problem which shows very clearly in his literature where he is far more assertive, more dogmatic in his rejection of 'bad' (non-scientific, non-zemstvo) doctors than he is of 'inauthentic' writers— the Treplevs and Trigorins who themselves search for an identity, fail, and in so doing evoke a considerable sympathy (I have considered this problem in relation to thematic structure in analysing *The Seagull*—the second of the chapters now omitted). Finally, I looked at the problem of Chekhov's dual roles more theoretically. Between primary socialisation (the values of ascription, mysticism, authority of his father), and secondary socialisation (the values of achievement, rationality, universalism of his medical group) Chekhov faced an almost total contradiction which could only be overcome by an experience almost akin to conversion (what sociologists have called a complete 'alternation of subjective reality'). People who have undergone this process of alternation typically reject totally their earlier values with 'nihilating' observations such as 'while I was still living a life of sin', or, 'while I was still caught up in bourgeois consciousness'—and we see this in Chekhov in his passionate rejection of his 'son of a serf' background. However, for Chekhov there was a complication: the very values of brutality and subservience which he rejected in his father, he saw reincarnated in the literary fraternity to which he looked for guidance and identity. It is not a coincidence that Chekhov's 'son of a serf' letter comes in response to criticism of his play *Ivanov* where he 'knew' as a doctor that he had at last pinned down the 'superfluous man' scientifically. He explains his failure as one of literary form—and he specifically ascribes *that* to his failure to throw off his brutalised past. So the contradictions between Chekhov's adult roles were deeply personal ones too, orchestrating the shifts and tensions in his own biography. And yet, as well as being personal, they were also global: the opposition between value systems (primary v secondary, literary v medical) was also that of Russia itself in the second half of the nineteenth century, the opposition between mystical authority and scientific rationality, the contradiction at the very heart of the 'modernising autocracy' which is the main subject of this book. Here there is only space to assert what I argue elsewhere more fully: that it was precisely *this* homology of oppositions at every level from personal biography to symbolic universe which made *this* doctor, Anton Chekhov, live so uniquely the contradictions of his time.

The effect this had on his literature, particularly in terms of what Lucien Goldmann has called the tension between the unity (coherence) and richness (multiplicity) of a text, there is no more space to discuss here, and in any case is properly the subject of another book. But the interested (or sceptical) reader can find some of my thoughts on this in a published article, 'Sociology of Knowledge and the Sociology of Literature' (*British Journal of Sociology*, June 1976), and of course in my Ph.D. thesis (where there are also analyses of far more Chekhov works than there is space for here).

While cutting the original manuscript I made a number of deletions from quotations. I have indicated these by five dots, and to distinguish these cuts from Chekhov's significant pauses in his works, I have normally signified the latter with three dots.

Finally, of all the people to whom I owe thanks, I should like to mention three in particular. To Professor Zev. Barbu I am in debt for supervising the original thesis. To Mrs Anna Smith I am in debt not only for an endless patience in guiding me through the refinements of literary translation beyond my quite ordinary competence in Russian, but also, as the daughter of a Russian doctor of Chekhov's time, for a contemporary glimpse of those lost values which form such an important part of this book. And I am in debt to my wife Marian for living, intellectually and emotionally, with Chekhov for the last ten years.

John Tulloch
March, 1979

1 The Chekhov Tradition

In April 1890, Anton Chekhov set off on a journey across a continent; literally a third of the way round the world. The journey was excruciating. Some of it was by boat and train, but nearly three thousand miles (and two months of travelling time) were covered by horse and carriage. The roads, deep with holes, were subject to the worst spring thaw in fifty years. Chekhov recounted his itinerary in letters home. First, a thousand miles of terrible cold; lashing wind and rain; roads that had become lakes that made jelly of his felt boots as he walked the horses through; entire days and nights spent in an uncovered cart on a desolate river bank waiting for the ferry delayed by gales and rain. Next, several hundred miles of impassable mud, 'my carriage and myself stuck in mud like flies in sticky jam', and of broken carriage shafts which necessitated several miles of knee-deep wading to the next horse station. Then, again, a thousand miles in the carriage, this time through intense heat, smoke from burning forests, and dust—'dust in your mouth, your nose, your pockets, so that, looking at yourself in the mirror, you appear to have a painted face'.[1]

Apart from the day and night burden of it, there were the especially dangerous times—like the night near Tomsk when he was hurled to the ground as two runaway carts smashed into his carriage; or another night, when the boat crossing the flooded river Tom came close to sinking in a storm.

Yet, if the journey was bad, the place he was going to was incomparably worse: Sakhalin Island, where the Russian government had established a penal settlement. Ostensibly this was a progressive move. The emphasis was supposed to be less on a prison, more on a self-supporting new colony. But this place, Chekhov pointed out in his report, was an 'absolute hell'; where any dignity—and the sense of independence necessary to colonisers—was driven out by brutal guards; where the best land was ignored and the worst densely populated; where convict women were bartered like animals, and the free women, so essential to the vigour of a new community, had to sell themselves daily while their husbands applauded in apathy; where cement was mixed into the prisoners' bread, causing fearful sickness; where girls became prostitutes before they first menstruated; and so on and on in a tale of corruption, murder, squalor, birchings and brutalisation.

Chekhov's survey of social change and human depravity at Sakhalin is modelled on the environmentalism he learned at medical school. He writes, in fact, of two colonies. The first, an ideal one, would flourish on a healthy symbiosis of all that was best in man and nature. A gentle and fertile environment would be found by properly scientific investigation, a colony would be set up, and prisoners would be taught the manual and mental skills necessary to the free farmer. A fine milieu and a progressive penal institution would thus combine in the creation of a free colony that would be a model for penal reform. The second colony was Sakhalin in reality: a froz n island, chosen purely for its remoteness, without surveys by qualified topographers, agronomists or meteorologists, and totally unsuitable as an 'agricultural colony'. From this initial, and reactionary, orientation an inevitable evolution followed. The weather 'froze the crops as well as the soul'. The prison institution, laying bare its underlying punitive intention, turned the would-be colonists into beasts of labour 'who worked waist-high in swamps, in the freezing cold, in chilling rain, lonely for their homes, subjected to all kinds of humiliation, and beaten by birch rods'.[2] Thus horrors which were both human and natural (in a reverse symbiosis) 'depress and brutalise the mind' of prisoners, settlers, guards and administrators alike. A community which was organic (because interdependent in every brutish part) had developed, and in it only the most degraded features of man had evolved. The contrast between the *potential* of life and what man had made of it could hardly be greater. The world, he wrote, is a good place; the only thing not good in it is ourselves.

Chekhov's journey and visit to Sakhalin took a heavy toll of him. He was already suffering from tuberculosis, and his health broke down as soon as he got home. It is possible that Sakhalin deprived literature of a post-*Cherry Orchard* Chekhov, at the height of his maturity. But in place of this Chekhov we have the report itself, *Sakhalin Island*—a 'rough prison garb' which he was intensely proud to hang in his 'literary wardrobe'.[3]

Why did Chekhov, whose literary reputation was beginning to flourish, suddenly submit himself to this ordeal? In the first place, he was driven there by his profound dissatisfaction with the condition of Russian writing, not least, with his own. His literary circle, he pointed out, gave itself over to trivial material, to pessimism, even to suicide, while great issues were left neglected. In a letter justifying his 'strange' decision, he wrote that the whole of Europe was interested in Sakhalin, 'yet to us it is a matter of little use!' What a gap there was between the great deeds of exploration in the early days of Sakhalin and the fearful deeds that went on there now. And how distant from the petty moralising of writers and literary critics who spoke of eternal causes, ignored explorers and convicts alike, and sat within their four walls grumbling about lack of inspiration and the dreariness of mankind.[4] If the literary entourage had anything to offer in the way of great truths, 'we would now know what to do, and Fofanov would not be in a lunatic asylum, Garshin would still be alive, Baranzevich would not be in the depths of pessimism, we would all be less dull and weak spirited than we are now . . . and I would not need to be drawn to Sakhalin'.[5]

Secondly, we have to realise that this bolt into environmental medicine was by no means an arbitrary or isolated phenomenon. Chekhov had been trained as a doctor; as most of his interpreters acknowledge. Few, however, give the matter a great deal of stress. For some it was a vocation quickly superseded as his 'essence' flowered more profitably in artistic creativity (cf. Maurice Valency in *The Breaking String*: 'he had no real taste for medicine and, in any case, it brought in little money'[6]). At most, it is admitted that his medical training remained with him in the guise of a 'clinical objectivity', that cool gaze that meets us from behind the pince-nez of his familiar photographs, and, somehow, informed his literary style.

This aspect of Chekhovian interpretation has, to say the least, been historically inadequate and sociologically naive.

(i) Firstly, because the account of 'clinical objectivity' assumes a certain psycho-social gestalt *inherent* in the medical role. It ignores history: the differences of personality structure and val system between different medical professions in different socie

(ii) Secondly because it is silent on the profound individual and society which makes up the process and in which a sense of self is formed which can thrown off. Thus Thomas Winner,[7] who is more Chekhov's deep attachment to science, still has world view well after the Sakhalin visit, as th

something freely chosen (or, in Valency's example, easily rejected).

Chekhov was, as I shall show more systematically later, deeply endowed with a faith in his first profession.

(a) He continued, *pace* Valency, to practice it with care and devotion until almost the end of his life when, to his great distress, sickness made him give it up.

(b) On more than one occasion he put aside the 'profitability' of writing for an extensive period because of medicine—to conduct a scientific study, to meet a cholera epidemic, and so on.

(c) He always had the idea of attempting a higher degree in medicine, and in the early days signed his stories with a pseudonym, reserving his name for his 'real' writing task, a medical doctorate. He still had hopes along these lines up to five years before his death and, in the late 1890s, raised the idea of getting a lectureship in the medical faculty of Moscow University.

Moreover, his was a very particular medical vision, very different indeed from either mere 'clinical objectivity' or the more conservative and mercenary position of later, capitalist, professions. Medicine, as Chekhov learned it, was an *active* force. It was fundamentally to do with social and environmental change—hence his interest in, and despair over, the Sakhalin project. I will discuss in a later chapter the constellation of values and assumptions which made up the world view of Russian doctors at the time, together with Chekhov's own deep and continuing attachment to them. But I want to bring forward a few examples here to throw more light on the inadequacy of so much interpretation of Chekhov and his works.

(1) TREES AND ENVIRONMENT

Chekhov, we are told endlessly, 'aimed at the evocation of a mood rather than the communication of an idea'.[8] Hence, we are not to expect any thing remotely resembling a positive hero in his works. He was far too 'sensitive' for that. 'He looked', Valency tells us, 'at the world with the innocent and penetrating eye of a child who, seeing it for the first time, finds it full of wonder and beauty, but not full of significance'.[9]

It seems inconceivable that anyone who has read *Sakhalin Island* could have said that. There Chekhov is sensitive indeed—but to the tragedy of depraved human action, not to the butterfly beauty of a ᷉c's aesthetic. But then *Sakhalin Island* is not 'literature', and in

Chekhov, Valency assures us, 'the artist saw further than the man'.[10] There are, however, very systematic continuities between Chekhov as 'artist' and 'man', which will become apparent as the book develops.

We can start with a critical interpretation of Dr Astrov in *Uncle Vanya*. One of the interesting things about Astrov is that he promotes the very same positive values which Chekhov does in *Sakhalin Island*. His vision extends beyond medical therapy to a scientifically ordered improvement of the climate, peasant economy, and general environment by means of planting trees, protecting flora and fauna, and applying 'the reason and creative power with which man is endowed' to the 'struggle for existence'. As with Chekhov's analysis of Sakhalin, Astrov has a dual vision. One is of a world in which man improves on what has been given to him, builds factories, schools, roads, railways, and a society in which people are 'healthier, more prosperous and better educated'. The natural environment will be modified, but creatively. Some trees will go for the rest to be saved; and man will live better. The other vision, as at Sakhalin, is 'a picture of gradual decay' caused by 'inertia, ignorance and total irresponsibility'—where the trees have given way, not to a modern community but to yet more 'swamps and mosquitoes, the same lack of roads and abject poverty, to typhus, diptheria and fires'. The fate of the people, as with Chekhov's Sakhalin colonists, is an 'insupportable struggle for existence'.

However, Astrov's rather systematic Lit. Crit. fate has been as an 'idealist'. Lines of *obvious* idealism (from the critic's point of view) are presented:

> And in countries with mild climates people have to expend less in the struggle with nature, leaving them more gentle and capable of tender feelings. There people are beautiful, sensitive and flexible spiritually; they speak elegantly and move gracefully. Science and the arts flourish. Their philosophy on life is optimistic, and they are courteous and refined in their attitude to women.[11]

If, however, these lines are intended to project Astrov as an 'abstract idealist', some of Chekhov's own letters from warmer climates should make us pause. From Venice, for example, where people are more polite, 'women are beautiful or elegant. In fact everything is devilishly elegant', where the people possess 'immense

artistic and musical taste', and a 'world of beauty, wealth and
freedom' is 'bathed from earth to sky in sunshine'.[12] So, too, should
his comments from Sakhalin where the arid soil, hostile milieu, cold
and fog 'depress and brutalise the mind'.[13]

In fact, if we look at Chekhov's medical socialisation we find that
there is nothing especially idiosyncratic or idealist about either Dr
Astrov or Dr Chekhov since it was perfectly *normal* for Russian
doctors to concern themselves with the social benefits to be derived
from a favourable environment. Various medical journals and
collections introduced doctors to psychological questions associated
with ethnographical, meteorological and topographical problems.
Chekhov learnt at medical school of vegetal and climatic influences
on the social, economic, mental and cultural life of a people. He and
his peers internalised the belief that doctors must communicate to
the people the idea of healthy evolution through a proper
understanding of the total environment. So much, then, for the man
of mood and innocent eye who communicates no ideas. So much for
Valency's amazing assertion that Chekhov believed people neither
learn nor change, are not affected by external circumstances, and
are defined irrevocably by nature as a kind of fate.[14] The traditional
distaste for exploring an artist's values along with his social world
has led to some surprising personal projections and blind spots in the
textual analysis.

(2) PSYCHOLOGY AND CHARACTER

Shiftless, whining and indecisive characters have, despite his
consistent objections, come willy-nilly to be associated with
Chekhov's works—an important ingredient of that 'Chekhovian
mood' which we think we know so well. Few critics actually identify
Chekhov with his 'cry-babies'.[15] But they *are* often seen as a kind of
soft side to his determined sense of 'absurdity'. Valency, for one, says
that the 'mood of indecision was Chekhov's prevailing mood', and
that 'philosophic apathy . . . was perhaps very much to Chekhov's
taste', tempered only by his attention to 'life itself'.[16]

It is true that the social psychology of the neurasthenic is central
to his perspective; but to begin to see *why*, it is again necessary to
look into his continuing medical affairs.

In January 1887, the Russian psychiatrist Merzheyevskii delivered a lecture which is generally regarded as the first develop-

ment of 'mental prophylactics' in Russia to the Medico-Psychological Association in Moscow. The lecture was basically an adaptation of Morel's degeneration theory[17] to Russian conditions. Having examined the familiar causes Morel gave for degeneration and neurasthenia in the West—heredity, alcohol, infectious diseases, working conditions, an over-heavy strain on the mind during education, sexual abnormality etc.—he turned to specifically Russian causes. He believed that the sudden reforms of Alexsandr II had raised people from their mental lethargy and had brought about a great demand for 'intellectual culture'. This had produced acute excitement of the intellect and then a corresponding reaction to the universally banal circumstances of social life. The tension between a highly active intellect and the unmovable object of Russian stagnation demanded 'more labour from the psychical mechanism, thereby conducing towards its greater deterioration'. In addition, many men with a university degree, who were accustomed to live amongst people of comparable intellect, found themselves, in the course of their occupations, condemned to live in the vast cultural backwaters of provincial Russia, where their yearning after 'higher ideals' met with incomprehension. The result, Merzheyevskii said, was disenchantment, mixed with excitable irritability, pessimism, debility, neurasthenia, even insanity.[18]

As will become clear from the following chapters, Chekhov always took close note of advances in medical knowledge, and was especially interested in psychological theory. It is no coincidence that within a very few months of the speech Chekhov, who attended the conference, had completed a play based precisely on this theme. Ivanov is a university man who returns to the country full of the ideals which the recent reforms had made possible—zemstvo activism, peasant education, scientific farming, liberalism etc. He involves himself in over-intensive mental and physical activity, becomes disillusioned in an alien and stagnant environment, and collapses into complete debility, exhaustion and pessimism interspersed with nervous irritability and excitability.

Disillusionment, boredom, nervous debility and exhaustion are a certain result of the excessive excitability which is so very characteristic of our young people. Russian excitability has one special aspect: it is rapidly overtaken by exhaustion. A man has hardly got out of the classroom before, in great excitement, he rushes in to shoulder a burden beyond his strength . . . But by the age of thirty to thirty-five he begins to become tired and apathetic. (Chekhov on *Ivanov*)[19]

Chekhov's analysis of Ivanov is close in detail to Merzheyevskii's report. So it is not really surprising that he could confidently say, 'the outlines of Ivanov are correctly stated. Even if the play may be bad, I have created a type that has literary value.'[20] 'Correctly', for Chekhov, meant 'objectively', true to the latest scientific principles. That is why he felt sure that his Ivanov was 'new to Russian literature and not yet touched on by anyone'.[21]

I have held to the bold dream of summing up everything that has been written up to now on the subject of whining, gloomy people, and, with my Ivanov, putting paid once and for all to these interpretations. It seemed to me that all Russian novelists and dramatists have felt compelled to depict depressed people, and that they have written from instinct without clear images or understanding of the subject. My plot more or less gets it right . . .[22]

The neurasthenic character appears again in the person of Uncle Vanya. And once again Chekhov is careful to inform us in the text that Vanya once was, like Astrov, a man of ideals and culture. But years of provincial spacelessness and stagnation have swallowed him up. As Chekhov once commented, degeneration and neurasthenia were attributable in provincial Russia, not to the cramped and festering life of the cities as in the West, but to the fact that there is 'so much space that man, in his smallness, cannot orient himself'.

So Vanya's psychological symptoms have social causes—and likewise could only have social cures. But modern critics tell it differently. Again Valency is fairly typical in seeing Vanya as a 'masochist who has taken every opportunity to deprive himself of the normal objects of man's desire, possibly because he prefers the pleasures of deprivation to those of satisfaction'.[23] Notably the author's definition of character, which has a sense of social praxis, is replaced by a static psychologism—this character an 'idealist', that one a 'masochist'—which then reinforces the *critic's* projection on to Chekhov of a sense for 'the mystery of things, to capture, not the answer, but the feeling of the unanswerable in all its charm and urgency'.[24] Ironically, this is the kind of empty rhetoric which Chekhov himself fastened on his most inauthentic characters (for example, the artist Ryabovskii in *The Grasshopper*, who alternates between a sense for the 'sublime mystery' of things and a belief that the world is 'completely relative and absurd').

(3) SOCIAL INSTITUTIONS AND CHANGE

Rhetoric *is* quickly spotted by Chekhov's interpreters when employed by revolutionaries (Chekhov, we are reminded, had far too much sense of the mystery of things to be taken in by crude dogmatists). Thus everyone recognises Trofimov's empty revolutionary abstractions in *The Cherry Orchard*, and scoffs at Soviet critics who derive an authentic vision of change from his rhetoric. In contradistinction to these Soviet 'literary processers' we are given the 'sensitivity', the mature wisdom of Chekhov who reveals the 'ultimate stupidity' of the whole human performance, on every level from the 'individual to the cosmic'. The plight of the *Cherry Orchard* characters 'is universal. Their heartbreak is resonant. It echoes from the uttermost confines of the universe.'[25]

The critics are right to point to Trofimov's rhetoric. It is their own self-confessed dedication to the universal and the changeless which is disturbing. Interestingly, when Trofimov himself denies change, his rhetoric tends to be forgotten and his words taken at face value—as in the following speech from Act 2:

> But it is clear to anybody that our workers are fed abominably and are forced to sleep without proper beds, thirty to forty to a room, with bed bugs, filthy smells, and a permeating damp and immorality. It's perfectly plain that all our high-sounding talk has the simple function of misleading ourselves and other people. You just tell me: where are these crèches everyone talks about, and where are the reading rooms? We write about them in novels, but in fact they simply don't exist. There's only filth, bestiality, Asiatic habits.

Chekhov could have told Trofimov that change *had* taken place, that his own medical group was establishing children's crèches, that libraries were being established (Chekhov himself was supplying a new one at Taganrog with books). The first part of the quotation, in fact, should be compared in detail with a statement by Chekhov's close friend and fellow zemstvo doctor, P. I. Kurkin (who had

provided Chekhov with the topographical maps for *Uncle Vanya*).
Kurkin points out that until 1889 the functioning of sanitary
surveillence in the local factories was unsystematic, but that it
received greater attention from 1890, when plans for construction
had to be submitted to the zemstvo,[26] to various medical assemblies
and sanitary councils, and factories were open to inspection once
built. He continues with a description strikingly close to Trofimov's:

> Erisman's research of 1880–1 showed that workers were living in
> very bad conditions—sleeping quarters that were ill-lit by day,
> badly constructed, overcrowded; these shanties were covered
> with bad straw, wet matting, earth floors, and in general such
> places resembled in no way human habitations.

But he continues:

> Now everywhere have been constructed vast, clean and dry
> barracks with proper floors and camp beds covered with straw
> mattresses. According to the research of 1880–1 factory owners,
> with few exceptions, paid no attention to the ventilation of their
> workshops. Now one can no longer find workshops without
> practical ventilators on the windows, and in some important
> factories mechanical ventilators have been employed to refresh
> the air.[27]

Kurkin was not, any more than Chekhov, an apologist for the
régime. What he was pointing out (and here he is typical of his
medical group) was that a better society was slowly evolving by
means of institutional change—in this case by the development of
liberal centres in the new zemstva (of which both Chekhov and
Kurkin were extremely proud). Chekhov was being taught by
Erisman at Moscow University at the time the latter was conduct-
ing his research into factory conditions, and (the pupil) took great
interest in his teacher's work after leaving university. Indeed, as a
zemstvo factory inspector himself, Chekhov was active in putting
into effect these same improvements in factory sanitation. He
continually discussed zemstvo medicine and sanitation with
Kurkin, had read his book from which the quotation above is taken,
and kept it in his library. It is inconceivable that, knowing these
facts, and, indeed, acting on them, Chekhov, who was always
punctiliously accurate in medical details, should have meant

Trofimov's speech to be taken at face value. Critics are certainly
right to point to the emptiness of Trofimov's vision of change, but
wrong to assume that Chekhov therefore sided with the 'immutable'
and the 'unanswerable'. Chekhov had, in fact, a very precise notion
of social evolution through institutional reform, and only a wilful
separation of his literature from the man, from his socialisation and
from his continuing activities on behalf of change can obscure that
fact.

It will probably be apparent by now that I am suggesting an
underlying consistency of assumptions and values beneath a great
deal of Chekhovian interpretation: an implicit ideology of 'universality', 'timelessness', the 'unanswerable', and so on—supporting, for example, the 'absurdist Chekhov' who has become
fashionable in our time. My examples have been taken mainly from
Valency, but the reader will easily find the same tendency in
numerous other cases. Indeed, this understanding is so well
established that we know immediately what is signified when a
reviewer of *another* writer refers to his 'Chekhovian mood'. Here are
two more examples: the first from a typical analysis of that special
'Chekhovian mood'.

> Chekhov seems to see the human condition as beyond remedy,
> writes from a profound disbelief. This permits him compassion,
> satire, even near-farce, but the whole is suffused by deepening
> sadness.
>
> (Derek Whitelock, *The Australian*, 12 Oct. 1974).

The second is from J. L. Styan's *Chekhov in Performance*. In
rejecting an 'optimistic' interpretation of the ending of *The Three
Sisters*, Styan says that Chekhov would never have been so naive as
to think that the problems he described would ever be solved, for 'if
it is hope for a better society, what could conceivably remedy the ills
Chekhov is concerned with in the play'.[28] Elsewhere Styan
interprets the flight of birds in the play as making us aware 'of the
infinite space and time which dwarfs us all'.[29] Together the key
concepts (and their underlying assumptions) form a pattern: the
'human condition' (as against class or group conflict), 'universality'
and 'fate' (as against social change and human praxis), 'timelessness' and 'infinitude' (compared with the active subject with an
active history), 'sensitivity', 'resonance', a 'sense for mystery' (as
against 'vulgar' ideology). Inevitably these values, which the critic

brings with him to the text, influence interpretation—as when
Styan dismisses Vershinin, who is committed to social change, (and,
as we shall see, was one of Chekhov's more positive characters) as 'a
marrowless colonel . . . a somewhat hollow man';[30] or when
Valency remarks that Chekhov's disbelief in change accounts for
the 'uncomplicated linearity' of his best plays.[31]

A pattern of interpretation so consistent and coherent (at the very
least, in terms of what it opposes) derives, needless to say, from
something more systematic and institutionalised than a disparate
body of Chekhovian critics. We should look instead at the implicit
assumptions with which literary critics operate, the values into
which critics *themselves* are socialised—which means looking at the
dominant literary tradition transmitted through schools and universities. Richard Ohmann has pointed out (in a penetrating study
of the literary institution) that the separation of the individual from
social change is central to the value system of the New Criticism,
which has dominated university (teaching) for so long. The outside
world, as the New Critics see it, is

> complex, discordant, dazzling. We want desperately to know it as
> unified and meaningful, but action out in the world fails to reveal
> or bring about a satisfying order. The order we need *is* available
> in literature; therefore literature must be a better guide to truth
> than are experience and action. But the specific truth to be got
> from literature is less clear than the desire for it; and the
> particular values that poetry advances are nebulous.[32]

The 'balance' to be achieved in the world is thus nothing to do with
the resolution of social conflict, nor with acting to change society.
Rather, it is to do with a process of expanding *consciousness*, as the
individual, isolated from all but the text, and prying the words loose
from their social origins, becomes sensitive to shades of feeling and
attuned to the need for pattern and order *within* the text. This
ordering, then, has nothing to do with the vulgar world of 'politics'
and social 'relevance'. Poetry 'lets us "realise the world" . . . by
freeing man *from* politics by putting him above his circumstances,
giving him inner control, affording a means of salvation, placing
him beyond culture'.[33] Ordering is achieved textually in a *heightened*
sense of the ambiguity, irony and paradox of things—terms, be it
noted, central to the interpretation, and high evaluation, of
Chekhov within the literary pantheon.

Strident assertions of textual 'autonomy' (cf. Valency's, 'It is quite unnecessary for the understanding of his drama to discuss his world-view. If he had anything of the sort, it was irrelevant to the subject of his art'.)[34] lead easily to the evaluation of literary significance *in terms of* the refusal to judge or to act. 'Immutable' social contradictions are thus resolved (through 'innocence' of vision and 'freedom' of thinking) within the coherence of the text, which, by drawing our finest senses to observe the ambiguity of life, mysteriously raises us up and beyond the 'imbalance of attitudes and impulses'.

At the same time, one might add, this accredited sensibility raises us into an intellectual élite, which is jealous of its position. Hence this 'letter to The Times' insisting against alternative approaches (in this case sociological and structuralist):

> Sir,—'Prac. crit.' cannot *afford* to lose favour . . . since it is the only 'approach' which justifies the continuation of literature as such . . . It is unpopular because it requires a great deal of personal effort. Questions about the social setting of literature can be relatively easily and swiftly answered with the help of an encyclopaedia; but questions about imagery, rhythm, style, verse form, ambiguity, symbolism etc. require concentration, reflection and patience . . . Thus practical criticism attempts to deal with literature at that level which is confronted after all the other 'approaches' have proved inadequate.
> Yours faithfully,
> Margaret Berg,
> Linacre College, Oxford.

(Letter to *The Times Higher Education Supplement* 19 March 1976.)

The trouble is, as we have noticed, that critics of 'literature as such' tend to let their own values obtrude into questions of rhythm, style, ambiguity and so on. And the placing of a work in its social context is, as the next section will demonstrate, rather more complex and demanding than Ms Berg allows.

My main complaint about the 'prac. crit.' tradition, whether at its most sophisticated, as in Leavis' work, or at its most (reductively) offensive (as above), is that it denies its own procedural principles to others (and ignores them itself when turning to social analysis). An immanent analysis of the text is sought, with a proper concern for the work's internal structure. Few critics, however, carry with them their concern for structure and systematic analysis when they finally make forays into the social context. None, I suppose, will actually look in Margaret Berg's encyclopaedia. But the social structure is raided, nonetheless, in a search for supportive data which is quite as gross in style as the more publicised 'quarrying' of literary texts by historians and sociologists.

I want to make two of my assumptions clear at this point, since they will underlie the rest that I write:

(1) Analysis of the social context of a work of art must be a structural analysis, because society, and human interaction within it, is systematic and structured. The starting point is hardly contentious. It is an assumption underlying almost any sociological perspective, and is presumably acceptable to the layman as well, since he speaks of the 'social structure'.

(2) Analysis of the text, and the *relationship* between society and text must also be structural. This is a less familiar assumption, and will need much greater exposition. To clarify it—and, furthermore, to consider the precise *level* of this relationship which the sociologist is most competent to analyse—I want to turn, in the next section, to the semiological theory of Roland Barthes, to Lucien Goldmann's genetic structuralism, and to the sociology of knowledge.

2 Structuralism and the Sociology of Knowledge

The major problem of traditional Chekhovian interpretation has been its impressionism and lack of system and structure—in the analysis both of the author's social context *and* of his works within that context. Recent trends in the analysis of art and literature offer an alternative. Structuralism promises, as its methods become more refined, a non-reductive reading of the literary text and a systematic location of the work in its broader context. 'Structuralism', however, still means different things to different people; and in particular to those with backgrounds in linguistics and sociology. So my primary concern in this section is to consider the main premises of the structuralist approach, and to see whether there can be a common meeting-point. A theory, in effect, which gives due weight to the systematic analysis of the work, of the social and cultural context, *and* of the author.[1]

The most influential by far of the contemporary group of structuralist critics is Roland Barthes, whose linguistic distinction of that which signifies (signifiant) and that which is signified (signifié) within all literary systems is important for any analysis of the arts.

(1) For Barthes, following Saussure, any 'message' (sign) is a 'compound of a signifier and a signified. The plane of the signifiers constitutes the plane of *expression* and that of the signifieds the *plane of content*'. Where we are considering a complex system of signification, such as literature, it has to be remembered that the signifier (plane of expression) is *itself* constituted by a signifying system (language). Thus, if we use E to represent the signifier, C the signified and R the *relation* of the two planes, we can describe the doubly articulated and 'staggered' system of literature:

2	E	R	C	Literature
1	ERC			Language

The first level (the system of language) is the plane of denotation; the second (the system of literature) the plane of connotation. The following example from Barthes will make this more clear:

> in a literary text, the primary signification, which is the language (for example, French), acts as a signifier for a second message in which the signified is different from what is signified in the language. If I read 'summon up the appurtenances for conversation', I am looking at a manifest ('denotative') message which is an order to get some armchairs, but I am also looking at a 'connotative' message in which what is signified is a French literary style known as 'affectation'. In information terms, literature is definable as a double system, both denotative and connotative.[2]

(2) Following Hjelmslev, Barthes introduces a further distinction since each plane (of expression, of content) can itself be divided into two strata: *form* and *substance*. At the basic level of language this will give us:

(i) a substance of expression: for instance the phonic, articulatory, non-functional substance which is the field of phonetics, not phonology;

(ii) a form of expression, made of the paradigmatic and syntactic rules . . .

(iii) a substance of content: this includes, for instance, the emotional, ideological, or simply notional aspects of the signified, its 'positive' meaning;

(iv) a form of content: it is the formal organization of the signified among themselves through the absence or presence of a semantic mark.[3]

More significantly for our present concern with literature, since he deals with a more complex system of signification, Christian Metz has extended Barthes' categories to the cinema.

> At the level of the film as a whole, the substance of the signified is the 'social content' of the cinematic discourse; the form of the signified is the profound semantic structure (sometimes called 'thematic structure') which organises the social content in that film . . . . The substance of the signifier (or rather the substances

of the signifier since film is a 'composite language') are the moving photographic image, recorded noise, phonetic sound, recorded sound—and all the consequences entailed by the fact that the film has recourse to these four substances rather than others (comparing it for example with cartoons, still photography, silent cinema, radio broadcasting, etc.). The form of the signifier is the set of perceptual configurations recognisable in these four substances: for example, the regular recurrence of a syntagmatic association between a particular phrase of dialogue and some visual motif, etc.[4]

Literature, as we have seen, is, like film, a 'connoted system'. The strata of substance (substance of expression) for 'literature' will presumably incorporate all the words in the language (including archaisms, features of dialect, etc.), since unless the substance of the connotator is coterminous with 'langue' the work of literature could not be readily understood (this is not to deny, of course, that some societies—and some genres—more than others will have a more specifically 'literary' register). Barthes, however, would not let us rest content with 'substance' in this sense of mere 'content'. The language of literature is itself 'coded', has its own form.

First of all, it is *written* language, the requirement of which (in contrast to the 'incomplete' and 'ill-formed' nature of spoken language) is that it finish its sentences . . . 'the sentence, in its closure and self-sufficiency, seems the fundamental goal of writing'.[5] This sense of closure, implicit in the language of literature, has the function of 'naturalisation' and 'domestication'. 'Language, as sentence, period and paragraph, superimposes on these discontinuous categories existing at the level of discourse an appearance of continuity . . . What could be more familiar, more evident, more natural than a sentence as read?'[6] Ultimately the function is an ideological one.[7] For example, however critical, depressing and apparently 'realistic' a 'slice of life' novel or story, may be (e.g. Chekhov's bleak tale of a life totally degraded in *Peasants*), there is the comfort of closure. The angst which we might feel if faced by the complete formlessness and alienation of a world of discrete words and objects is in fact avoided by an immediate taming of existence within the comforting convention of an ordered narrative of completed sentences. By this form of closure at least, man imposes his order on the world. At the same time, the words, deriving from the first level of the semiotic system, appear 'natural', thereby disguising the fact that this is not only an ordered and *conventional* code, but one which contains an ideology.

Once we have defined written language (and Barthes admits that the task is only just beginning), we can begin to consider what distinguishes *literary* from other forms of written language (scholarly writing, administrative writing, journalism and so on). This draws us further into an analysis of the connotative form of expression, which Barthes calls 'rhetoric'.

In *Elements of Semiology*, Barthes, adopting the distinction between strata of form and strata of substance, argues that: 'rhetoric is the *form* of the connotators'.[8] Barthes is concerned that rhetorical analysis should proceed in structuralist terms (that is, analysis of the way in which the message is composed) before being related to society (i.e. in terms of what the message says), and points to two legitimate modes of procedure.

The first derives from Jakobson's distinction within every message of six factors, each with their appropriate linguistic functions according to emphasis: that is, any one utterance is a combination of most of these functions, but derives its particular characteristics from the domination of one or other function over the others:

> for example, if the emphasis is put on the sender, the expressive or emotive function dominates; if it is put on the receiver, it is the connotative function (hortatory or supplicatory); if it is the referent which is emphasized, the utterance is denotative (as it is in the present case); if it is on the connection (between the transmitter and the receiver) the phatic function of all those signs is designed to maintain communication between the people engaged in interaction; the function which can be termed metalinguistic, which is concerned with elucidation, puts the stress on the code itself; finally, when it is the message itself, its pattern, the physical presentation of its signs which are stressed, we are dealing with the poetic utterance in the broad sense of the term. This is obviously the case with literature: one would specify a literary work or text as a message which *puts the emphasis on itself*.[9]

In other words, what distinguishes literature from other forms of writing (all of which employ most of Jakobson's six factors— transmitter, receiver, context or referent, contact, code, message) is that its emphasis is not so much what is said (context or referent) but *how* it is said (message).

Nevertheless, 'the consistency and the intent of the poetic function can vary through history, as well as synchronically; the same function can be swallowed up by other functions, a phenomenon which in some ways reduces the specific literary qualities we can attach to a piece of writing'.[10] Thus, without abandoning an internal analysis of rhetoric, it would be possible to relate it to social difference and change. Certain literary conventions ('Naturalism', for example) reflect a movement away from the 'poetic' to the referential and contextual, and this difference can be analysed sociologically.

An approach to poetics of this kind would help us to locate theoretically the difficulties which Chekhov had in adapting a naturalistic style to the conventions of the theatre. Naturalistic conventions rejected the melodramatic forms which had dominated the Russian stage during the period up to Chekhov on the grounds that they were not 'true to life'. Since, however, in 'real life' deep emotions are frequently not articulated, naturalist dramatists were faced with a problem. Either they had to limit themselves to visible surface emotions which the audience could see for itself without theatrical devices (and thereby miss much that was humanly dramatic), or they had to find a form which could express the inarticulate without conventional 'artifice'.

Two traditional conventions for expressing hidden emotions and values—the chorus and the soliloquy (which foregrounded the phatic and poetic functions)—were unacceptable because of their lack of 'vraisemblence'. Chekhov's works are marked, as Geoffrey Borny[11] has shown, by a struggle to develop a new form which did not subvert the referential and contextual emphasis of naturalism. The development is marked by the artistic gap between an early work such as *Ivanov*, in which Chekhov simply could not make his central character understood *without* adding monologues and soliloquys, and a late work like *The Cherry Orchard* where the now familiar Chekhovian solution of the 'sub-text' reached its culminating form. In his stories, Chekhov reacted in a similar way against conventional modes of 'explanation' and 'resolution' (as, for example, found in Turgenev)—authorial apostrophes, elaborate prologues, digressions and epilogues, and conventional melodramatic climaxes. In their place he developed a concise 'objective' style,[12] the 'zero ending' (since unresolved tension is 'more true to

life') and sub-textual 'comment'. In his plays and his stories
Chekhov looked for a style in which the 'poetic' was not at the
expense of the 'contextual'.

Barthes' other procedure for investigating rhetoric is also helpful
in understanding Chekhov's works. Here Barthes draws on the area
of linguistics which 'deals with the definition of words less by their
meaning than by their syntactic associations . . . very broadly
speaking, associations between words occur according to a certain
scale of probability: dog is fairly straightforwardly associated with
barking, but pretty improbably with "meowing"; even though
syntactically there is nothing to forbid the association of a verb and
any subject'. This approach helps us in defining fundamental
aspects of literary language. 'In "the sky is blue like an orange",
there are no deviant associations between words; but if one moves
to a higher level of unit, a level corresponding with connotation, . . . it is statistically rare to associate blue with being
orange. Literary messages can thus be defined as deviant association
between signs.'[13] Literature, then, in the terminology of cyber-
netics, is

> essentially a system of high-cost information. However, if litera-
> ture is consistently a matter of 'luxury spending' there are several
> 'luxury economies' which can vary between historical periods
> and between societies. In classical literature . . . syntactic asso-
> ciations occurred largely within the normal range, so far as the
> denotative level is concerned, and it is precisely at the rhetorical
> level that high-cost information occurs. On the other hand, in
> surrealist poetry (to take the other extreme) the associations are
> unpredictably deviant and, even at the level of elementary units of
> speech, information is very costly.

It should thus be possible, Barthes argues, to make 'connections
between a particular society and the economy of information
assigned to it by its literature'.[14]

There has been no analysis of Chekhov in these terms, but
Thomas Winner's book, *Chekhov and his Prose* provides a number of
useful insights which could be considered within Barthes' perspective. Since this is not my main purpose here, I can do no more
than suggest, in a fairly schematic way, the kinds of problems that
should concern us at this level. The following are a few of the 'high-
cost' aspects of Chekhov's style which may derive from literary

language as such, and yet, as we shall see, are consistently undercut through emphasis on a referential function.

(1) Semantic deformation: Winner gives as an example from *The Steppe* the moment when the waggon train stops by a silent grave which, to Yegor, seems 'audibly' silent. This surprising and 'literary' association is an example, as Winner sees it, of the device of 'making it strange', 'a peculiar semantic shift which transforms a depicted object to a different plane of reality . . . causing a perceiver to see the object in a fresh light, as though for the first time.'[15] The device achieved its most systematic theatrical expression, of course, in Brecht's 'alienating' techniques. My point is, though, that in Chekhov, no less than in Brecht, the transformation has a specifically referential function. The silent crosses in the steppes suggest, metonymically, Chekhov's central theme of the isolation of man from man, and from the social and natural world. According to the evolutionary vision which (as we shall see in a later chapter) was the central strand of Chekhov's world view, man had only two possibilities of interaction. Either he might relate with the social and natural world on a basis of scientific understanding, or he might not, in which case the world would be a place of stark, mute and incommunicable objects. The distance between the harsh and the humanised world, between silence and the organic community, was one of potential—the future lay in man's hands. Hence wherever the separation expressed itself in reality, there could only be a sense of loss and pathos at man's neglected potential. A familiar device which Chekhov adopted to express this lost potential was a form of 'pathetic fallacy': nature, as in the old epics (and in Tolstoi), was seen to grieve at the loss of community between man and the world. Thus in *The Steppe* (through another Chekhovian device— using sound to convey melancholy) nature is heard to cry out of its 'waste', and to call for a poet and man of understanding. The pathos is expressed as a tension between man's muteness and isolation (silent graves) and nature's audible cry of neglect. It is in this context that the 'audible' silence of the graves should be understood: as a trope compressing, with a sense of precision and closure typical of literary language, man's vast potential and at the same time the pathos of his loss. It is the same tension which Chekhov expresses less 'poetically', more denotatively, in the following remarks:

> What riches, what treasures of beauty are as yet untouched; and how much spaciousness still exists for the Russian artist.[16]

I was pained to see these wide open spaces—which you'd have thought had all the conditions for a richly civilized life—positively smothered in ignorance.[17]

(2) Rhythmic repetition, counterpoint and antistrophe: Another feature of 'high-cost information' is the rhythmic counterpointing of oppositions which can be used to develop the emotional intensity of a work. Winner, for example, describes how the contrapuntal interplay of lyrical imagery and the dry style and banal imagery of 'poshlost'[18] (smells and sounds from the kitchen, etc.) in Chekhov's last story, *The Betrothed*, acts like a musical discourse to channel affectivity. This rhythmic counterpointing is, however, integral to the referential and contextual emphasis of the Chekhovian sub-text. The even tenor of life in these works (social occasions, as in *Ionych* and *The Three Sisters*, dull scenes of artifice and conventional interaction in *The Betrothed*, *Uncle Vanya*, etc.[19]) are penetrated by sounds, smells, sights, objects presenting the two worlds of human potential and banal degradation. Thus, for example, in *Peasants*, immediately juxtaposed with the dirt, smell and overcrowding of life in the village, we have this expansive and lyrical scene:

A vivid green meadow lay below—wide and level and mown already—where the village herd wandered. The river was nearly a mile from the village and meandered among fine tree-lined banks. Further on there was another wide field, with a herd of cows and straggling lines of white geese. Beyond that was a rise as steep as on the near side. At the top of the rise there was a large village, a church with its five onion-shaped domes, and, further away still, the home of gentry. 'It is so lovely here!' Ol'ga said, crossing herself as she saw the church. 'Lord, how far I can see!'

In this story, the two worlds of human potential and conventional closure penetrate the degraded intercourse of the village in a passage of ironically juxtaposed *imagery* (Ol'ga responds to the potential openness the images establish with a gesture that ties her to the closure of a mystical and exploitative religion). In *The Three Sisters*, by contrast (and more appropriate to drama) the escapist conventionality and complacency of the ballroom world is penetrated by alternatives of *characterisation* and *action*, through two characters (Vershinin and Natasha) who polarise and subvert the dreams of the party. So by means of ironic juxtaposition, polarising action and (as in the extract from *Peasants* above) shift in point of view, Chekhov presents an evaluation (without the authorial comment, soliloquy, etc. inappropriate to the conventions of Naturalism) both of the relationships of the social/natural world, and of individual characters within it.

(3) Sub-text: A repeated Chekhovian device is the informal (and therefore naturalistic) 'chorus', whereby characters give apparently superfluous information, but compositely comment on the action. A well-known example is the apparently inconsequential sequence of comments from the other side of the stage in Act I of *The Three Sisters*[20] which in fact throw light on the inadequacy of the sisters' dreams, without resort to the 'unreal' device of a formal chorus. In addition to the sub-textual devices already mentioned (rhythmical opposition, superfluous dialogue, etc.) characters may be presented in relation to natural images (Tuzenbakh to a dead tree, Vershinin to the flight of birds) which, by association with the counterpointing of themes (Vershinin—the potential of nature/Natasha—cutting down of trees) locate them (and those with whom they interact most closely—e.g. Tuzenbakh/ Irina) in relation to the authorial point of view.

(4) Literary allusion: A familiar kind of literary 'excess' is, as Barthes points out,[21] its development of pre-existing forms (proverbs, previous literature etc.). Mainly, this drawing upon the cultural 'memory' operates at an unconscious level—what Barthes calls the recording of life through a body of formulae. Some writers, however, consciously play upon inherited forms, previous styles, and conventional characterisation—thereby foregrounding them in a reflexive way. Chekhov's work is studded with conscious literary allusion, from the stylistic parodies of his early works, to the mythical and literary exempla of his mature writing.

Winner points to the frequent subversion of myths and the stylistic parody by means of which Chekhov (again without authorial interjection) comments on his characters. Thus, in *Ariadne*, the 'scheming, egotistical Ariadne is an inversion of the Greek Ariadne, the personification of spring, and her lovers are also antithetical to their Greek prototypes'.[22] And in *The Darling*, 'Those whom Olenka loves successively are but absurd shadows of the god of love. Had Chekhov's Olenka held a light to her lovers, as did Psyche to Eros, Olenka's lovers might also have vanished. It was, however, their prosaic attributes, not their godlike qualities, which could not bear close inspection'.[23]

Among the literary types which Chekhov draws on, those of Tolstoi, and particularly Anna Karenina, are especially important. There is close and conscious irony (through unfulfilled expectations of plot line and inversions of character) in stories related to Tolstoi's Anna—*Anna on the Neck, Lady with a Little Dog, The Betrothed*. Winner points to the very close parallel, for example, between the lives of the Annas of *Anna on the Neck* and *Anna Karenina*, and then contrasts the somewhat overblown and novelettish presentiment of the first Anna of 'a terrible power moving on her as a cloud, or as a locomotive ready to crush her' (reference, of course, to the death of Anna Karenina) with the more prosaic reality, in which adultery leads to ascendancy in the hierarchical society that Chekhov knew so well.

But the significant point, as I see it, is the way in which Chekhov uses this kind of ironic reversal and 'zero ending' to comment on the stale conventionality (i.e. betrayal of originality and objectivity) of *both* vision and style. Time and again his searching (but 'inauthentic') characters are marked by theatrical and clichéd responses which the text specifically relates to melodrama and popular novels. For example, Konstantin Treplev, in *The Seagull*, a seeker, like Chekhov, after new artistic forms, traps himself in the well-worn Hamlet stereotype (which in Russia had conventionally been interpreted as that of the 'superfluous man'[24]). Thus Konstantin betrays originality of form *and* (because of the overlaying of his own relationship to his mother with the Hamlet/Gertrude one) spontaneous interaction.

Again, in *The Cherry Orchard*, the student Trofimov is, like Konstantin, a seeker after new forms—in this case, political ones. However, the theatricality of his famous message, 'Onwards! Let us march irresistibly towards that bright star shining there in the distance! Onwards! Don't lag behind my friends!' links him in conventionality, for all his optimism, to Anna on the Neck. An even closer comparison with Anna's 'terrible power moving . . . . . as a cloud' is Tuzenbakh's 'The Time has come: a tremendous thundercloud is advancing on us. A great storm is coming to wake us up!' In each case, grandiose sentiments are subverted from the start by the shabby style of cheap fiction (a point ignored by Soviet interpreters who, ignoring both style and structure in the plays, take Tuzenbakh and Trofimov as visionaries of authentic revolution). The author's ironic comment, frequently conveyed by an abrupt lowering of style (e.g. Chebutykin's 'I'm not going to work' in response to Tuzenbakh's oratory), is, in Trofimov's case largely conveyed by metonymy (for example, Trofimov's absurd little beard and down-at-heel shoes which contrast with his pretentious language) and by slap-stick action (Trofimov falls downstairs after a particularly sustained bout of oratory).

Simplistic, conventional and theatrical responses betray themselves in an excess of style, and contrast with Chekhov's more restrained sense of hope and suffering. Indeed, one of the most beautiful of all his stories, *Lady with a Little Dog*, unfolds within this contrast, from the conventional gossip and stale, stereotypical patterning of the first line—'It was rumoured that a new face had appeared on the embankment; a lady with a little dog'—through the expected and degraded ritual of seduction, to the final peripety, and the mature conclusion:

> And it seemed that a solution would appear in just a few moments more, and that a new and beautiful life would then begin for them. Yet both knew perfectly well that the end of the road was still a very long way away, and that the hardest and most complicated part of their journey was only just beginning.

The distance of vision, in terms of freshness and objectivity, between this final recognition of hope and suffering and the stale and simplistic response of 'a new and beautiful life' in just a few moments more, is a mark of the lovers' progress beyond Anna, Konstantin, Trofimov and Tuzenbakh *and* the rhetorical conservatism they represented.

I have been suggesting a few devices of rhetoric that the research which Barthes projects might include as aspects of literary language; and at the same time I have remarked on Chekhov's personal *usage* of this language. Obviously the analysis is fragmentary, but it is interesting that, in all the examples I have given, what at first appears as literary 'excess', or the reflexive concern of the literary 'message', has an underlying *contextual* emphasis, within the acceptable parameters of the conventions of Naturalism. A structural analysis of Chekhov's 'rhetoric' would need to consider much more completely the relative emphasis of the various functions which Barthes isolates.

Meanwhile, this analysis, mainly at the level of Barthes' form of the signifier is intended to demarcate the level which, as a sociologist, I feel most competent to contribute—the form of the *signified*—while emphasising the equal importance of structural analysis at all the other levels. I have dwelt, inadequately, with the plane of expression for the last few pages because the rest of my analysis will not be concerned with this level. This, as I have said, is a matter of competence, not sense of significance or priority, and I wanted to make that quite clear.

Barthes' distinction between strata of form and substance is particularly important for research at the level of the connotative signified, if only because most neglected. It is here that literary critics' relegation of 'social content' to a perusal of encyclopaedia can be most damaging, leading, as Metz has remarked,[25] to a fairly unsystematic enumeration of 'human problems'—a reductive interpretation which takes no note of the effect the *form* of the content has on the events described.[26]

This significant absence (of analysis of form) is, however, filled. It is at this level that we find the tendency of critics to read their own values, or those of their social group and culture, *into* their thematic analysis of Chekhov. And so we have the interpretations of Astrov as idealist (interestingly enough, Astrov becomes less of an idealist as *our* societies move towards a greater concern for the environment, as in Magarshack's *The Real Chekhov*[27]), Vanya as masochist, and the Freudian analyses of Konstantin Treplev. This is not to say that these analyses are uninteresting; simply that they ignore the structuring principle of ideology in Chekhov's works. As Barthes has said, the signified of connotation is 'a fragment of ideology'. The connotative signifieds 'have a very close communication with culture, knowledge, history, and it is through them, so to speak, that the environmental world invades the system. We might say that *ideology* is the *form* (in Hjelmslev's sense of the word) of the signifieds, while *rhetoric* is the form of the connotators.'[28]

Mention of ideology, however, raises a new problem, and a fundamental distinction between Barthes' approach and the theoretical orientation of this book. When Barthes talks of ideology, he tends to do so in a global and diffuse sense, as, for example, when he describes the avant-garde in general as 'a somewhat exuberant, somewhat eccentric portion—of the bourgeois army . . . a kind of vaccine intended to inject a little subjectivity, a little freedom under the crust of bourgeois values . . . sooner or later it returns to the bosom which had given it, with life, a freedom of pure postponement.'[29] It would, of course, be perfectly possible to analyse Chekhov's values in terms of a more global connection—as part, for example, of a new guard among the bourgeoisie in Europe, dedicated to science, 'truth in art and life', the positivist method, freedom (of a strictly limited kind), and so on. However, that would be to miss the more intimate textures of life—not only Chekhov's personal sense of identity as writer[30] and doctor, but also the struggle of a very particular social group in a very particular time and place. Moreover, the distinction between Barthes' approach and my own is much more than a matter of emphasis. It derives from a fundamental difference of assumption about structuralism itself.

For Barthes the defining characteristic of structuralism, 'in its most specialized and consequently most relevant version', is its methodological basis in linguistics. This has profound consequences for the task which structuralism sets itself, particularly in relation to ideology, since linguistics is concerned to explain not what we mean when we speak but *how* we mean. Linguistic structuralism, as Jonathan Culler defines it in his *Structuralist Poetics*, is not so much concerned with hidden, unknown or 'true' meanings of texts, but with poetics—how do texts make sense?

> the task of criticism . . . is purely formal; it does not consist in 'discovering' in the work of the author something 'hidden' or 'profound' or 'secret' . . . the critic is not called upon to reconstitute the message of the work, but only its system, just as the business of the linguist is not to decipher the meaning of a sentence but to determine the formal structure which permits the transmission of its meaning.
>
> (Barthes[31])

> Poetics bears, as Barthes says, not so much on the work itself as on its intelligibility.
>
> (Culler[32])

The refusal to approach literature in order to recover there a central 'meaning' which governs its structure thus derives from basic methodological assumptions, and accounts for the emphasis in Barthes and Culler on the text as process and on *reading*. For Barthes the 'closing' of a work's possibilities by the 'definitive' commentary is an act of bad faith. In Culler's words,

> a structuralist poetics would claim that the study of literature involves only indirectly the critical act of placing a work in

situation, reading it as a gesture of a particular kind, and thus giving it a meaning. The task is rather to construct a theory of literary discourse which would account for the possibilities of interpretation, the 'empty meanings' which support a variety of full meanings but which do not permit the work to be given just any meaning.[33]

In this perspective ideology, broadly determined, is only one 'code' one order of determination, among many which mediate the textual encounter and enable the reader to give it meaning.[34] At the same time, for Culler the excitement, the 'pleasure' of literature as an institution, come from 'the moments of indeterminacy, un-certainty, excess' which subvert the conventional coherence of a text, and force us to reconsider our own action in giving meaning to things according to codes external to us and normally beyond our control. Criticism thus focusses on the 'adventures of meaning'. The 'type of ultimate recuperation towards which a structuralist criticism moves' is 'to read the text as an exploration of writing, of the problems of articulating a world. The critic comes to focus, therefore, on the play of the legible and the illegible, on the role of gaps, silence, opacity . . . The reader learns to cope with these contradictions and becomes, as Barthes says, the hero in the adventure of culture.'[35]

All of this is of obvious importance to the literary critic, and much of it to the sociologist too, because the way in which readers decode a text and overlay its meanings with their own should be a central part of the sociology of literature. There is, however, a fundamental problem with this perspective from a sociologist's point of view. For the linguist, as for the language user, the meaning of any given basic sentence is already known. The same is not true, the sociologist would argue, of basic social institutions, which, in any situation of competition for power, tend to hide behind a legitimating rhetoric. Thus sociology *is* fundamentally concerned with latent and un-known meanings beneath surface phenomena, and with *values* which expose and express social forces and contradictions. For Peter Berger, for example,

the first wisdom of sociology is this—things are not what they seem . . . To ask sociological questions . . . presupposes a cer-tain awareness that human events have different levels of meaning, some of which are hidden from the consciousness of

everyday life . . . Sociological perspective can then be understood in terms of such phrases as 'seeing through', 'looking
behind' . . . the facades of social structures.

This, for Berger then, is the *defining* characteristic of sociology.[36]

The sociologist who accepts these fundamental assumptions
about his discipline will be worried by an absent centre in Culler's
examples (of both opening and closure) of the possibilities of
'meaning' through reading. He will, for example, accept Culler's
stress on the importance of genre in enabling the reader to
'naturalise' (make understandable in terms of his taken-for-granted
conception of the world) discrete information. But he will also want
to know something about the latent values which structure a
particular genre and therefore pre-set the reader's perception
within an existing ideology. An example here would be the Social
Darwinism (underlying a 'frontier' morality) central to the Western
film genre. The sociologist will also accept Culler's point that to
reduce Balzac to a critic of capitalist society is to miss his uniqueness,
his 'strangeness'. But then what accounts for the moments of
'indeterminancy, uncertainty, excess' in Balzac? In what way for
instance do these relate to the very conservative socialisation of this
'critic of capitalism'? If the gaps, silences and opacity in Balzac's
text subvert our conventional readings, we can hardly explain them
in terms of those readings. In each case there is a centre of values in
the text which Culler skirts round.

These differences of assumption between linguistics and sociology
account for a further difference which is more precisely related to
the purpose of this chapter. Linguistic structuralism seeks to expose
'distinctions and rules operating at an unconscious level'[37] which, in
Culler's version, make up the ideal reader's 'competence', and
hence his ability to understand discourse. Meaning is thus explained
in terms of conventional systems beyond the individual's consciousness. Far from being the Cartesian thinking reed, creator of his
works and his world, man is here no more than a point of nexus for
'codes' which 'speak' his activity. The coherent, thinking subject
disappears wherever we used to find him:

(i) from the role of author, where 'the self comes to appear more
and more as a construct, the result of systems of convention';[38]

(ii) from the author's characters since 'Stress on the interpersonal and conventional systems which traverse the individual,
which make him a space in which forces and events meet rather

than an individuated essence, lead to a rejection of a prevalent conception of character in the novel';[39]

(iii) from the subject who reads, who 'is constituted by a series of conventions, the grids of regularity and intersubjectivity', and who is no more than 'the track or the furrow left by the experience of texts of all kinds'.[40]

Hence it seems logical for the great French structuralists, the anthropologist Lévi-Strauss and the historian Foucault, to posit the disappearance of man altogether: 'The goal of the human sciences is not to constitute man but to dissolve him' (Lévi-Strauss);[41] 'man is only a recent invention, a figure not yet two centuries old, a simple fold in our knowledge, and . . . will disappear as soon as that knowledge has found a new form' (Foucault).[42]

A sociological approach to structuralism would also deny the independent, conscious subject, and would be as ready as the structuralists mentioned above to insist that 'to be located in society means to be at the intersection point of specific social forces'.[43] Thus, as this book will make clear, Chekhov was not—could not be—the autonomous and sensitive creator, untouched by the grossness of ideology and world view, which traditional interpretation has given us. He was the product of very specific social forces operating at different strengths, at different times and at various levels during his continuing process of socialisation and identity-formation. Moreover these specific forces of interaction were only possible because of certain historical events—without these, I am suggesting Chekhov's works would have been entirely different.

However, the elimination of the conscious subject is not at all the same thing as the elimination of *man*, as Culler implies. If the structuralism derived from linguistics defines its parameters in terms of man's disappearance, the sociological perspective I shall be adopting here most certainly does not. The belief that sociology's primary concern is with man is deeply held by sociologists of many different persuasions. Thus Peter Berger: 'We would say then that the sociologist . . . is a person intensively, endlessly, shamelessly interested in the doings of men . . . His consuming interest remains in the world of men, their institutions, their history, their passions'.[44] Peter Worsley likewise capitalises the centre of interest— 'Man'—while emphasising that our concern is not with 'natural', Romantic man: 'What we may claim for sociology, at its ideal best, is a distinctive *perspective*: . . . it is a way of looking at Man's behaviour as conditioned by his membership of social groups.'[45]

A structuralism deriving from sociology will thus be centred on the actions and beliefs of men—hence the unashamedly 'biographical' remarks with which I opened. But, equally, it will concern itself with 'Man's behaviour as conditioned by his membership of social groups'. This will be to give proper recognition to what Berger has called the 'persistently Janus-faced paradox of our social existence': that society defines man, but is in turn defined by him. A sociological structuralism consequently has to provide a theoretical refutation to Jonathan Culler's common sense assertion (on which he bases his rejection of the author as 'subject'): 'if the self is a construct and result it can no longer serve as a source'.[46] In place of Culler's stark opposition of the active phenomenological subject and the subject 'dissolved' in interpersonal systems, the theoretical construction of this book will be the dialectical one: 'Society is a human product. Society is an objective reality. Man is a social product.'[47] Since this formulation of Berger and Luckmann's will underlie—most of the time implicitly—the perspective of what follows (and, of course, my divergence from a linguistics-derived structuralism), I should explain, as briefly as possible the relevant part of their theory.

(1) Externalisation: Man, as Berger and Luckmann see it, *creates* his world as a process of 'externalisation'. The human being, they begin, 'occupies a peculiar place in the animal kingdom'. Unlike other higher mammals, he has 'no environment firmly structured by his own instinctual organisation'; there is a lack of direction to his 'drives'. Precise ontogenetic reasons account for this: crucial organismic developments, which in the animal have been completed before birth, take place in the human infant after separation from the mother's body. Thus the human organism is still developing biologically while it is inter-relating with an external environment which is *cultural* and *social* as well as natural. Biologically as well as geographically man has many possibilities of relationship;

. . . there is no human nature in the sense of a biologically-fixed substratum determining the variability of socio-cultural formations. There is only human nature in the sense of anthropological constants (for example, world-openness and plasticity of instinctual structure) that delimit and permit man's socio-cultural formations. But the specific shape into which this humanness is moulded is determined by these socio-cultural formations and is relative to their numerous variations. While it is possible to say that man has a nature, it is more significant to say that man constructs his own nature, or more simply, that man produces himself.[48]

It is this diversity of social construction that constitutes the place of man's freedom. Men, like Eichmann, can say, 'I have no choice'; but this is a lie. Unlike animals who cannot say 'no' to their instincts, Berger argues that men '*can* say "no" to their society, and often have done so'.[49]

There is, however, nothing Romantic about man's 'freedom'. 'Man's self-production is always, and of necessity, a social enterprise. Men *together* produce a human environment . . . Solitary human being is being on the animal level . . .' Lacking 'the necessary biological means to provide stability', the human organism, quite unlike the Romantic hero, seeks social *order* to ward off chaos. 'One may say that the biologically intrinsic world-openness of human existence is always, and indeed must be, transformed by social order into a relative world-closedness'. Nonetheless, social order is an on-going production of human action. 'Both in its genesis (social order is the result of past human activity) and its existence in any instant of time (social order exists only in and in so far as human activity continues to produce it) it is a human product.'[50]

(2) Institutionalisation: 'All human activity is subject to habitualisation. Any action that is repeated frequently becomes cast into a pattern, which can then be reproduced with an economy of effort and which, *ipso facto*, is apprehended by its performer *as* that pattern.' Thus a person A, alone on a desert island, having learned to draw fire from twigs, wood and a piece of stone will habitualise the process until it becomes 'second nature' to him. Habitualisation makes it unnecessary for man to define each situation anew every time he meets it.

'Institutionalisation occurs whenever there is a reciprocal typification of habitualised actions by types of actors.' In other words, if A is now joined on his island by B, the latter will soon observe the daily similarity of A's actions in making fire, and will be able to attribute motives in seeing A use the fire each day to cook food. Thus actions which are at first strange are quickly reduced to trivial 'normality', and become part of B's taken-for-granted view of the world. Similarly A will in due course no longer be terrified by the initially disturbing observation of B hunting, killing and slicing up birds and animals. Not only will these actions become ritualised and trivial. They will also become the basis for role-taking. A and B will begin to see each other as encumbents of specific roles: B hunts and prepares the food, A lights the fire and cooks it. Prediction of the other's activity—and, therefore of interaction—becomes possible. Psychologically this is beneficial, since a world reduced to more and more taken-for-granted routines is no longer a source of astonishment and fear. And economically the division of labour releases energy for innovation, and thus further habitualisation. The significant point that Berger and Luckmann are making is that, during this reciprocal process of observation, attribution of motives, typification and ordered action, A and B are *constructing* a world. Moreover, though this construction may soon become 'taken-for-granted', it remains transparent to them. They can understand the world that they themselves have made in the course of a shared biography that they can remember.

When A and B have children, however, all this begins to change, since what were the *ad hoc* conceptions of two individuals, now become *historical* institutions. For the children, the world of their parents becomes *the* world. A transmitted world cannot be so easily transparent. The world 'thickens' and 'hardens' into something not subjectively constructed, but objectively 'there', a facticity. 'To take the most important item of socialisation, language appears to the child as inherent in the nature of things, and he cannot grasp the notion of its conventionality. A thing *is* what it is called, and it could not be called anything else. All institutions appear in the same way, as given, unalterable and self-evident.'[51] Thus is born the paradox that language, institutions, the world produced by man acquires an ontological status apart from the activity which produce them. Man creates the world in a process of externalisation. The world is 'objectivated' during habitualisation and institutionalisation. Finally, it is internalised as a 'facticity' during socialisation. The three processes of 'externalisation', 'objectivation' and 'internalisation' together produce the human dialectic: Society is a human product. Society is an objective reality. Man is a social product.

In this context it becomes clear that to reduce man to a passive cipher where languages and systems of signs interact is to focus arbitrarily on only the last stages of the dialectic. However, it could be argued that the abstraction of the model invalidates it. Society and its conventions pre-date any relationship of A and B we can know, and Berger himself admits that 'society is an historical entity that extends temporally beyond any individual biography . . . society is the walls of our imprisonment in history.'[52]

To this Berger and Luckmann have two different kinds of answer:

(i) As an explanatory strategy the relationship of A and B has significance in reminding us that though it may appear to us as 'facticity', the world is nonetheless man-made.

> No social structure, however massive it may appear in the present, existed in this massivity from the dawn of time. Somewhere along the line each one of its salient features was concocted by human beings, whether they were charismatic visionaries, clever crooks, conquering heroes or just individuals in positions of power who hit on what seemed to them a better way of running the show. Since all social systems were created by men, it follows that men can also change them.[53]

Moreover, for any *one* individual, the process of identity formation is an ongoing activity of creating new 'worlds' and negating old ones. The process never stops.

(ii) the starting assumption that man makes his world encourages us to examine empirically the sociological circumstances in which he does so. Since it is the *alternatives* of action which define man's uniqueness and freedom, the proliferation of alternative roles within one society must expand man's potential for 'deviance'. Modern industrial society has in fact vastly multiplied the number of roles man can, and must, play. At the societal level this is likely to have a subversive effect. As Berger and Luckmann put it,

> In advanced industrial societies, with their immense economic surplus allowing large numbers of individuals to devote themselves full-time to even the obscurest pursuits, pluralistic competition between sub-universes of meaning of every conceivable sort become the normal state of affairs . . . Pluralism encourages both scepticism and innovation and is thus inherently subversive of the taken-for-granted reality of the traditional *status quo*.[54]

For the individual, pluralism of roles is likely to increase awareness of the conventionality of any one of them. Social mobility has become a feature of advanced industrial society enabling many people to sample both the experiences and the associated values of non-ascribed social positions. People in these societies of high mobility, Berger argues, 'seemingly spend years of their life reinterpreting their own background, retelling over and over again (to themselves *and* to others) the story of what they have been and what they have become—and in the process killing their parents in a sacrificial ritual of the mind . . . But what is distinctively modern is the frequency and rapidity with which such reinterpretation often occurs in the lives of many individuals'.[55]

Two theoretical considerations (important to understanding Chekhov) are apparent here:

(a) The model of society which emerges from Berger and Luckmann's analysis displays man as the dramatic interpreter of his part, and not as an empty space activated by codes and conventions. The model does not deny

> that the actors on the stage are constrained by all the external controls set up by the impresario and the internal ones of the role itself. All the same, they have options—of playing their parts enthusiastically or sullenly, of playing with inner conviction or with 'distance', and, sometimes, refusing to play at all . . . The institutions of society, while they do in fact constrain and coerce us, appear at the same time as dramatic conventions, even fictions. They have been invented by past impresarios, and future ones may cast them back into the nothingness whence they emerged.[56]

The self, in a sociological perspective, is not 'given', but 'is rather a process, continuously created and re-created in each social situation that one enters, held together by the slender thread of memory'.[57] Since the self is created continuously in the process of exchanging roles and the related 'constructions of reality', a sociology of man inevitably implies a sociology of knowledge.

Moreover, stress on the interaction of man in terms of a pluralism of world views gives due weight to the potential of systems of thought to 'deconstruct normality'—to act back, in other words, on the world. Instead of the 'mechanistic' Marxian notion of a one-way causality between economic 'base' and ideational 'superstructure', the sociology of knowledge emphasises the role of everyday 'knowledge' in man's ability to distance himself from the 'facticity' of the world. Knowledge, then, re-creates the world that made it. The relationship is dialectical: knowledge is a social product *and* knowledge is a factor in social change.

(b) Emphasis on the alternation of social roles in modern society implies a fuller concern for man's uniqueness and individuality.

(i) The social world is, in the first place, transmitted to the child by parents who have themselves been exposed to a multiplicity of experiences. In mediating the world to the child they modify it according to those experiences.

> They select aspects of it in accordance with their own location in the social structure, and also by virtue of their individual, biographically rooted idiosyncracies . . . Thus the lower class child . . . will not only come to inhabit a world greatly different from that of an upper-class child, but may do so in a manner quite different from the lower-class child next door.[58]

Acceptance of the importance theoretically of this 'double selectivity' (of class and idiosyncratic parental background) enables us to take up, in the analysis of individual writers, Sartre's objection to the simplistic determinism of traditional Marxism, which, he complains, is unable to explain why *this* bourgeois, Flaubert, wrote *these* particular books, and not those of the Goncourt brothers.

> Marxism has nothing to say about this all-important phrase: 'to belong to the Bourgeoisie'. Children are not born at the age when they earn their first wages or own their capital and exploit their first worker. The child does not experience his alienation and reification first of all in the course of his own work but in the course of the work of his parents . . . like all families, that of Flaubert was a particular family, and it was in the face of the particular contradictions of this family that Flaubert served his apprenticeship as a bourgeois.[59]

(ii) The understanding of modern man as a being wrestling with a multiplicity of roles foregrounds the problem of socialisation and individualism. In the first place, there is the problem of consistency between succeeding phases of socialisation. Secondary socialisation always has to work on an already existing 'internalisation' of the world (the process of primary socialisation). The quite considerable chance that the modern child will try to internalise contradictory values to those of his parents during secondary socialisation raises the problem of unsuccessful or ambivalent socialisation. The relationship between the parents' choices which determined the value transmitted during primary socialisation and the potential sets of choices available to the child facing further socialisation is an important aspect of the *particularity* of any one individual which Sartre is concerned with. Secondly, the disparate possibilities of the modern world may face the individual at *both* stages of socialisation in the form of competing groups of 'significant others'. An important example of this at the primary level is the case of many Russian writers in the nineteenth century who were influenced by the alternative values of their class and of the peasants who brought them up. An example at the stage of further socialisation, which we will consider below is the competition of discrete reference groups associated with simultaneous dual roles—in Chekhov's case as writer and doctor.

In all of these cases unsuccessful socialisation may result from the interaction of 'acutely discrepant worlds'. And, as Berger and Luckmann put it, the 'possibility of "individualism" (that is, of individual choice between discrepant realities and identities) is directly linked to the possibility of unsuccessful socialization'.[60]

I have argued at some length elsewhere that Chekhov's aesthetic as a writer was profoundly positivist.[61] To put it another way, Chekhov never found an acceptable literary reference group (or literary identity) which could impinge upon the strength of his attachment to current medical values. Hence it was these latter values which organised his conception of literary 'authenticity'. However, this was no simple problem. As I have also suggested elsewhere,[62] the values he associated with his theatrical and literary peers—subservience to authority and other people's ideas, cynicism and brutality to inferiors, mysticism, hypocrisy, injustice—were also those which had patterned his *own* primary socialisation, as the son of his father. This earlier cluster of organising values, which he had consciously suppressed during secondary socialisation as a medical student (Berger's 'killing of parents in a sacrificial ritual of the mind'), was endlessly with him as a writer, as any consideration of his many 'who am I, and for whom do I write?' letters will show. For most of his life he continued to worry about his 'son of a serf' connection which, he believed, vitiated his 'art' in the early play, *Ivanov*.

There was, then, sufficient uncertainty about the interaction of Chekhov's two roles to prevent his complete identification with either one of them. He had, in Berger's sense, sufficient 'role-distance' to ponder, not so much on the 'human condition', as on the nature of 'role' itself. In a sense the tension between his roles *became the subject of his art*;[63] and *that* was the scope of his individualism. Further, the tension between his primary and secondary socialisation (translated, as I have said, from one of biographical succession to one of simultaneity), the tension between ascriptive and achievement-oriented roles was, as we shall see in the next chapter, precisely the central tension of Russia itself in the second half of the nineteenth century. By playing out this tension through the mediation of his literary identity crisis, Chekhov was relating the most intimate and personal features of his life with the most global. It is *this* dynamic between 'the man', 'the artist' and the social structure which we know as 'Chekhov'.

There are a number of aesthetic issues which follow from this that there is no space to develop here.[64] What I do want to stress at this point is more strictly sociological: that the concepts of role alternation in modern society, 'double selectivity', discrepant reference groups, ambivalent and unsuccessful socialisation which I believe to be central to understanding Chekhov, have two important implications for the structuralist analysis which follows. On the one hand, the continuous tension between individual biography and social group which makes up the socialisation process creates, at the same time, an *active subject* who is much more than the structural linguists' intersection point of determining codes. On the other hand, individualism (and therefore 'creativity') in the sense developed here has nothing to do with the 'autonomous subject', but with the dialectic of man and society.

Thus far we have been discussing some of the differences of assumption underlying contemporary forms of structuralism and the sociology of knowledge. Is there any way of bringing the two theoretical perspectives together?

Clearly, some of the differences *are* fundamental, particularly over the notion of the 'subject'. However, there is one version of structuralism which *could* be developed within a sociology of knowledge framework—the genetic structuralism developed by Lucien Goldmann. Goldmann calls it *genetic* structuralism because he discovers the genesis of literature in the interaction of social groups, and not within its own formal structure. This sociological orientation of Goldmann's places him at the margins of contemporary structuralism, dominated as it has been by the study of language. But by the same token, it relates him more closely to the sociology of knowledge tradition. There are a number of features in common:

(a) For Goldmann art works are products of an inter-subjective process—the interaction of individuals with social groups (he speaks of the 'trans-individual subject'). However, Goldmann's specific formulation of structuralism develops the sociology of knowledge within a Marxian framework which differs in certain essentials from the perspective I have used. Following the Marxian distinction between 'actual' and 'potential' class consciousness, Goldmann distinguishes the uniqueness and creativity of the 'privileged individual' who is the artist (or philosopher) by his ability to derive the purest 'essence' (potential consciousness) from the day-by-day, frequently contradictory, ideas, aspirations and emotions (actual consciousness) of his social group or class. Since the individual group or class cannot go beyond the ultimate coherence of its own world view without entering the plane of quite another class, there is a natural closure to the possibilities of any artist's consciousness. His uniqueness can thus be defined in terms of his mediation between the actual (often 'reactionary') consciousness of his own class and the authentic expression of the progressive class which will replace it. Something very similar to this notion can be seen in the familiar Soviet interpretation of Chekhov as the champion of the small man, close to but not quite within the proletarian consciousness. This understanding of Chekhov as a progressive of the 'Not Yet' (Lukacs), relies on a deterministic notion of history which I cannot accept, and which finds no place in my analysis. I believe the concepts which I have described above—internalisation, socialisation, role distance, 'double selectivity', and so on—to be more useful in accounting for the unique clarity and coherence of Chekhov's position *within* his social group.

(b) Goldmann's work (and that of his few followers) has been especially concerned with social mobility, identity crisis and the creation of 'knowledge'. Thus, as in the sociology of knowledge of Berger and Luckmann, a central concern is with man reconstructing his world during the crisis of role alternation. For example, in his major work, *The Hidden God*, Goldmann accounts for the world view of Racine's plays according to a Jansenist 'tragic vision', itself related homologously to the fall from grace and power of the noblesse de robe at the court of Louis XIV. Similarly, Roger Pincott, analysing the dramas of Aeschylus has accounted for the new construction of reality, a 'tragic vision', according to the downward mobility of a privileged aristocratic group in Athens in the fifth century (B.C.).[65] This notion of social mobility, marginality, and new constructions of reality will be a central one in this book.

(c) As a sociologist Goldmann rejected what he called the 'elimination of the psychological and sociological subject' (and with it, he believed, 'history' and diachronic analysis) at the hands of structural linguistics. Like Berger and Luckmann, Goldmann had a humanist notion of man as the creator of his world, of man as defined by his possibilities, and yet continuously threatened by the world as 'facticity'. In arguing with Barthes, Goldmann insisted that by pushing the determining nature of language too far, linguists exaggerated the determined nature of man. It was true that man did not pre-exist language; but equally true that his language did not pre-exist man. The *dialectical* relation of these two moments was the significant fact, not the one-sided determination of one by the other: 'there is still an I who *becomes*'.[66]

So Goldmann's genetic structuralism can be incorporated in, and be extended by, the sociology of knowledge. But is it genuinely structuralist? The structuralist approach, as Culler sees it, is founded on the insight that social and cultural phenomena are 'defined by a network of relations, both internal and external'. Structuralism is based 'in the first instance' on the understanding that for human actions or productions to have a meaning there must be an underlying system of distinctions which makes that meaning possible. 'The object is itself structured and is defined by its place in the structure of the system, whence the tendency to speak of "structuralism".'[67] This double articulation of structure—both within the object under analysis, and in its relationship with a greater structure—is significant at every level, from the relationship of phonological marks within a language to the global relationship of complete works within an entire social system (which is the level at which Goldmann works). Genetic structuralism is, as I have already said, sociological in its understanding of human products and objects in terms of a wider structure (group, class and social system). Most sociological and Marxist analyses of artistic products are 'structuralist' in terms of the second part of Culler's definition. What is unique to genetic structuralism, in comparison for example with the Marxist interpretations of literature by Lukacs, is its *equal* concern for the first part of the definition: 'the object is itself structured'. It is worth comparing Goldmann's approach with Culler's own basic principles of a structuralist approach to see how far it fulfills them.

(a) Since meaning is dependent on underlying systems of distinctions, structuralism proceeds on the assumption that it is 'possible to break down larger units into their constituents until one eventually reaches a level of minimal functional distinctions'.

(b) By this process a grid of units will be exposed, in syntagmatic relations with each other, and each, at the same time, in a paradigmatic relationship with any other units that might be put in its place.

(c) Thus the emphasis of a structuralist analysis is not on the substantive characteristics of independent entities (e.g. specific characters in a plot), but on the functional *relationship* between items. 'The notion of relational identity is crucial to the semiotic or structural analysis of all kinds of social and cultural phenomena, because in formulating the rules of the system one must identify the units on which the rules operate and thus must discover when two objects or actions count as instances of the same unit'.[68]

Two examples which Culler takes from among the classical works of structural analysis will make this more clear. In his analysis of Russian folk tales, Propp argued that if you take a motif of the plot, such as 'a dragon kidnaps the king's daughter', one has a syntagmatic chain of elements which make up a certain kind of action which can be differentiated from other kinds of action. But the sequence can also be considered in terms of its paradigmatic relations, since the motif can be broken down into four elements, each of which can be substituted without altering the plot. 'The dragon could be replaced by a witch, a giant, or any other villainous force; the daughter by anything beloved; the king by other fathers or possessors, and kidnapping by any version of disappearance'.[69] Thus Propp was able to break down apparently independent and specific themes of content into sets of minimal functional distinctions, according to profound syntagmatic and paradigmatic relations.

Similarly, in his analysis of Racine, Roland Barthes looked for relations and oppositions rather than substantive features or themes . . . Thus when he maintains that there are three formal 'spaces' in Racine, the Chamber or seat of power, the Anti-Chamber where characters wait and confront one another and the Outside, which is the locus of death, flight and events, the claim is not that each of the plays contains, specifically, a chamber and an anti-chamber and no other spaces but the outside world. The claim is rather that the two oppositions, between the actual seat of power and the space where people talk, and between the place where characters are isolated and the external world which exists only potentially as a space where other things happen, have a central function in producing the tragic situation. The space in which characters find themselves is, functionally, an Anti-Chamber: 'trapped between the world, the place of action, and the Chamber, the place of silence, the Anti-Chamber is the place of language' whose enclosure enforces the tragic destiny . . . . The contrast which produces the dramatic situation and defines the roles of the protagonists is the opposition between he who weilds authority and he who is subject to it. These functions . . . are not defined by identity of substance but by the presence of an opposition which is taken to be functional in the system as a whole.[70]

Despite analysing from a different perspective (historical and sociological as against Barthes' linguistic and psychoanalytical approach), Lucien Goldmann's own study of Racine adopts similar structuralist principles.

(a) He reduces the diffuse themes, plots and characterisation of Racine's tragedy's to a set of minimal functional distinctions. As with Barthes, he finds three fundamental units in Racine's works:

(i) the world, which, in the absence of values greater than individual selfishness and isolation, is totally 'degraded';

(ii) a hidden God, who is both absent from the world (in so far that man cannot have any theoretical certainty that he exists) and present (in the realisation of certain men that a 'totality' greater than the compromising and inauthentic values of the world must be insisted on);

(iii) the tragic hero, characterised by a realisation that the world cannot be changed to reveal any terrestrial 'authenticity', yet at the same time, in the absence of God, by the understanding that the world cannot be left behind while the hero seeks refuge in the city of God. Admitting only the clarity of absolute and unambiguous values, yet placed between a blind world and a hidden God, the tragic hero upholds human authenticity in the moment of conversion to an 'essential existence' (associated with the tragic death) when he finally refuses to accept the limitations of the world.[71]

(b) These fundamental units are then analysed in terms of their paradigmatic relations throughout Racine's corpus, since out of the many different kinds of absent value, heroes, heroines and actions in his works, 'objects or actions which count as instances of the same unit' are disclosed.

(c) Goldmann also analyses these units in terms of their syntagmatic relationship within and between plots, and shows that the existence of the tragic universe within a text depends on the specific three part chain in which they are opposed. Thus he claims that in *Bajazet*, unlike the pure tragedies, *Britannicus*, *Bérénice* and *Phèdre*, the absence of one of the units of the chain must alter the meaning of the other units, since they *only* have meaning in relation to each other.

For the Triad of God-Man-the World . . . constitute a coherent whole, in which a change in any one of the three must inevitably produce changes in the two others . . . But, in this Triad God-Man-the World it is perhaps the third element which undergoes the deepest change in *Bajazet*. In the three earlier tragedies there was an infinite and qualitative difference between the world and the hero. Faced with the absolute purity of tragic man, for whom there are no relative values, the world which did not satisfy his ethical demands became a purely negative reality . . . . The situation inevitably changes as soon as the hero tries to reconcile himself with the world and live in it. His increased closeness to the world necessarily affects the structure of the play's universe. As the human level of the hero sinks, the moral level of the world rises, and the qualitative difference is replaced by a difference of degree. If the hero is no longer wholly good, then the world is no longer wholly evil, and they finally completely coalesce in *Mithridate*.[72]

Thus though there are Gods and heroes in *Bajazet*, they betray the presence of quite another genre—the 'historical play', not tragedy.

In the former the structure is characterised by a fusion of the hero, the world and the Gods; in the latter, by their opposition. I have quoted Goldmann at length here because it is a clear example of the emphasis of structuralist analysis on the functional relationship between distinct minimal units (here at the level of theme), and not on independent items of content (e.g. the 'content' Gods of *Bajazet* are reduced to more fundamental units and related to other minimal units of the genre's structure).

It would seem, then, that a sociological structuralism can be a genuinely structuralist undertaking by Culler's own definition, and it is this kind of structuralism (a subsumption of Goldmann's genetic structuralism within the sociology of knowledge) which will be adopted in the analysis of Chekhov. Like Goldmann, I discovered three minimal units underlying the complete corpus I studied:

(i) once again, a fundamentally degraded world—the hierarchical world of the 'autocratic-bureaucratic' regime, characterised by relations of brutality and subservience, ascription and mysticism, and the misuse of science;

(ii) the epic visionary, characterised by an understanding of the *historical and material* possibility of an authentic world, but constantly overburdened by existential pressures. In the absence of any possibility of sudden conversion to the new epic world, the only authenticity of the epic visionary is the suffering of endurance and the 'hope that when we lie at rest in our graves we may see visions, which may even be pleasant ones' (*Uncle Vanya*);

(iii) the inauthentic hero, distinguished from the people of the degraded world in his choice to reject its boredom and depravity, and distinguished from the epic visionary in the inauthentic nature of that choice.

These minimal units are only meaningful in relation to each other—for example, the inauthentic hero has dramatic point only in relation to the authentic position he neglects, and to the world he rejects but which inevitably claims him in the end. Though all three elements may not be evident in every work of Chekhov (*Peasants*, for example, portrays explicitly only the degraded world), no work can be meaningfully separated from their chain of relationships. Even in *Peasants* the depravity of the world is *characterised* in terms of what it lacks—education, the potential for rejection, choice and authenticity.[73]

As well as examining the distributional relations of these elements in terms of their rules of combination (opposition *and* ongoing interpenetration of epic vision, degraded world and inauthentic choice), it will also be important to identify all the actions and characterisations which together constitute the paradigm for any one unity. For example, inauthentic heroes are, at the level of content, of many varied types in Chekhov's works: bored young provincial women who reject the world and break out traumatically, but only into the arms of empty bureaucrats personifying the degraded world; scientists and doctors who despise the world but, despite their potential to change it, are sucked back into it by their egotism, materialism and desire for power; artists who, sick of the vulgarity of the world's conventions, seek new forms, but end up painting landscapes of the world they reject; intellectuals who, sickened by the injustice of the world, take its weight upon their shoulders through empathy and emotion, and are crushed by it. Each of these can be chosen in a particular work to provide variations of plot and theme, but they are all members of the one paradigm which is in a functional relation with the other units of the structure.

The analysis of the internal structure of Chekhov's works will thus be synchronic in the sense that Culler has defined the term: the 'attempt to reconstruct the system as a functional whole'. Culler points out the importance of synchronic study to structural analysis since it 'constitutes a break with the notion of historical and evolutionary identity'. The latter, diachronic, kind of analysis must be kept strictly separate lest it falsify the synchronic analysis. 'For example, historically the French noun "pas" (step) and the negative adverb "pas" derive from the single source.' But, 'To try to incorporate the historical identity into one's grammar would be to falsify the relational identity and hence the value that each of the words has in the language as now spoken. Language is a system of interrelated items and the value and identity of these items is defined by their place in the system rather than by their history.'[74] A similar contrast between diachronic and synchronic analysis can be made in the case of Chekhov's *Ivanov* between those critics who trace the characteristics of Ivanov within the line of 'superfluous men' in Russian literature and my own analysis which suggests that the identity and value of Ivanov in the play is derived from his place in its structure (i.e. the minimal unit 'inauthentic hero') and not from his historical identity.

But while agreeing with Culler that synchronic and diachronic analysis must be considered separately, I cannot accept the exclusion of the latter altogether from structural analysis, since that would be to suppress history and the active subject.

The portrayal of Ivanov *objectively* (and not, like other writers, 'instinctively') *empirically* (as an example of 'life as it is') and *typically* (as a deviation from the norm of physical, mental and social health) is, as I have shown elsewhere,[75] a convenient summation of Chekhov's literary method. It is at the same time, however, significantly related to Chekhov's world view as a doctor. Here I am arguing for a diachronic analysis, separate from, but at the same time *explaining*, the synchronic relations in the text.

I will conclude with a summary of what has been, inevitably, a complicated argument. In this section I have introduced Barthes' typology for the analysis of literary systems, and have suggested that while every level of the typology still requires appropriate analysis in the case of Chekhov, the specific contribution of the sociologist will be at the level of the connotative signified. In particular, I will be concerned with structural analysis of Chekhov's works mainly in terms of the *form* of the signified (form of expression) a level which is almost entirely unexplored in the case study of any writer. However, I have also suggested that Barthes' notion of ideology operating at this level is inadequate to the understanding of literature in terms of process and interaction. Writing, like life itself, should be considered as a dialectical process of externalisation, institutionalisation, and internalisation, of the writer (in his various roles), his society, and his conventions. Genetic structuralism will take us some of the way towards this fuller analysis, without neglecting the basic premises of a structuralist perspective. However, genetic structuralism itself needs to be considered within the framework of the sociology of knowledge if due weight is to be given to the specificity of the individual writer. This established, we can turn to a deeper analysis of the life and art of Anton Chekhov.

3 Chekhov the Doctor

In chapter 1, I suggested that attempts by literary critics to relate writers and societies, where attempted, have generally foundered because their analysis of the social context of works has not been systematic. In chapter 2, in considering the issue of structuralism, I suggested the particular level of the relationship between text and society at which the analysis of this book will be operating, and introduced the reader to the theoretical framework within which the structural analysis is set. Both these suggestions from the first two chapters posited the need for a properly *sociological* understanding; and it will be the task of the present chapter to provide that understanding of Chekhov's social context.

There can be no short cuts here. It is simply not enough to infer from a few fragmentary statements that Chekhov was, or was not, committed to medicine as a career and as a world view. Nor is it satisfactory to heap a little bit of Chekhovian medical wisdom on an otherwise discrete artistic vision—a knowledge of psychology here, a 'clinical' clarity there. What precisely do we *mean* by 'a professional doctor's world view'? Our answer in this chapter will certainly involve an essay in the sociology of professionalism. Further, what was *unique* about medical professionalism in Russia at this time? Surprisingly little has been written about this; historians of the period having been more interested in tsars and revolutionaries. Finally, what *evidence* is there to suggest that Chekhov held this particular world view? The chapter needs to be sociologically systematic because it seeks to demonstrate conclusively that an historically specific medical perspective was *essentially* the basis of Chekhov's world view, determining, as later chapters will show, the *structural coherence* of his works.

An important assumption of Goldmann's 'world view' approach is that the structural configuration of a work functions in a rather *direct* way to express a social group's reaction to historical change. According to Goldmann, world views are, on the one hand, the expression of the concepts, actions, aspirations and feelings bind-ing together the members of a social group in a common 'psychic structure' in opposition to other social groups.[1] On the other hand, they account for the inner coherence of the text. Thus, as Goldmann sees it, a series of transformations take place between the social structure and the textual structure. In the first place, significant works of art frequently appear at moments of social and political crisis, since it is then that men tend to become acutely aware of their relationship to the external world. Secondly, it is the quality of the significant artist to embody with coherence and clarity his social group's *essential* perception of the change. Thirdly, this 'world view', which hitherto existed only as an abstraction of 'potential consciousness', becomes *form* as the internal structure of a literary work.

It will be noted that Goldmann's definition of a social group is in terms of *struggle* and conflict with other social groups. This is important, since by avoiding a harmonious or 'organic' model of social interaction, he also avoids a gross and static analysis of literature as expressing (in the sense of passively *reflecting*) the 'spirit of an age'. Instead, he emphasises the importance of the dialectical interaction of material circumstances and human consciousness in creating the world within a nexus of inter-class conflict (though, as I suggested earlier, he does collapse the interaction of individual and society beneath notions of group determinism).

However, if this stress on art works as social *action* seems to escape the tendency to circular argument of 'reflection' theories (where art is said to reflect its age, which, in turn, is in part defined *through* its art), in fact it only transfers the problem to another level. If art works express the 'essential' perception of a social group or class, how do we define, independently of the works, what that essence is? As Richard Wollheim has argued,[2] sociological explanation of art of this kind must not only show the connection of the work with the various expressive manifestations of the group, but must demonstrate that these expressions are *intrinsic* to the group as such.

Goldmann's attempt to meet this problem by asserting a *homological* relationship between the various structural levels is not entirely convincing. There is a danger (which Goldmann does not avoid) of the analyst projecting a structure which he finds within a corpus of work onto the wider social infrastructure (or vice-versa): in which case 'homologies' are little more than intellectual abstractions in the sociologist's own mind.

For example, one of Goldmann's central homologies in *The Hidden God* is the parallel between, on the one hand, the tragic vision of 'essential' Jansenism (that of Pascal and Racine) according to which man must remain in the world (because the existence of God is no more than a wager) yet at the same time refuse the world (which is inauthentic and degraded), and, on the other hand, the double-bind situation of the noblesse de robe who had to remain in the world (because as officiers they were dependent on the King) yet opposed the world (in which they were being irreversibly outmoded by the new intendents). The homology is attractively elegant, but rests on a number of questionable assumptions. For instance, even if the increasing centralisation of the monarchy was inevitable (and that is *very* questionable), it is by no means clear that the 'essential' response of the noblesse de robe was the Jansenist 'tragic vision' which Goldmann finds in the works of Pascal and Racine. Rather, the 'typical' strategy might have been for the officers themselves to become members of the new centralised bureaucracy (and Goldmann admits that *most* of them did this). Or, it might have been to side with the class reaction of the Third Estate, from which the noblesse de robe had originally come (and from which many historians, including some Marxists, do not distinguish them at this stage). Moreover, it has been pointed out that more of the noblesse de robe were in fact sympathetic to the Jesuits than to the Jansenists—a problem which Goldmann responded to by arguing that the 'essential' values of a group are often carried by a minority. Possibly so, but hardly proven in this case. Goldmann does say that his analysis of the noblesse de robe was no more than a preliminary and tentative hypothesis, and that 'the only thing which can decide which is the significant structure in any one particular case is empirical research'. But it is research he never in fact followed up, while meanwhile placing a heavy weight of interpretation upon it.

The search for values intrinsic to a group will become more systematic if, instead of resorting to 'homology of structure', we analyse the values into which members of a group are in fact *socialised*. This will, of course, mean dropping some of the essential distinctions which Goldmann makes between actual and potential consciousness, but does not necessarily reduce the art work to the 'average' expression of a group or class (there are other ways, as we saw in chapter 2, of understanding the special acuteness and coherence of vision of the artist in relation to his social group). In taking this alternative approach, we can draw on a much more empirically based area of sociology—socialisation within the family, occupational consciousness and professional ideology. Here, a specific value system depends less on 'homology' than on competing constructions of the world within an arena of social conflict and exchange.

I have claimed that the values which structure Chekhov's works were essentially those of the contemporary medical profession. To justify this claim, I have to do more than show that Chekhov was trained in medicine, and that (despite many critics' assertions to the contrary) he was seriously involved in medical affairs until the end of his active life. These things are important: but I have to prove too that the *specific* medical values which he internalised as a student continuously and fundamentally organised his perception of the world.[3] And I also have to show how this perception established the thematic structure in his literary works. This will be the task of the remaining chapters. In the first place I intend to analyse *independently*[4] of his works, the values which structured Chekhov's literature.

*   *   *   *   *

There is a substantial sociological literature which we can draw on to analyse the intrinsic values of a professional group. But there are also some initial difficulties. A good deal of the so-called 'sociology' of the professions does little more than add up, quite unsystematically, a list of 'typical' attributes said to be inherent, at all times and in all places, within the professions. This listing approach is blindly a-historical. Or, more precisely, it isolates what appear to be typical features of a narrow range of professions located in recent or contemporary *capitalist* societies, and project these traits as essential in all kinds of society. This is not only to give a spurious significance and universalism to culturally-bound norms and values, but also, since the 'essential' traits are more often than not those which the professional practitioners themselves isolate, is to underpin professional ideologies.

An alternative to the listing approach is to analyse professionalism from within a specific theoretical perspective. There are, of course, a number of these, even within sociology; so to avoid the charge of selecting my theory to fit my evidence, I intend to draw on *several* of the main ones which have been central in the literature.[5] If Chekhov can be shown to adhere to the identity, attributes and values of professionalism according to *all* these

perspectives. I shall consider the first part of my case conclusively
demonstrated.

'Professionalism' (following Terence Johnson[6]) I shall take to be
that specific mode of professional control based ultimately on
occupational authority (as against direct control from another social
group or institution). The perspectives which will be used to analyse
professionalism are:

(i) a 'functionalist' perspective, which relates professionalisation to the *division of labour* intrinsic to modern societies;

(ii) a 'symbolic interactionist' perspective which explores the
career constituents out of which the individual professional constructs his *identity*;

(iii) an historical perspective which, following Thomas Kuhn,[7]
explores professionalism in terms of the development of *scientific
paradigms*;

(iv) a 'conflict' perspective, which analyses professionalism in its
ideological context, as part of the struggle for power between rival
groups and classes.

I

The rise of professionalisation has been associated almost universally in the literature with industrialisation. A more complex
division of labour, it is said, assured the differentiation of roles in
industrial society and the emergence of specialised occupational
skills. This accounted for a new demarcation of the professional role,
in which the doctor's close attachment to the classes which could
afford to pay him was replaced by a degree of autonomy. According
to MacIver, each profession became, at this time, 'a functional
group in a society whose tendency is to organize itself less and less in
terms of territory, race or hereditary status, and more and more in
terms of function'.[8]

As a corollary, the division of labour ensured the replacement of
the patron, whose values and culture the doctor had once adopted,
by the 'ignorant layman' who was highly vulnerable to exploitation.
'Functionalist' sociologists, such as Talcott Parsons, have shown
how fundamental aspects of professional organisation, such as the
control of training and an apparently altruistic code of ethics, are
related to this new demarcation of the doctor/patient situation, in so
far as they protect the latter from his ignorance. They assure the

patient of an 'honest' and scientifically competent service in critical areas of human concern. In return, the patient offers the doctor a unique status in terms of prestige, material rewards and a carefully prescribed physical intimacy. According to the functionalist, 'professionalisation' is equivalent to the striking of a bargain which integrates the roles of doctor and patient in a reciprocal way: unique status is accorded to the professional in return for unique services. Crucially, then, professionalisation occurs when there is a service/ status bargain depending on the emergence of new functional roles.

This broadly functionalist approach does, however, pose a number of theoretical problems. In the first place the notion of a producer/consumer bargain as a response to the division of labour tends to suggest a *natural* reciprocal relationship based on an *equal* position of power; whereas the profession, by exploiting what is, in effect, a relationship based on uncertainty, may well be able to establish the 'contract' in a more unilateral manner. Secondly, the notion of a contract between the occupational group and society tends to suggest that *all* classes in society gain in the same degree from the relationship, which is clearly not the case.[9] However, while keeping these reservations in mind, it still seems to be the case that the functionalist perspective applies a little better to doctors than to some other professions, since medicine is seen, in all modern societies, as a uniquely significant service and does, by and large, have a society-wide, fully heterogeneous public. It is in fact precisely because it provides such a crucial service to such a wide clientele that the profession has a functional power not so readily accessible to most other occupational groups.

A third problem is that the belief that industrialisation inevitably *precedes* professionalisation seems to be based on the assumption, true of certain western societies only, that industrialisation and modernisation go together. As David Apter has shown,[10] modernisation and the development of new roles can occur *before* the industrial infrastructure. Indeed, for Apter, the growth of career roles, 'professionalism', is fundamental to the concept of modernisation itself. Whereas he defines industrialisation according to the development of roles specifically related to the manufacturing process, modernisation is an aspect of development which takes place predominantly in non-industrial societies, and is related to the growth of career roles inclined to an ideology of rationalism and the scientific method. For Apter, then, it is the modernising society which is the professionalising society (and it may, in addition, be the case that 'professionalism' is incompatible with the demands of corporate industrialism). This is to put the emergence of new roles, on which the functionalist case depends, into a more specific historical context.

Tsarist Russia in the second half of the nineteenth century was a modernising society of Apter's type. The emancipation of the serfs around the middle of the century led to the creation of new functions within the new rural administrative units, the zemstva. Long before the beginnings of large scale industrialisation in the 1890s, new service functions become available, because the abolition of bondage suddenly threw the peasants onto the mercy of the local authorities. Three important features of this new functional space for professionals should be noted:

(i) The zemstvo reforms were carved out of a dispute between the Tsar and the liberal gentry,[11] who were seeking wide-ranging reforms at the national level which would signal their independence from autocratic control. The Tsar in turn bought off the gentry by conceding greater local control than he had intended in two crucial areas: education and medicine. It was out of this 'accident' that the relative autonomy of the medical profession was to grow. The zemstva, in fact, took over from the assemblies of gentry as a basis for political liberalism in Russia, thereby providing a focus for aspiring and idealistic medical students (who, until then, had often eschewed a medical career altogether rather than sink into attachment to the aristocracy). The new zemstvo service role was clearly an environment of great public need where universalistic ideals could be directed to practical tasks. If, as MacIver suggests, one sign of professionalisation is when 'activity of service replaces passivity of station', and when educated men move from a culture of patronage to one of functional specificity of competence, then this was certainly taking place among Russian zemstvo doctors who, by a conscious decision, rejected the class nature of 'city medicine'.

(ii) Although new functional space was emerging in Russia, facilitating professionalisation and decreasing alienation among aspiring doctors, it was at the same time heavily circumscribed by political, economic and social factors. On the one hand, government suspicion necessitated a constant struggle by doctors to preserve the measure of autonomy the reforms had given them. On the other hand, because economic and social maturation was extremely slow in Russia (at least until the 1890s) rapid social mobility was more or less *confined* to the professions. As a result, an aspiring and idealistic professional class was faced with a weak, backward and vulgar trading class, and, beyond that, an ignorant peasantry which as often as not totally ignored professional advice. Hence professionals could feel politically victimised *and* encounter social isolation and a considerable degree of job frustration all at the same time. By vocation, zemstvo doctors often exiled themselves to cultureless rural areas where superstition, ignorance, lack of visible rewards, and a general stagnation defeated much of their professional endeavour.

(iii) I noted earlier that medicine and education were the two areas of potential autonomy which emerged from the zemstvo reforms. Any hint, however, of local or professional participation, let alone leadership, in *educational* matters led to nervous reactions from the government. From 1874 the Ministry of National Education assumed control of teacher education and heavily restricted zemstvo supervision of teachers and school boards. The official state policy was to ensure that 'not one talent will be lost to the country or turn out harmful to society'.[12] 'Enlightening' courses for teachers were discouraged on the grounds that they 'encourage them to think for themselves, an activity incompatible with the modest position of primary schoolteachers'.[13]

The repressive part of the policy seems to have been supremely successful. Alston remarks that 'after 1871, the majority of teachers in both the gymnasiums and the realschulen remained petty officials of the educational bureaucracy'.[14] Constant government supervision of pedagogical associations (which were only allowed at the primary level anyway), appalling material conditions for teachers, and the lack of any institutional or social basis for education as a distinct and autonomous discipline, made any real professionalisation impossible. The Moscow Pedagogical Society, which Alston sees as a 'turning point in the development of the secondary teachers as a self-aware professional class', was not founded until 1899, and improvement was slow thereafter.[15] This greater bureaucratic suspicion of the 'science' of education than that of medicine ensured that of the two areas of potential autonomy squeezed from the Tsar during the reforms, it was only that of medicine which was able to achieve professionalism in Chekhov's time. Thus even *within* the ranks of 'professionals' zemstvo doctors were isolated.

What I have been analysing here is the 'social space' in which professionalism developed in Russia, and it remains to see what

Chekhov's relationship was with this necessary infrastructure of a new career identity. Since this social space had very precise parameters, and was subject to very specific pressures, it will be possible to analyse in detail the degree of Chekhov's identification with it. What I need to show is:

(a) that Chekhov was very closely attached, in work and ideals, to the zemstvo and to its criterion of 'progress' through professional activity (which distinguished its ideals from the more global ones of the 'alienated intelligentsia');

(b) that Chekhov responded to the frustrations of zemstvo ideals, and particularly to the professional isolation of doctors, in a manner typical of the new medical group.

Chekhov spent virtually all his medical career with the zemstvo; and it was, in the words of his friend Dr Al'tschuller, 'under the influence of the zemstvo medical circles that Chekhov became more concerned socially'.[16] Although he respected the moral fervour and ideals of the 'sixties' Chekhov nevertheless identified with the more pragmatic values of zemstvo doctors. In 1890, for example, he wrote to Suvorin: 'if I were given a choice between all the "ideals" of the famous "sixties" on the one hand, or the most wretched zemstvo hospital on the other, I would choose the latter without any hesitation at all'.[17] In fact he worked very hard throughout his active life for the zemstvo, and was quick to defend it from cynical or disillusioned criticism. In 1888 he wrote, 'I do not conceal my respect for the zemstvo, which I love';[18] and both Kurkin and Chlenov[19] emphasises his enormous attachment to zemstvo medicine, and his pride in being a zemstvo doctor. Chlenov comments that Chekhov singled out zemstvo doctors 'from the general mass of doctors and put them on an unreachable height. One only had to say, in Chekhov's presence, something against zemstvo doctors, and he would get cross immediately, and with, for him, unusual severity, say, "drop it; you just don't know zemstvo doctors".'

His high evaluation of zemstvo medicine was not just based on ideals, but also on tough practical experience. The way ahead, he knew, was hard:

Doctors have the most awful days and hours. Heaven forbid anybody going through the experience they do. It is true that it is possible to find coarse and ignorant brutes among them, but then so do you among writers, engineers and the public in general. Yet *only* doctors suffer the frightful days and hours which I mentioned, and for that reason one should, to be fair forgive them a great deal.[20]

But without denying the severity of the task, Chekhov placed his hopes of future success in the progress *already* achieved. Medicine, he writes in 1890, has advanced enormously since the days of the sixties, and he damns everyone—from the socialists to the right wing Suvorin, from Zola to Tolstoi—who abuses it:

> I put my trust in Koch and in Spermine . . . A huge amount has been done . . . Surgery alone has advanced so much that it leaves one bewildered. To the contemporary medical student the period up to twenty years ago seems insignificant.[21]

His high praise for the activity of zemstvo workers and doctors during the cholera campaign of 1892 is in sharp contrast to his frequent criticism of the lazy 'molluscs' among the intelligentsia:

> The doctors and educated people in Nizhni have performed miracles. I am simply overcome with delight when I read about their handling of the cholera. In the old days, when people used to get ill and die in thousands, no one could have dreamed of the great triumphs which are being won right in front of us now. It is a pity you are not a doctor and therefore cannot share my gratification.[22]

All these quotations present a very different Chekhov from the 'innocent-eye-observing-the-mystery-of-things' caricature which I criticised earlier. In fact his optimism in the achievements of social engineering becomes all the more understandable the closer we look at his particular zemstvo background. In his definitive *Médicine du Zemstvo*,[23] Osipov writes that Moscow regional Zemstvo was the most progressive in organising public medicine in Russia at that time; and that it was *Chekhov's own Serpukhov district Zemstvo* which was the most advanced of all the Moscow region. Chekhov, then, was working in perhaps the most forward-looking zemstvo in Russia: a good basis for his optimism.

> Miracles are being performed at the Nizhni Fair which might even make Tolstoi take up a more respectful attitude towards medicine and towards the general participation of educated

people in social life. It looks as if the cholera has been held . . .
In an enormous area like the Moscow region it will not mount
above fifty cases a day, whereas in the Don thousands will catch it
every day. That is an impressive difference. We district zemstvo
doctors are ready. We have a definite programme of action and
may perhaps get the percentage of deaths even lower in our
districts.[24]

Chekhov admired the work of Serpukhov Zemstvo—'the zemstvo people here are intelligent, friendly, educated and active'[25]—
and he certainly worked hard and with great conviction on its
account. In preparation for the cholera epidemic of 1892–4, he
studied in detail both the histories of previous epidemics and the
latest therapeutic and preventive measures. When, on 6 July 1892,
Serpukhov Zemstvo Council asked for his full-time help, he gave it
free of charge, despite his inability as a full-time doctor to make
much out of his writing. Between August and October, 1892, he
controlled an area which covered twenty-six villages around
Melikhovo, where he lived, and saw something over a thousand
patients, as well as sending detailed statistical reports to the sanitary
bureau. In addition, he spent his days travelling, organising
medical points and barracks, delivering lectures on hygiene to the
peasants, looking after sanitation measures at several factories,
schools and a monastery, and all without adequate feldschers and
sanitary workers, or even decent transport. He was also appointed a
member of the Serpukhov Sanitary Committee which he attended
regularly, and delivered reports to it on school and factory
sanitation in his area. The pattern is repeated in 1893—with one
significant addition. At the Twelfth Extra Congress of Moscow
Zemstvo Doctors, Osipov had called for a new observatory in the
Melikhovo area to monitor the migration of disease at an especially
critical point. The observatory was set up, and it was Chekhov who
was asked to supervise it.

During these two years of overwork (vitiated by ill health)
Chekhov knew all the frustrations of a zemstvo doctor: the
bureaucratic and aristocratic disdain of the powerful, the complete
ignorance and resistance of those he had to treat, the long distances
to travel, the loss of sleep, the harsh conditions of work, the
disgusting diseases. Sometimes he writes in despair of medicine; yet
he continued to put it before his writing. In 1892 he wrote to
Suvorin, 'While I serve the zemstvo, don't think of me as a literary

man.'[26] In October 1892 he wrote, 'Life has been nothing but hard work this summer, but I have the feeling now that I have never passed a summer so well'. Partly this was because of his work as a farmer and planter of trees; partly because 'I have served the zemstvo, have presided at the Sanitary Committee and have visited the factories. And I have liked it all.'[27] In January, 1893, the painter Repin wrote to Tolstoi's daughter about Chekhov: 'Isn't he marvellous. Even with his writing work, he doesn't leave medicine. He is a zemstvo doctor with a large practice and huge area, and he is very happy with his activities'.[28]

It was positive experiences like these that reinforced Chekhov's faith in the gradual improvement of life through the application of science, and enabled him to write, near the end of his life, to the medical graduate Bernshtein, 'I wish you every success and satisfaction. Both are perfectly possible for a doctor who believes deeply in his work.'[29] The letter suggests that Chekhov's commitment as a zemstvo doctor was not simply an emergency measure, quickly forgotten: and the evidence supports this. To his years of zemstvo work before and during the epidemic, Chekhov added several years after it. Between 1894 and 1897 he went on working as a zemstvo doctor, carrying out instructions from the Serpukhov medical sanitary organisation, editing its annual reports and sending in medical statistics to the sanitary bureau. He also continued to attend the medical congresses which, *Médicine du Zemstvo* pointed out, 'had such a great importance in the medical development of the zemstvo, in throwing light on the needs of the organisation, in showing means of improving them, and in unifying the ideas of the doctors and their work activities'.[30]

In addition to this zemstvo work, Chekhov maintained a close relationship with leading members of the zemstvo medical movement throughout his later years. The sanitary doctor P. I. Kurkin, one of the founder members of zemstvo medicine and co-author of *Médicine du Zemstvo*, was one of Chekhov's closest friends, and their correspondence suggests their mutual concern for zemstvo work. The distinguished zemstvo psychiatrist, Vladimir Yakovenko who, according to the Soviet *Large Medical Encyclopaedia*,[31] counts as one of the most significant names in Russian science, was another of Chekhov's friends whose psychiatric hospital near Melikhovo the writer often visited. Other zemstvo doctors of considerable standing with whom he had a lasting friendship included Chlenov, Zhbankov, Rossolimo and Vitte. Among leaders of zemstvo medicine who were obvious points of reference for Chekhov were his teacher Erisman, whom Chekhov wrote of with respect,[32] and Osipov, to whom he sent a telegram congratulating him for his twenty-five years of work in the Moscow region. In 1900 Chekhov contributed to a medical prize dedicated to him.

Even after bad health drove Chekhov from the Moscow region, his attachment to zemstvo medicine continued. For example, in November 1898 I. V. Popov, the third co-author of *Médicine du Zemstvo*, sent a telegram to Chekhov at Yalta on behalf of 'his colleagues, the Moscow Zemstvo doctors'; and when Chekhov was elected an honorary Academician in 1900, he wrote with satisfaction that the honour had delighted the Moscow region doctors.[33]

But secure though he was in his attachment to the new functional areas for medical service, Chekhov was acutely aware of the problems of an *isolated* professionalism. The failure to professionalise of the other area of potential zemstvo autonomy, education, was not going to make the task of doctors in communicating with an ignorant peasantry any easier, as the zemstvo physicians were well aware. Chekhov did a lot for local education—building schools out of his own money, planning public collections, acting as a schools examiner, helping to establish public libraries, projecting a statistical analysis of the poor conditions of Serpukhov district schools 'for the use of zemstvo workers'.[34] But he realised that little could be achieved by this piecemeal action. Behind the bad teaching and the continuing cultural backwardness of the provinces there lay the full weight of state policy.

Chekhov understood that education would be bad as long as teachers were unprofessional, as long as they were ignorant of theory, had no autonomy, suffered appalling conditions of service, and had the ideals crushed out of them by an unsympathetic state. The Russian village, Gork'ii recalls Chekhov saying,[35] cried out of its stagnation for an educated teacher. Instead,

Our teacher, for eight or nine months of the year, lives like a hermit: he has no-one to speak to; without company or amusements, he is growing stupid, and if he invites his colleagues to visit him, he becomes politically suspect—a stupid word with which crafty men frighten fools. All this is disgusting; it is the mockery of a man who is doing a great and tremendously important work . . . '

In his literary works, Chekhov portrayed the teachers he *knew*:

frequently ignorant and brutal, and at best absurdly pedantic petty officials. Often he portrays them with humour, but his laughter conveys a serious critique. The timid schoolmaster, Medvedenko, in *The Seagull*, is not simply ridiculous: 'there's me, my mother, my two sisters, my small brother, and my salary is only twenty-three roubles altogether. We have got to eat and drink, haven't we? And then what about tea and sugar? What about tobacco? One has to scrape along and put kopecks by.' In fact he reformulates Chekhov's serious concern for the actual teachers he described to Gork'ii: 'He's married . . . has four children . . . his wife is ill . . . Himself consumptive . . . his salary is twenty roubles'.[36]

It is a noteworthy fact that professional doctors were, both individually and as an organisation, in the forefront of the drive for professionalisation of teachers; and Chekhov's awareness of the *professional* demarcation between doctors and teachers is typical of his group. Like other doctors, he called for more autonomy for teachers, and more scientific knowledge. In place of the teacher-journeyman, 'ill-educated, who goes to the village as though he were going into exile . . . starved, crushed, terrorized'[37] and tied by the state to his school during the holidays, Chekhov suggested that zemstvo teachers should, like doctors, be sent to Moscow during holidays for refresher courses. There they would learn about the applications of science, about horticulture, and the potential of the natural environment: 'Teachers ought to know everything—everything . . . .'[38] It was certainly a far cry from Count Tolstoi's remark that thinking was incompatible with the needs of pedagogy.

II

Most of the perspectives which I adopt in this chapter for analysing essential characteristics of professionalism tend to focus at the macro-level, with a resulting underplaying of the individual professional. Yet professionalism is not *just* a 'functional pre-requisite' of a modernising society, nor yet *merely* a system of occupational and ideological control. It is also integral to the individual practitioner's *concept of himself* as a professional. Sociologists of a 'symbolic interactionist' persuasion would suggest that an individual's concept of himself, whom he really is, what he is like, is 'derived from his perception of the reaction of others to him, especially those reactions that arise in the context of significant situations'.[39]

There are two parts to this definition:

(i) There is the understanding of the self concept as intimately related to *interaction* with others' perception of oneself. The assumption here is that for the regularity and predictability of co-operative social behaviour to be possible, man must first predict, to some extent, the reaction of others—which he can do by empathising with them, and considering his own actions through *their* perspective. The effectiveness of this kind of interaction will, of course, depend on a shared nexus of meanings and symbols. But the significant point is that though this sharing of symbolic 'cues' is culturally transmitted, it nevertheless depends on consistent day-by-day interaction by individuals if the meaning of the social world, and of the self within it, is to remain coherent.

(ii) In many cases—and generally in the case of the more pervasive aspects of the individual's self-image (as, for example, with the highly salient role of doctor)—there are very *specific* others (e.g. the medical profession) acting as a reference group for one's self-concept. Socialisation within the medical group will establish common norms of conduct, values, characteristic attitudes towards professional status and career, etc., which will provide an organised perspective to which the individual doctor may refer with confidence. At the same time it will facilitate his detachment from alternative reference groups by providing an 'in-group' with a culture of its own.[40]

Shibutani's reference group theory suggests that 'common perspective—common cultures—emerge through participation in common communication channels. It is through social participation that perspectives shared in a group are internalised'.[41] And since the boundaries of each social world are set 'neither by territory, nor by formal group membership, but by the limits of effective communication', we can readily understand why institutionalised channels of communication—periodicals, scientific journals and the co-ordinating professional association—are so essential to the professional identity of each practitioner. Without them the self-concept we have associated with professionalism would not be possible.

In Russia these channels of professional communication began to appear for medicine just before and during Chekhov's medical career. The first congress of Russian naturalists and physicians took place in St Petersburg in 1867, and by 1897 there were more than 100 medical-scientific societies. The first congress of zemstvo doctors was in 1871, and by 1905 there had been 298 of them. The journal *Physician*, which was to be a crucial channel of communication for the very widely diffused body of Russian doctors, was founded by Manassein in 1880. The first psychiatric journals, *The Archives of Psychiatry* and *Clinical Psychiatry and Neurology*, were founded in 1883, and the first surgical journal, *The Surgical Messenger*, in 1885.

The professional association which was to be particularly significant in providing a common focus and reference group for zemstvo doctors, the Society of Russian Physicians in Memory of N. I. Pirogov, began life in 1885. It was organised around national congresses and had local branches throughout Russia. The Society co-ordinated the zemstvo tradition of preventive medicine, social welfare and liberal activism. Recognising that no amount of technical improvement in the medical field would improve the lot of the people without large-scale economic and social reform, the Pirogovists actively campaigned in the political as well as the medical field, strongly criticising the government's cautious and static policies. Between 1900 and 1905 there was a distinct 'turn to the Left' among the Pirogovists, culminating in overt demands for universal suffrage, a secret ballot, political freedom, and transfer of the police force to local zemstvo control. The resolution of their 1905 congress claimed that 'Only when these preliminary conditions are met, will it be possible to organise a realistic, planned struggle against national calamities and epidemics; only then will our country be able to conquer plague, cholera and other epidemics.'[42] Despite their increasing radicalism, however, the Pirogovists clung firmly to the *peer group* identity and autonomy typical of professionalism. They were, for instance, as opposed to Bolshevik as to Tsarist control. During Chekhov's lifetime the Pirogovists, acting in a markedly political context, were able to establish a corporate identity and a near monopolistic position for the emerging medical profession, becoming thereby the most significant reference group for progressive doctors.

Professionalism, as Johnson points out, creates occupations with a considerable degree of self-consciousness and 'complete identity'.

The core meaning of life is central to the work situation, and occupational skills are regarded as non-transferable—the property of a specific community . . . That is to say that periods in which it is claimed that charlatanism is rife and needs to be stamped out are just those periods when an occupation is attempting to establish or struggling to maintain a monopolistic position.[43]

The self-concept of the practitioner is, in these circumstances, deeply involved with an upgrading and universalising of skills on the one hand, and equally concerned with denying the legitimacy of alternative skills on the other. We would expect, then, during a period of rising professionalism to see:

(i) a considerable significance accorded to raising the quality of service through improved training, to encouraging research and theoretical advances, to promoting new specialisms—all of which will increase the distance between the supplier and consumer of services on which the autonomy of professionalism is erected;

(ii) the replacing of alternative sources of service, and the warding off of private and state patronage—thereby ensuring peer group solidarity and the individual's 'professional' identity.

The Russian medical profession was developing rapidly in all these directions in the latter half of the nineteenth century. A British observer remarked in 1862 on the astonishingly low level of medical qualifications before the zemstvo reforms,[44] and Pirogov speaks of the deplorable standard of medical teaching:

I received a physician's diploma and had mastery over life and death without ever having seen a single typhus patient and without ever having had a lancet in my hands! My entire medical practice in the clinic was limited to writing the history of an illness, having seen my patient only once in the hospital![45]

It was not until after the new zemstvo administrative units were set up, creating new needs, that 'scientific' medicine began to establish itself. By 1879, when Chekhov entered the medical faculty of Moscow University, clinical medicine was on a level with that of Western Europe. When British doctors visited Moscow for the Ninth International Congress of Medicine in 1897, they were impressed with the depth and scope of medical teaching, and with the new specialisms, covering nervous and mental diseases, gynaecology, diseases of the skin, children's diseases, hygiene and veterinary study. A special supplement of *The Lancet* noted that: 'Nowhere are the needs of scientific medicine more fully recognised or more generously satisfied than in the Russian capitals.'[46] The Pirogovist Society played an important part in the campaign for better medical education, and called for further training institutions for practising doctors to augment the Lenskii institute (which, when established in 1885, was the first foundation for the improvement of doctors in the world).

The promotion of research and theoretical knowledge was also foregrounded as an essential feature of professionalism, to the extent that in certain specialisms, such as prophylactics and mental illness, Russia came to the front in European medical science. The link between theory and medical practice quickly became a marked feature of the Russian medical profession and was stridently propogated both by university scholars like Pavlov and Bekhterev and by Pirogovist and other medical congresses. Many leading research scientists such as Erisman and Mechnikov had been zemstvo doctors, as were many famous surgeons, and close links were established which led to rapid implementation in the rural areas of the latest discoveries in microbiology, bacteriology and surgery. The Pirogovist Society led campaigns for the co-operation of university clinics with rural medical institutions, and for research centres to be situated in the zemstva; while, on the other side, the zemstva themselves increasingly recognised the need to give doctors frequent extended leaves (contrasting notably with the attitude to teachers) so that they could be 'refreshed and complete their knowledge in the centres of medical instruction'.[47] Hence it was zemstvo doctors who carried modern medical knowledge to the villages and who provided, through their systematic statistics, feedback of important field information to the research institutions. It was certainly a far cry from the time before the zemstvo reforms when there was not a single independent department of hygiene at any university in Russia, nor any eminent hygienist, to the situation by the end of the century when public health departments proliferated at the universities, sanitary congresses, organisations and bureaus with modern statistical sections proliferated in the zemstva, and public lectures on hygiene, demography and statistical research multiplied both in the universities and the rural areas. This was a tremendous growth time for Russian medical science, and the identity of zemstvo doctors was closely bound up with it. Chekhov's belief in scientific change and dedication to even the 'most wretched zemstvo hospital' was based on a confidently expanding professionalism.

The other area of medical research in which Pirogovist doctors were prominent in uniting theory and practice was psychiatry. In the official history of zemstvo medicine (prepared for the International Congress of 1897) Osipov compares the steps made in the treatment of the mentally sick since 1879, when the zemstva were first given control over them, with the abysmal record of the previous hundred years of state inactivity, during which time 'the idea that it was necessary to look after and treat the mentally sick in a special manner did not occur to anyone'.[48] The zemstva had begun to open mental hospitals situated in pleasant natural surroundings where the patients were treated according to the latest theories of psychiatrists such as Kovalevskii, Korsakov and Merzheyevskii. The enormous gulf noted by Chekhov in his story of a mental institution, *Ward Number Six*, between on the one hand the prison-like *non-zemstvo* institution with its brutal warder, and on the other, zemstvo mental hospitals of the 1890s with their specialist alienist doctors, is a measure of the growth of medical consciousness in Russia. Chekhov's portrait of ward number six in fact seems to derive closely from *Medicine du Zemstvo's* own findings. In their report, Osipov, Popov and Kurkin speak of the 'state of great dilapidation' of the hospitals before the zemstvo ones:

> roofs in a bad state, walls cracked and leaning, floors rotten, smoking stoves; one was struck by the absurd constructions of the places and by the infections they spread.[49]

And Chekhov describes ward number six thus:

> The roof has rusted, the chimney has half collapsed, the steps of the porch are rotten and inundated with grass. Only the odd patch of stucco remains on the walls . . . . . The walls are coloured a dirty blue, and the ceiling is as filthy with soot as any peasant's hut: the stoves obviously smoke in the winter-time, and fill the room with their charcoal fumes.

'In these establishments', says the report, 'everything was directed by supervisors who had no medical knowledge, who engaged servants incapable of looking after the sick.' In ward number six the medical work is done by an incompetent feldscher and the violent servant Nikita. Report and story alike speak of the spread of disease, the lack of distinction between forms of sickness, the filth, bedbugs, foul stifling atmosphere, incorrect diet, bars on the windows, straight jackets, and utter neglect of science and psychiatry.

Inevitably the advances in scientific theory and services within the zemstva were accompanied by a struggle by the profession to create and maintain a medical monopoly; in the face of 'superstition' on the one hand and state interference on the other. Monopoly demanded, first of all, the elimination of alternative 'lay' services provided by the 'wise old women', who had traditionally been a mainstay of peasant treatment, and also by the ill-trained medical assistants (feldschers) who, because of the huge size of the country, were the most advanced source of medical aid the poor could expect in the rural areas. The problem was fought on a number of fronts. Improved care in the hospitals (which hitherto had justifiably been viewed by the peasants as death traps) began to lure people away from more traditional remedies. In the face of considerable financial restrictions the number of zemstvo physicians was increased threefold between 1865 and 1910. And though feldschers were still needed because of the sheer physical extent of Russia, efforts were made to improve their quality, while strictly demarcating their competence from that of professional doctors. Osipov wrote that to identify the activity of feldscher and professional doctor was to slight the progress of science, and he insisted on the adequate training of medical auxiliaries as one of the zemstvo's most urgent tasks. The issue was mainly a financial one, and, as such, was never fully resolved. Time and again Pirogovist congresses returned to the thorny issue of 'feldscherism'.

It was, however, state interference which most threatened professional monopoly, and which the doctors were most united in resisting. After the forced concessions of the 1860s which had allowed the medical profession to come into being, the government made increasing attempts to invade zemstvo, and therefore professional, autonomy. The state appointed officers to vet all medical congresses, consistently opposed the setting up of sanitary organisations and, after 1900, sought more control over the Pirogovist Society itself. Osipov, as the spokesman for the zemstvo doctors, wrote very critically of state interference, claiming that it threatened to take the care of the people's health out of the competent hands of the zemstvo and back into 'the old domain of administrative fictions'. This would, he said, 'lead inevitably to the suppression of popular scientific medicine which the zemstvo has created with so much love and is now so well established'.[50] It was this professional and anti-bureaucratic attitude which led the Pirogovists to call for the transfer of factory medicine to the zemstva, and to oppose the findings of the Botkin Commission (1886) and later the Rein Commission (1913) which suggested setting up a central government department to unify sanitary-medical matters.

I have tried to establish in this section the constituents of career identity and self concept within the professional role—not as some a-historical essence, but in terms of an historical phenomenon, 'professionalism', and, more particularly, professionalism in Russia at the time of Chekhov. The features I have emphasised (and to which I want now to relate Chekhov's own position) are (i) the existence of common communication channels (journals and professional associations) which established a very specific career identity in terms of (ii) scientific theory and service (improvement of medical training, promotion of research and of specialisms such as prophylactics and mental illness), and in terms of (iii) monopoly control (particularly the problems of 'feldscherism' and state interference).

(i) Chekhov was in close and continuous contact with the communication channels of his profession. He read *Physician* regularly and played a particularly important role in attempts to save certain surgical journals. In the early 1880s there were no surgical journals in Russia, despite the needs of a rapidly expanding field. By 1891 there were only two. One died in 1895 and in that same year, the other journal, *Annals of Surgery*, edited by two of Russia's most eminent surgeons, P. I. D'yakonov and N. V. Sklifosovskii, also ran into financing problems. It was a critical moment for a journal performing an important role in acquainting zemstvo doctors with the latest research in the field. On 21 October 1895 Chekhov wrote to Suvorin about the matter:

> When I heard that the journal was in danger I got very angry. It is scandalous that such an essential journal, which could manage to make a profit in three or four years, should go bankrupt. To be ruined over such a paltry amount! The nonsense of it all got me into a rage. I have looked around diligently, humbled myself, gone from place to place and had dinner with the devil knows whom—but haven't achieved anything . . . But for the 1500 roubles I am spending building a school, I would offer to publish

it at my own expense—it is so painfully difficult for me to accept
such an obvious absurdity. On 22 October I will come to Moscow
and suggest to the editors that they apply, in the last resort, for a
state subsidy—about 1500 to 2000 annually. If they agree I'll
dash off to St Petersburg and get things under way. How should I
do it? Can you advise me? To save the journal I'm ready to go
anywhere, and wait in anyone's waiting room. If I succeed it will
give me enormous pleasure and relief. To save a surgical journal
is as useful as performing two thousand successful operations.[51]

For the normally restrained Chekhov it is agitated comment, and is
followed by an ebullient letter to Suvorin when the latter offers a
loan.

Later D'yakonov began publishing his own journal, *Surgery*, in
Moscow with the active help of Chekhov, who dealt with problems
of censorship and advertising. Though well received in medical
circles, this also soon ran into financial difficulties, and Chekhov
was again writing to Suvorin that he must save the journal, and
would stand barefoot for a week outside the Minister of Finance's
house if necessary to get a subsidy. In fact, an industrialist came to
D'yakonov's aid with a large subsidy, and the journal was to survive
until 1914. D'yakonov wrote jubilantly to Chekhov, thanking him
for his constant support and help in times of stress: 'You alone
among men deeply and truly understood the journal's significance,
and without you it would not have appeared.'[52] Chekhov's support
was all the more welcome, D'yakonov writes, because of the general
apathy surrounding him. 'You encourage my belief in my strength,
and in the success of this matter, which I consider vitally necessary
for the development here of a scientific rather than an artisan
surgery'. The words of one of Russia's most eminent surgeons speak
for themselves about Chekhov's understanding of the relationship
between professional communication channels and scientific
development.

As well as taking a keen interest in medical journals, Chekhov was
concerned with various types of medical association and congress.
In August 1897, the Ninth International Congress of Medicine met
in Moscow, bringing together leading scientists, doctors and
psychiatrists from many countries. Chekhov's close friend Kurkin
was co-author of the official history of zemstvo medicine presented
at the Congress, and Chekhov himself wrote to Dr Sredin in May
that, health permitting, he would attend the proceedings.[53]

Chekhov was in continuous contact with both the regional and central zemstvo and Pirogovist congresses, taking part in some, and generally acquainted with the main items discussed. His correspondence with Kurkin, Chlenov, Zhbankov, Vitte and others kept him in touch with the main events, and the 'turn to the Left' which Soviet interpreters like to see in Chekhov after 1900 can in fact be linked closely with the increasing radicalisation of his reference group, the Pirogovists, between 1900 and 1905. Chekhov, nearing the end of his life in Yalta, paid close attention to these events, and instructed Yelpatevskii and other members of the Ninth Pirogov Congress to keep him informed immediately of what took place. Several of his friends noted his keen concern with political events at this time, and his hopes that a constitution would soon be established. But like the Pirogovists, whose leaders without exception rejected an alliance with the Bolsheviks, Chekhov was never a revolutionary. His move to the Left was simply the articulation by events of the chasm which separated the medical profession from the Tsarist state.

The Pirogovist Society was, in fact, a reference group for Chekhov in each of the senses in which sociologists normally use the term. It was a group to which he aspired, which served as a source of ways of seeing and evaluating, and, finally, it was an audience towards which he oriented his conduct and his work, a fixed point against which to assess his own status and position. Chlenov reports how pleased Chekhov was when the editor of *Physician*, Manassein,[54] at last recognised him as a doctor who was also a great writer; and in January 1902 he was extremely eager to impress the Eighth Pirogovist Congress which was meeting in Moscow. He put on a performance of *Uncle Vanya* for the Pirogovists—a play in which there is, of course, strong emphasis on the typical ideals and frustrations of zemstvo doctor Astrov. Chekhov wrote excitedly to Ol'ga Knipper that the cast must act especially well on this occasion, and he was delighted with the praise he received after the play was performed. The Pirogovists sent him two telegrams: 'Your colleagues, members of the Eighth Pirogov Congress of Russian Doctors, today attending the performance of *Uncle Vanya*, send their dearly beloved author and dear colleague expression of their profound respect, and they wish him health'; 'The zemstvo doctors from remote corners of Russia who saw the work of the doctor-artist greet their comrade and will keep the memory of January 11 ever fresh.'[55] This was recognition indeed for the 'doctor-artist', and

Chekhov joyfully wrote to Chlenov thanking him for all the attention they had given him: 'During the Congress I felt like a prince. The telegrams raised me to heights I had never dreamed of.'[56] He also received a telegram from Osipov, and wrote about it with evident pleasure to their mutual friend Kurkin: 'I neither did nor could expect such an honour, and I accept this reward with the greatest pleasure, though I know I don't deserve it'.[57] Today, the name of E. A. Osipov, founder member of zemstvo medicine and leader of the Pirogovists, may not strike a profound chord compared with the name of Chekhov. But at the time, and certainly for Chekhov himself, it did, standing for a scientific professionalism compared with which contemporary art was, as Chekhov puts it in *The Seagull*, like the peasant who missed the train.

(ii) Chekhov was particularly anxious to raise the standards of medical proficiency. Dr Chlenov[58] speaks of a conversation with Chekhov about the still unsatisfactory situation in Russia of specialist improvement courses for doctors. Chekhov responded by setting out to raise money to build a specialist institution, and wrote to Chlenov, suggesting that they might try to build a second one as well.[59]

The degree of Chekhov's commitment to bringing together the practical and theoretical sides of medicine only seems remarkable if taken out of the context of his medical reference group. He in fact kept in touch with medical advances by following professional journals, and noted with interest research in microbiology and bacteriology, such as that of Mechnikov and Koch. His effort to found a research institute for skin diseases in Moscow was not an isolated one, since he also took part in the creation of a biological station in the Crimea, and had a keen interest in the Russian zoological station at Villefranche in France. (Thus when he wished to show that Van Koren in *The Duel* was not an 'authentic' scientist, he could give precise reasons as to why the Black Sea, which Van Koren chose instead of Villefranche for his research, was a poor area for marine study: Chekhov was always scrupulously accurate in his scientific details.)

The two specialisms which were advanced most successfully by the medical profession—prophylactics and mental illness—were also ones with which Chekhov had a special concern. He of course did a lot of practical work in spreading up-to-date sanitary and hygienic knowledge in the rural areas in his capacity as a doctor, and was naturally keen to get hold of the most recent articles and books in the field by specialists like Erisman and Kurkin. Like Osipov, who stated that the doctor who worked to improve sanitary conditions among the people must at the same time develop the people intellectually, Chekhov stressed the importance of popularising science on properly rigorous lines. For example, he wrote to Kurkin and other zemstvo doctors to 'energetically take that place in the popular press' which their competence as medical men, and particularly as sanitary doctors, should give them by right.[60] He also pressed publishers, such as Suvorin of the *New Times*, and editors like Evreinova of the *Northern Herald* to print articles on hygiene, forestry and scientific agriculture by 'learned and able' scientists like Erisman.[61] In the psychiatric field, Chekhov combined his practical work as a doctor with constant reference to the advice of specialists among his friends, such as the leading zemstvo psychiatrist Yakovenko and G. Rossolimo (who was later to become a prominent neuropathologist), and also kept up with the latest psychiatric works, like Korsakov's, which he bought immediately on publication. Chlenov and Rossolimo, who were both professors of medicine at Moscow University, seem to have thought highly of Chekhov's own research works, such as the embryonic *Medicine in Russia* and the completed *Sakhalin Island*; and Rossolimo and the psychiatrist Dr Nikitin were later to write articles emphasising the scientific originality and significance of Chekhov's psychiatric ideas.[62]

(iii) Chekhov was often critical of infringements of professional monopoly. His main response to 'feldscherism' came in his stories, where he satirised their ignorance, stupidity and incompetence.[63] But his letters[64] show his concern with the problem too, and his work at Voskressensk, Serpukhov and Sakhalin frequently brought him into contact with the problem which Osipov called 'a crime against the life and health of the people'.[65] Like Osipov, he argued for further training of medical assistants.[66]

Chekhov's overt response to threats to professional monopoly from the state had necessarily to be more cautious. Many of his early stories, such as *Death of a Government Clerk*, *Sergeant Prishebeyev* and *By the Patient's Bed* were as unsparing in their attacks on bureaucratic denial of autonomy as other Russian satirists, such as Shchedrin; and though it was impossible to speak out too openly, Chekhov's *Sakhalin Island* was a crushing indictment of state care for the sick and unfortunate. One reads in his letters of his hatred for an imperial regime which, unlike the British one, did not even bring its servants the advantages of roads and modern technology.[67] As we have seen, he was excited in 1904 by the Pirogovists' demand for greater individual, local and professional freedom from state control.

In fact, Chekhov opposed lay interference from any quarter in medical matters. He once wrote to Sulerzhitskii, 'Are you treating sick people? That won't do. You should send the patient to the doctor';[68] and during the famine he wrote to the zemstvo worker, Yegorov, that 'the snap opinions of laymen on diptheria annoy me, as a medical man'.[69] On another occasion we find him writing angrily to the Pirogovist doctor, Rozanov, about the sacking of the head doctor of Odessa city hospital, Dr P. E. Gryaznov. He had earlier read and admired Gryaznov's medical-topographical dissertation, and was scandalised at the action of a board composed of 'shopkeepers, property owners, and a doctor who is not a stranger to commerce'.[70] His words echo the Pirogovists' frequent criticism of those 'city doctors' who treated people 'according to the rules of commerce and trade'.[71] In 1897, Osipov, Popov and Kurkin wrote with some satisfaction that 'free treatment as a principle is spreading increasingly within the zemstvo',[72] and Chekhov echoes these sentiments when he writes angrily to the zemstvo doctor Orlov about 'doctors who own villas, rapacious officials and thieving engineers'.[73] In many of his works (*Intrigues, General Education—the Latest Conclusions of Dentistry, At the Chemist, Belated Flowers, Three Years, Ionych*), Chekhov attacked private city doctors and other medical personnel who put their concern for money before their professional duties. It is significant that Ionych, beginning as one of the mercenary types who, in the early days of zemstvo medicine, mixed public and private work (but who, according to Osipov, had been completely phased out by the 1890s), ends up as a purely mercenary doctor with zemstvo ideals long forgotten.

Chekhov's criticism of the medical group was invariably from within the value system we have related to professionalism. He criticised absence of scientific service, lack of autonomy, infringement of monopoly, and the related absence of medical universalism. On the other hand, the positive development of all these things was a source of identity and considerable optimism. At the beginning of his career he wrote to his brother Aleksandr, 'I shall throw myself into medicine; there is salvation there'. And at the end of his career he preferred to register Ol'ga as the wife of a doctor rather than an honorary Academician, because 'it is so much pleasanter being the wife of a medical man'.[74] From first to last his self concept responded to the development of professionalism in Russia.

III

Any list of 'essential traits' of a profession includes a 'systematic body of theory'. The importance of theory, it is said, is in precipitating 'a form of activity normally not encountered in a non-professional occupation, viz. theory construction via systematic research.'[75]

'Theory' has indeed been significant historically as a feature of professionalisation; but as with other 'trait' approaches to the professions there is a tendency to derive from culture-bound professional attributes a very a-historical essence. It is quite apparent, for example, that the corporate patronage under which many professionals in capitalist societies work today emphasises the day-to-day needs of the patron rather than (and often at the expense of) the pursuit of basic knowledge.[76]

Still, there have been certain historical times, and specific professions, in which scientific theory *has* been an essential part of occupational consciousness. 'Professionalism' (as we have defined it) can be said, roughly, to be an historical phenomenon existing between two periods of patronage control of the professions: that of an aristocratic élite (as in the eighteenth and early nineteenth centuries) and, in our own time, that of large-scale corporations. And it is no coincidence at all that this was also the time when the first 'scientific' paradigm came to be integrally associated with the new concept of the professions, since the claim to autonomy was invariably based on possession of new expertise.

Kuhn has described the development of science from 'early fact gathering' to the development of the kind of unifying paradigm which 'transforms a group previously interested in the study of nature into a profession'.[77] It is this common paradigm which gives meaning to the notion of 'scientific objectivity' by providing a group with a body of belief with which to assess particular questions, types of evidence and research methodology. Thus the nineteenth-century French physiologist, Claude Bernard, claimed that medicine would become scientific only when there was a move from 'mere' empiricism to an 'objective' understanding of physiology: 'It is not enough for experimenting physicians to know that quinine

cures fever; but . . . what fever is and accounting for the mechanism by which quinine cures, i.e. they must define the human
mechanism in its normal as well as its pathological state'.[78] The
evolution of a scientific paradigm of this kind took place in Russia in
the second half of the nineteenth century. It was only then, the plant
physiologist Kliment Timiryazev insisted, that medicine turned
from 'the sterile provinces of empiricism and speculation' to become
a science founded on physiology.[79]

Alexander Vucinich has analysed in considerable detail the development of a scientific paradigm in Russia,[80] and its acceptance
and institutionalisation by the broader society (the latter an
essential feature of professional claims to occupational control and
autonomy). A wider acceptance of science in Russia had begun in
the first half of the nineteenth century, but progress was always
faltering because of the traditionally ambivalent attitude of the
Russian government. The ruling élite saw the need for science as a
source of economic and military power, but rightly suspected that
its spirit of critical inquiry might have wider ramifications, and
threaten the social and political status quo. Any scientific special-
ism, such as physiology or medicine, which threw into doubt the role
of divine interference in spiritual life, or which, in its social
implications, disturbed in any way the values of the autocratic
regime, was particularly closely supervised and heavily restricted.

The Russian defeat in the Crimean War, however, marked a
turning point. The débacle was generally interpreted as a result of
Russia's technological underdevelopment, and a massive shift
towards science quickly took place in the curricula of schools and
universities. In 1853 only twenty-two students graduated in the
natural and exact sciences in all universities; by 1855 there were
328, and by 1860, 508. In the 1820s, the Minister of National
Education, Aleksandr Shishkov had claimed that 'Science . . . is
not a national asset unless it is allied with religion and
morality . . . science, like salt, is useful only when used and taught
within proper limits.'[81] Now, in 1855, the new Minister of
Education made the radical change of policy official: 'Science . . .
is our first need. If our enemies are superior to us, it is only because
of the power of their knowledge.'[82] From the scientists' side,
Timiryazev was able to announce the legitimation of science as a
state institution: 'Until this time science developed despite government erected barriers . . . From this point on, it benefited from the
government's co-operation.'[83]

Vucinich remarks that a

> typical university professor of the new generation differed
> tangibly from his predecessor . . . He was usually guided by
> Claude Bernard's laconic pronouncment that 'a theory is merely
> a scientific idea controlled by experiment', and by the principle
> that a scientist must not generalize until he has considered the
> actual data in detail. . . . the new professor stuck closely to
> experimental results and the general ideas that gave them
> coherence and larger meaning.'[84]

So it was that during the last four decades of the century large
numbers of impressionable young Russians spent their formative
years internalising the modes of rational inquiry associated with the
scientific method of Claude Bernard and the Western positivists.

Indeed, if science were *no more than* a mode of inquiry, we might
conclude from our survey that the 'time for science' had come in
Russia, determined, in some inexorable way, by the Crimean War.
In fact, of course, science is not simply a mode of inquiry: as
Vucinich remarks, it is also 'a unique system of knowledge built
upon certain metaphysical assumptions', as well as being 'part of a
specifically national culture and . . . a world view'.[85] More is said
in other sections of this chapter about the cultural and ideological
implications of science in Tsarist Russia. At this point it is worth
remarking that if we analyse historically the development of science
as an epistemology, that notion of a simplistic, relatively unproblematical development from the early fact gathering to 'objective'
analysis seems less than satisfactory. Rather, we are confronted in
Russia with a conflict of *rival* epistemologies (defined by their
opponents in turn as a reactionary idealism and a 'decadent'
materialism), and a far from unproblematical movement from one
to the other.

For thirty or so years up the middle of the nineteenth century,
Schelling's Naturphilosophie had dominated Russian intellectual
circles, much given to idealistic emphasis of the 'soul' and of the
'inner' and 'living' forces which were said to be quite opaque to
'mechanistic' and 'purely external' material methods. The intellectuals' concern for soul, religion, morality, and the assertion
that 'matter' was a product of 'spirit' thus did little to shake the
official policy of state theologians and Ministers of National
Education who in opposition to Western materialism, 'dedicated

the temple of national education to God's throne, the Cross, and the prayer'.[86] This legacy, Shevyrev noted in 1855, 'was the most burdensome problem of our education during the thirty years preceding the middle 1850s'.[87]

In contrast, the dominant epistemology of the second half of the century was a materialist one.

> Until the end of the nineteenth century the Newtonian system of mechanics was the dominant and most general paradigm; its chief elements were the concepts of continuity, external causality, the absoluteness of space and time, the indivisibility and immutability of atoms, and the ontological primacy of matter. The Newtonian paradigm was flexible enough to allow both for limited transgressions and for the emergence of subparadigms in the form of special traditions in individual sciences. In broad terms, however, it held absolute sway over the main lines of scientific development.[88]

What this meant, in effect, as Vucinich points out, was that, on the one hand, Timiryazev could become a champion of Russian science by bringing together Newtonian mechanism and Darwin's historicism (since the latter, with its emphasis on materialistic and external casuality operationalised the master paradigm in widening areas); yet, on the other hand, N. I. Lobachevskii, the founder of non-Euclidian geometry, was ignored by the scientific community because he challenged central principles of the mechanistic view.

This is, of course, typical of 'paradigm articulation' within 'normal science' as Kuhn defines it, and it suggests that a new paradigm had been definitively established. However, its institutionalisation, and further development from the 1860s on, were neither 'natural' nor unproblematical. For the rest of the century (even while the process of extending the blend of Newton and Darwin to more and more fields went on apace) war was waged between those who 'saw men as permanently dependent on the mysterious forces of nature' (the 'idealists') and those who took up 'the task of explaining the relationship of man to nature, of unveiling the laws governing the latter, and of eradicating the conditions unfavourable to social progress'[89] the 'materialists').

For example, in 1871 a conservative historian, K. D. Kavelin strongly criticised the 'determinism' and 'materialism' of Ivan Sechenov's physiological work, and stressed instead the importance of introspection as the source of psychological knowledge. There followed decades of controversy. As Vucinich remarks, 'the growing ranks of neovitalists, theological anti-Darwinists, and all kinds of spiritualists viewed Sechenov's work as the mainstay of materialism and the source of inspiration for social rebels'.[90] The admirers and followers of Sechenov found their chief spokesman in I. P. Pavlov who argued that the 'application of the reflex principle to explain the activity of the higher nervous centres is proof that causality can be applied to the highest forms of organic nature'.[91] The most 'spiritual' of man's activities was, in fact, subject to the 'material method'.

Pavlov, however, felt himself to be working in a wilderness of subjective, introspective psychology, which he was unable to accept as a science, and Vucinich points out that the *majority* of academic psychologists merely bolstered up the 'ideological crusade against the underlying materialism of modern experimental psychology'.[92]

In this context, the scientist's claim that 'There is nothing in the world that is outside the concepts of matter and force'[93] assumed the urgency of an ideological challenge; and it is not in the least surprising that when Timiryazev himself was attacked by the new wave of vitalists and anti-Darwinists towards the end of the century, he chose to centre his counter-attack on his critics' *ideologically* suspect dismissal of 'natural-scientific materialism'. Even Mendel's genetic laws were at first suspected by the embattled Timiryazev as the way back to metaphysics and idealism in science and society.

Timiryazev's notion of materialism was not separable, as we shall see in the next section, from an extreme environmentalism; and since he was both the spokesman for scientific Darwinism in Russia *and* one of the scientists whom Chekhov professed to admire most, his position is of more than passing interest here. Vucinich points out that Timiryazev's evolutionism combined three ideas: the Darwinian concept of natural selection; Newton's mechanistic notion of causality and continuity in the work of nature; and the Comtian extension of ideas of progress from organic life to the world of human society and culture. This blending of 'natural-scientific materialism' with progressive social philosophy was typical of Russian scientists at this time, and brought them close to the Nihilist 'men of the sixties' who had adopted the 'scientific method' and the 'primacy of matter' as weapons against conservative ideology and an idealist metaphysics.

The *difference* between the 'ideologues' and the 'scientists' is not always easy to discern. Vucinich remarks that in Sechenov's case it was partly a matter of tone, partly of strategy. But most of all it was to do with the scientist's refusal to over-emphasise a materialist ontology at the expense of professional caution and careful experiment. All 'materialists' at this time stressed the primacy of matter, the importance of the experimental method and the urgent need to spread a knowledge of science among the public. The difference between the professionals and the amateurs, Vucinich suggests, was that the former had the skills to adhere equally to the second of these, while not neglecting the first and the third.

The widespread development and intellectual dominance of a new paradigm which combined a materialist ontology with notions of public service provided a natural basis for the take-off of medical professionalism. But it also brought difficulties. In the first place, there was the danger that experimental method would take second place to 'progressive' ideology. The rapid emergence of medical specialisms dependent on intensive research reduced that risk. However, the rise of specialisms in turn raised another problem. In particular, the central significance of physiology both to the development of experimental science *and* to the paradigm debate between 'spirit' and 'matter' created problems for professional authority. Certainly the development of scientific specialisms provided a solid 'objective' underpinning for claims to professional autonomy, and the institutionalised ineffectiveness of consumer control which goes with it. On the other hand, suspicion of medical science in its ideological ramifications existed among the ruling class from the start. State mediation threatend to determine the orientation and content of medical affairs, thereby encroaching on the doctors' professional autonomy. Persistent attempts were made by the Russian ruling class to confine medical science to therapeutic concerns alone (a futile attempt, since the major epidemics which swept Russia were vitiated by appalling social and economic conditions) because medical *prophylactics* (implying social reform) threatened the status quo.

In addition to these difficulties, the development of specialisms also potentially threatened occupational authority from within the medical group. As Johnson points out, professionalism is likely to emerge only where specialisation is relatively low, since high levels may result in fragmentation of occupational identity. There may, for example, be a considerable gap between the perspective of the individual practitioner applying routine cures (and therefore committed to the 'scientific ethos' in only the most indirect way) and that of the scientific researcher in a university. Typically, fragmentation leads to the formation of sub-groups with competing ideologies within the profession.

The stimulus to occupational authority and professionalism provided by the development of 'objective science' was therefore threatened from three different quarters. Firstly, the overlapping of ontological and epistemological values between the scientific group and the general intelligentsia threatened to weaken and diffuse the identity and authority of the professional cadre. Secondly, state intervention in central areas of concern threatened professional autonomy. Thirdly, developing specialisation potentially threatened to fragment the profession from within.

To some extent, the different threats to autonomy offset each other. On the one hand, state intransigence drove Russian doctors to subsume new specialisms within reformist politics, and therefore towards a wider corporate identity. Since for example, the state sought to hinder the development of environmental research, the doctors, as we have seen, sought to change the state. On the other hand, the intense development of specialist science, and the years spent at university internalising experimental methodology, tended to distinguish the hard-headed professional pragmatists and social engineers from the 'men of faith' of the sixties.

Further, specialist theory *was* in fact of immediate concern for practising doctors in Russia. Those frontiers which were pushed forward the most were often the ones of greatest practical urgency. Hence the 'material method' was constantly vindicated by hard practice. And frustration and failure generated further research. For example, the considerable advances achieved in Russian microbiology were related to the zemstvo doctors' experience of ravaging epidemics which frequently swept the rural areas; and Vucinich remarks that the 'emergence of soil science as a distinctive Russian discipline' was intimately connected to the concern over 'the depletion of the cultivated soil, the drastic annual fluctuation in agricultural output and the perennial threat of famine'[94] (a concern which Chekhov drew on in *Uncle Vanya*).

The real distinction between the true man of science and the materialist ideologue, as Claude Bernard saw it, was that the former, steeped in years of experimental work, could never suppress the hard fact beneath systematic ideals. The hard facts of science in effect extended well beyond the Russian doctor's laboratory years.

They were the stuff of his daily activities and frustrations. Further, the continuous flow of communication, which we have noted, between practising doctors and scientific research centres upheld in full Timiryazev's demand that the worlds of pure and applied science should constantly refresh each other, avoiding on the one hand overspecialisation, and on the other the élite's attempt to divert science to the solution of 'appropriate' technical problems.

In this brief overview of the historical development of science within Russian society during the nineteenth century, I want to recapitulate and emphasise three central points:

(i) Corresponding roughly with the Russian defeat in the Crimean War, there was a shift from an 'idealist' to a 'materialist' paradigm which dominated not only scientific ideas, but also the main body of intellectual thought in the second half of the century. This development, however, was far from 'natural' or unproblematical. Although science received institutional recognition after the war, the association of 'idealism' and 'materialism' with social and political centres of power provided the focus for continuing paradigm debates among men of ideas and scientists alike.

(ii) Though the 'material method' was favoured by most of the intelligentsia, it was a trained adherence to experimental modes of inquiry which distinguished professionals from amateurs, 'scientists' from 'ideologues'.

(iii) Although the danger was thereby avoided of a loss of professional identity by too wide a diffusion of central ideas throughout the intelligentsia, there were still two other threats to the in-group autonomy and occupational control which we associate with professionalism. Both these threats—over-officious state mediation and internal fragmentation—were countered by the development of specialisms only within a broad reformist perspective which emphasised the inter-connectedness of new scientific and sociological developments, and related laboratory science to applied science in the most pragmatic way.

We can now examine Chekhov's position in relation to each of these features of the professional community: the materialist ontology, the experimental mode of inquiry and the adherence to theory within a global social compass.

(i) In the paradigm debate between 'materialists' and 'spiritualists' there is no doubt at all that Chekhov came down on the side of Sechenov and the 'material method'. Many of his remarks recall

Sechenov's quite closely. For instance, Sechenov had complained about the false wars constantly being waged against men of science and said one 'should recall what mankind gained from the medieval thought which gave rise to alchemy. It is terrible to think what would have become of mankind if the rigid medieval guardians of public opinion had succeeded in burning and drowning as sorcerers and evildoers all those who worked hard at imageless ideas and who were unconsciously creating chemistry and medicine'.[95] In letters to Suvorin, Chekhov makes the same point: 'Right through medieval times alchemy was gradually, in a natural and peaceful way, being transformed into chemistry, and astrology into astronomy. But the monks, unable to understand, saw it as a matter to fight a war over'.[96] An equally futile war, he felt, was even now being waged over 'materialism':

> Where is the enemy? What danger do we fear from him? Firstly, the materialist movement is neither a school nor a tendency in the restricted newspaper sense. It is not something which is arbitrary or sudden. It is necessary, inevitable, and beyond man's power to change. Everything that lives on earth is necessarily materialistic . . . Creatures of a higher nature, thinking men, are also materialists of necessity. They search for truth in matter, because there's nowhere else they can look for it—since they can see, hear and sense only matter. They must necessarily search for the truth precisely where they can use microscope, lancet and knife. If you deny man the materialist philosophy, you deny him the chance to seek the truth. There is no experience or knowledge, and therefore no truth, outside matter.[97]

It is significant that Chekhov raises this issue in the context of man's 'higher nervous centres': like Sechenov and Pavlov he rejects the currently dominant academic psychology as 'a fiction, not a science'.[98] Sechenov had argued that 'There are no clear distinctions whatever between the obviously somatic, i.e. bodily, nervous acts and the definitely mental phenomenon'.[99] Chekhov adopts the same position: 'mental phenomena and physical ones are so remarkably similar that one can't make out where one begins and the other ends'.[100]

Suvorin, in a letter which Chekhov refers to, seems to have sided with the 'idealist' psychologists who believed that only the corporeal, and not the spiritual, being of man was subject to the laws of nature. At any rate, in his reply Chekhov indicates that, like Timiryazev, he fears the crusade against materialism: 'You write, "Let the science of matter go on its way, but leave us somewhere we can take refuge from absolute matter". In fact, though, if anything is under threat, it is the natural sciences and not the holy places where you would hide from them'.[101] Suvorin, like the hero from Dostoyevskii's *Notes from Underground*, seems only to have wanted to 'scatter rationalism to the winds' in the face of a *hegemonic* materialism. For him, the 'science of matter' should have an appropriate, not total place. But Chekhov's reply was that science *had* to be hegemonic, or it was nothing. Like Sechenov and Timiryazev, he considered that to separate 'spirit' or 'soul' from material analysis was to deny science itself and bolster up the dualistic position of the Orthodox élite. Science, he insisted, not Orthodoxy, must underpin modern culture. Truth would be found 'not by seeking in Dostoyevskii, but by clear knowledge, as one knows that twice two is four'.[102]

Attacking the 'spiritualists', Sechenov had commented that 'Should man be able to create combinations containing at least one genuinely *non-terrestrial* element, the independent creative activity of the spirit would undoubtedly be proved'.[103] Similarly Chekhov comments that if these people could actually point to an incorporeal origin of things so that materialists could see it, their case would be proven. Meanwhile, 'I believe that when we dissect the corpse of even the most ardent spiritualist, we will *of necessity* be faced with the puzzle: where do we look for his soul'.[104]

(ii) Like many other 'materialists' among the Russian intelligentsia, Chekhov believed in the close relationship between science and moral 'truth', and himself extended the scientific method to wide areas of social inquiry, such as sociology and penology. He once wrote to Dr Kurkin of the importance of statistics as 'the science of the large organism which we call society, and which lies like a connecting bridge between biology and sociology';[105] and it was this 'science of statistics' which underpinned his own medical and sociological analysis of the penal settlement at Sakhalin.

Nevertheless, as a professional doctor, Chekhov clearly separated himself from 'ideologues of whatever tendency. He was quite pragmatic in his evaluation of the 'men of the sixties': 'The famous sixties did absolutely nothing for the sick and imprisoned . . . In our age something is being done for the sick, but still nothing for the prisoners. Our jurists are simply not interested in penology. So, I assure you, Sakhalin is of use . . .'[106] Nor was there to be anything amateur about his methods there. Though, like other intellectuals, Chekhov was a great believer in the popularisation of science, he insisted that this work should be done by professional doctors and scientists. He did a lot of studying in preparation for his visit to Sakhalin, and was not impressed by what he called the pseudo-scientific methods of 'false philosophers'.

In the event 'false philosophers' could come in a number of guises. As well as the Nihilists of the sixties, and the Populists of the seventies, there were also the apathetic 'intellectuals' who surrounded Chekhov in the eighties. Chekhov adopted Bernard's distinction between those who trusted in science too much, like the intellectuals of the sixties who were prone to put generalisation before method, and those who trusted in science too little. Of the latter Bernard had written:

> The sceptic disbelieves in science and believes in himself . . . The doubter is a true man of science; he doubts only himself and his interpretations, but he believes in science. A sceptic who believes in nothing no longer has a foundation on which to establish his criterion and consequently finds it impossible to build up a science; the sterility of his unhappy mind results at once from the error of his perception and from the imperfection of his reason.[107]

Chekhov often criticised in his letters people who 'disbelieve in science and disbelieve in everything'; and in 1889 was to present an extended analysis of the sterility of one such 'unhappy mind'. In *Dreary Story*, Professor Nikolai Stepanovich loses his belief in the powers of science. One of the clearest signs of the moral collapse which parallels his physical decline is his seduction by the enervating pessimism and cynical platitudes of the 'intellectuals' to whom he resorts in his last days.[108]

Writing an obituary for the Russian geographer N. M. Przheval'skii, Chekhov attacked the debilitating scepticism of contemporary intellectuals, and praised 'positive' types like Livingstone and Przheval'skii for their practical and active commitment to science. Scientific scepticism, he suggested, differed from the apathetic version of many intellectuals mainly in its concern for positive inquiry. These two great explorers make us aware that apart from trivialising pessimists, sceptics and mystics of various kinds, 'there are also people of quite another type: men of faith, action and a goal in life'.[109] In the sixties, he implied when writing about his own exploratory trip to Sakhalin, there had been too much faith and not enough action; in the eighties there had been too little of either. Faith had its place, because without it one was rapidly brought to the cold cynicism of the eighties. But faith without science was foredoomed from the first, as was the case with so many of Chekhov's Ivanovs who believed they could shift social mountains and instead were crushed by them.[110] In his Notebooks Chekhov wrote, 'When one longs for a drink, it seems as though one could drink a whole ocean—that is faith; but when one begins to drink, one can only drink altogether two glasses—that is science.'[111]

The distance between a 'whole ocean' and a 'two glasses' understanding is an experimental one, similar to the one Sechenov perceived between the global 'understanding' of intuition and the much more limited knowledge of science: 'As a science based on experiment physiology will not affirm as an incontestable truth that which cannot be confirmed by precise experimentation . . . Huge gaps may appear in . . . actual knowledge; instead of explanations we will get in most cases the laconic phrase "We do not know".' And yet science will have made a huge advance, and in place of intuitive speculation will be based 'on positive facts, on verifiable propositions'.[112]

Chekhov, of course, *had* known and worked in the laboratories which Bernard said distinguished the man of scientific method from the false generaliser. Bernard's *Introduction to Experimental Medicine* had been a basic textbook in all the university medical faculties for some time. Chekhov's teacher, G. A. Zakhar'in had worked with Bernard in Paris, and passed on to his students his principles of accurate observation and constructive scepticism as a basis for scientific procedure. Apart from the examples mentioned already, there are often positive echoes of Bernard's position in Chekhov's letters—sometimes written long after he had left university: affirmation, for example, that for a scientist 'method is half of talent', that the essence of medicine (and of art) is to go beyond the empirical detail to the general, and that in seeking the truth, which man might never know in its entirety, the observer must employ an absolute freedom of mind, honesty and objectivity which together would produce doubt but never cynical disbelief.[113]

We can find a clear example of the continuing importance of the scientific method to Chekhov in his published criticisms of scientists who abused it. In 1891 Chekhov and the biologist V. A. Wagner jointly put out an article[114] supporting and extending Timiryazev's attack on the Moscow Zoological Garden for its departure from strictly scientific methods. Drawing on his training in Bernard, Chekhov pointed out that the scientific observations collected in the station records and diary should be systematic and continuous, and generalised so that one could see a clear purpose behind the work. Instead the reports were discontinuous, laconic and certainly not redolent of a concern for pathology or physiology. 'September 21, the elephant is ill; September 22, 23, 24 etc.—he is still ill; September 28, he is healthy again'. Not a word, Chekhov remarks, about the nature of the illness, its symptoms, the cure; but plenty about visitors to the gardens swearing at the ticket office, and poking the animals. Scientific observation does not extend beyond brief comments about animals coughing in the night, 'but in the darkness we could not decide which'. 'Since the gardens are designed for strictly scientific research on strictly scientific methods', Chekhov writes, 'we should find spacious buildings full of the necessary equipment, very specialised personnel, a well-equipped library etc., such as we find abroad.' But there is no library, the laboratory is closed, and inside it, in place of specialised equipment, there is a litter of 'logs, broken cases, heaps of bones, broken dishes, old galoshes, torn reports and rotting specimens' which, for lack of trained personnel, were acquired but never dissected. 'Not a single article concerning scientific work has appeared, apart from the unsuccessful attempts to infect a dog with disease.' The paper is full of Chekhov's humour, developed during a decade of work on his stories. But the intent is completely serious, and the method of research behind it both systematic and exceedingly time-consuming. The severity of the article, Chekhov writes to Suvorin, is explained by the 'need for truth based on documented data'.[115]

(iii) 'To work for science and public ideals, that is personal happiness',[116] Chekhov once wrote to his friend Chlenov, who remarks that he has rarely met anyone whose attitude to science was so deep and who believed in its importance so much for the moral health and well-being of humanity. In 1889, Chekhov wrote to Suvorin, 'science . . . must be above suspicion'; in 1894 he wrote, 'the natural sciences are achieving miracles now, and may rush upon the public and conquer it by sheer size and splendour'; in 1899 he wrote to Dr Orlov, 'science is constantly pushing forward'; and to

Dyagilev he wrote in 1902 that modern culture based on science is the beginning of a quest for truth and a great future—a real god, whereas religion is a system of the past.[117]

The quotations suggest that Chekhov's dedication to a materialist ontology and to the scientific method had wide reformist implications. Unlike his professor in *Dreary Story* who spent a lifetime dedicated to the 'bone medula', Chekhov's interest in science managed to be both specialist *and* global—all aspects being linked, as we shall see, within a subsuming evolutionary paradigm. As evidence for the first point we have his concern as a practising doctor for specialist journals, his argument that doctors should encounter the latest research through periodic refresher courses, and his care in returning statistical data to the research bureaus. As evidence for the second, there is his concern for the application of Western European technological achievements—scientific agriculture, shipbuilding, radium and X-ray—in Russia. In 1891 his very wide commitment to science was recognised. On the recommendation of D. N. Anuchin (whom Vucinich describes as the most productive and influential Russian geographer before the twentieth century) Chekhov was appointed to membership of the Society of Lovers of Natural Science. It was another example of something which has been becoming clear in this chapter: Chekhov's ability to win the professional respect and friendship of a surprising number of men who either were, or were to become, important specialists and leaders in a wide range of Russian sciences. They were all, needless to say, champions of the materialist paradigm.

IV

It has been becoming increasingly apparent in recent years that traditional definitions of the professions have been excluding an essential element of their day-by-day proceedings. As certain professionals have dedicated themselves not to some abstract concept of public service but to the whims of corporate organisations, often rising to positions of considerable influence on their controlling boards; as other professionals have utilised their status, their influence in political circles, and their economic resources to oppose legislation introducing 'socialised' medicine, it has become clear that no analysis of the professions can be complete which ignores their power relations in society. Far from being engaged within a system of natural reciprocity, professions are seen by 'conflict' theorists as competing on a societal battleground: a place where social groups and classes which are differentially located in relation to the ownership of the means of production, and therefore in their degree of access to positions of influence, struggle for power over each other. In this final section I want to examine Chekhov's professional identity in terms of this 'conflict' perspective.

For the 'conflict' theorist the struggle for power is the 'natural' state of society: hence he has to explain why it does not manifest itself more often, or at least appear more overtly. This accounts for his concern with agencies of socialisation which help maintain the hegemony of ruling class values. Social groups or classes which are socialised, in one way or another, into acceptance of these hegemonic values approximate to what Marx called a 'class in itself'; that is, a body of people which may be nominally coherent, but which does not struggle for, indeed has no accurate notion of, its 'real' interests. To act in its own interests (to become a 'class for itself'), it must be *conscious* of what its true interests are. Action on the political level implies the formulation of group consciousness as an *ideology*, since the group will need to justify its actions not only to itself, but also to other powerful groups in society. As Krause has pointed out, the 'reasons for acceptance or rejection of a group's ideology may tell us much about the trend of the group's power in the future, the degree to which it can influence its own fate'.[118] Today, in the capitalist world, we are accustomed to see occupational ideologies at work bolstering up a privileged position of power and status.[119] But historically they have been equally important in the struggle for the very beginnings of upward group mobility among doctors and other professionals. This, we will see, was the case for Russian doctors in the second half of the nineteenth century.

From a 'conflict' point of view, the growth of professionalism could only take place in Russia once doctors had shorn off their client/patron relationship with the ruling class. Under these subservient conditions the doctor was, as Johnson has argued, little more than a kept man, a courtier, who had to share the social manners and graces of his betters. However, even after the emergence of a new occupational consciousness, as we have seen, the 'autonomy' achieved was a very problematical one. On the one hand there was a professional group dedicated to social engineering, since it was only through broad scale social changes that the nation's health could be improved. On the other hand there was a modernising autocracy with the aim of maintaining the existing political structure and system of stratification while carrying out a scientific and economic transformation.

One of the central problems of any modernising autocracy is the absorption of new élites into the political hierarchy.[120] Where the modernising roles are based on an ideology of science, and are social in application, the trend will be towards planning, calculation and rationalistic goals oriented to the future, while recruitment will be of the 'achievement' type, according to merit. This kind of development may, however, endanger the traditional political élite since it will require absorption of values antagonistic to their own 'ascriptive' ones.

In Russia, the political élite, unable to integrate the new scientific groups easily within the system, tried to separate directly *instrumental* modernising roles from those new roles which might threaten the élite's most central values. In practical terms, this meant separating science as a technological force from science as a spirit of inquiry, and encouraging vocational and technical institutions at the expense of the universities, which were considered to be breeding grounds of 'free thought'. In medicine it meant encouraging therapy at the expense of prophylactics. Given the attempt by the state not simply to determine the content of their practice, but to eliminate effective preventive medicine which was the very core of their professional identity; and given their diffusion across thousands of widely separated localised bases in the zemstva, there was a very real danger of the disintegration of corporate identity among zemstvo doctors. Unifying features which I described earlier, such as the role of the professional associations, helped with this problem. But even more important was the existence of an alternative *ideology* strong enough to prevent disintegration. Darwinism provided Russian doctors with this counter set of values.

In the West 'Social Darwinism' had been quickly adapted to the 'tooth and claw' ethics of a burgeoning capitalism. In Russia, on the other hand, its reception was visionary and radical. Kline points out that evolutionary theories 'were received not as academic or technical theories, but as total world views—indeed vessels of consolation or instruments of salvation. Darwinism was viewed by the positivistically and materialistically inclined intelligentsia as the support of their "realism" (that is anti-idealism and antiromanticism) and their "nihilism" (anti-traditionalism).'[121] From the 1860s on, Darwinism was fervently popularised by critics such as Chernyshevskii and Pisarev, and among scientists, by Sechenov, Mechnikov, Timiryazev and Pavlov. Darwin's major works were quickly translated, and the complete works (by Timiryazev) by 1909. Glagol'ev, writing after the turn of the century, confirmed the spirit that had been abroad since the sixties—in Moscow and Petersburg, he wrote, one hardly dared mention Darwin's name without doffing one's cap: 'To express doubts as to Darwin's scientific competence on any of the questions investigated by him was to defy truth itself.'[122]

What interests us is less the 'spirit' than the *ideological* assimilation of Darwinism as a two-fronted oppositional consciousness: opposed, that is to say, not only to the values of the traditional 'autocratic-bureaucratic' élite, but *also* to an élite-in-potential as well—that of capitalism. At the time that the values of the Russian intelligentsia, and later of the medical profession, were developing a Darwinist orientation, the social infrastructure for an ideology of progressive capitalism (which accompanied the growth of the professions in the West) was missing. The cultural and economic backwardness of Russia was responsible for the absence there of developed entrepreneurial interests and the dominant laissez-faire ideology typical of ascendant capitalism.[123] In fact a strong tradition of anti-capitalist theory was present among thinkers of all convictions.

So it was not very surprising that the 'tooth and claw' variant of Social Darwinism was almost unanimously rejected. In its place Darwin's emphasis on *co-operation within a species* took firm hold, through the works of Nozhin, Timiryazev, Kropotkin and others. The Russian extension of Darwinism to social concerns, and the stress on 'symbiosis' between man, the natural and social worlds, was related not simply to the question of creating a new life, but one different in essential features from that of the West.

Russian scientists took up this oppositional orientation of Darwinism, rejecting the pessimistic and fatalistic accretions of the West almost as a matter of course. Vucinich remarks that a 'typical Russian naturalist adhered to the Darwinian theory but was inclined to ignore or disclaim its Malthusian "bias"'.[124] Spencer was admired for his application of the theory of evolution to society, his rejection of tradition and his belief in progress; but though many scientists accepted his Lamarckian belief in the inheritance of acquired characteristics, few could share his belief in the *inevitability* of perfection through evolution (with its accompanying laissez-faire values).

A clear gap existed for Russian scientists and doctors between the theory of perfectibility and *actual* social evolution. Sechenov in physiology, Mechnikov in embryology, Timiryazev in botany, Merzheyevskii in psychology, Chekhov in his scientific, sociological and literary works, all referred to that distance between human potential and the existing social reality.

Most scientific thinkers agreed with Mechnikov that one must not think of human nature as immutable, but each must try to modify it for the advantage of mankind.[125] At the Moscow International Medical Congress in 1897, Mechnikov rejected the claim that science was sanctioning the 'Law of Might' by tabulating the laws of the struggle for existence. Instead it was a great ethical force:

> Science, by revealing the laws of nature, applied to humanity the benefits derived from them, while striving to counter-balance their cruel or harmful effects. The struggle against plague and other diseases was a concrete example of this, for here medical science opposed itself to the cruelty of natural selection! . . . Just as, in order to satisfy his aesthetic tastes, man revolts against the Laws of Nature which create races of sterile and fragile flowers, so he does not hesitate to defend the weak against the laws of natural selection.[126]

The Russian physiological school, accepting Spencer's extension of evolutionary theory to psychology, treated the human organism as an entity, in which physical and psychological phenomena were alike subject to the co-operation of two factors: a definite but variable organism and external influences. Russian doctors were in fact unique in Europe for rejecting the localised approach to individual organs which Virchow had established. Their working concept of the nervous integration of the whole organism naturally unified therapeutic work with prophylactics, and brought physiology into close contact with sociology. The mainstream of Russian physiological thought, inculcated into a generation of medical students, considered the nervous system within a biological and social evolutionary framework.

The notion of progressive evolution through the active reciprocity of 'scientific' man and his milieu provided the focus for

Russian doctors' ideological solidarity. The emphasis on long-term evolution and social engineering rather than immediate and revolutionary solutions, enabled them to work *within* the system, despite the frustrations they faced. So, whereas originally the reception of Darwinism in Russia was rooted in the ideals of the 'alienated' intelligentsia, it soon was embodied in the values of a more socially secure group of technical and scientific experts with meaningful work roles.

Instead of the orientation to radical political change so typical of professionals in underdeveloped societies of the twentieth century,[127] Russian doctors concerned themselves with a host of environmental sciences. Professional journals directed them to problems of psychology, ethnography and topography as well as to biological and statistical material. *The Medical-Topographical Collection*, for example, was designed to give doctors the wide ranging knowledge of the interrelationship of nature and culture (the reciprocal influence of the climate, inhabitants and soil, and 'the results that man can attain by cultivating nature intelligently'[128]) which the profession felt should underlie sanitary measures. E. A. Osipov outlined a programme for every hygienist doctor which included a knowledge of the medical topography of the environment: its geological properties, proportions of land and water, vegetal influences and environmental diseases, its climate and related illnesses.[129] In addition he emphasised the importance to the doctor of understanding the economic, social and cultural conditions of the people, and of precise statistical knowledge of births, marriages, illnesses and deaths. Only with this breadth of understanding, Osipov insisted, could the doctor put into practice the 'truths stemming from science'. Medicine must apply to the whole man in all his social and natural relations: and it must apply to *all* men. Chekhov's work at Sakhalin was closely formulated according to Osipov's kind of programme, and, as I have suggested already, Dr Astrov's concern for the environment in *Uncle Vanya* reflected the evolutionist ideology of his profession.

To come to grips with Chekhov's world view more closely it is important to look in some detail at his period of adult socialisation as a doctor, because it was then that he internalised a perception of reality which he was never to alter. The Russian therapeutic school into which he was inducted emphasised the central role of the nervous system within the total organism, and the mutual relationship between organic forms and their milieu.[130] All of

Chekhov's teachers followed Darwin's understanding of the organism as an entity in adaptive relations with its environment, and defined illness as a *normal* occurrence under environmental conditions unfavourable to an organism.

Chekhov's main teachers at the medical faculty of Moscow University were G. A. Zakhar'in and A. A. Ostroumov for therapy, F. F. Erisman for hygiene, A. Ya. Kozhevnikov for nervous diseases, A. B. Fokht for anatomical pathology, N. V. Sklifosovskii for surgery, and V. F. Snegirev for women's illnesses—all of them leading specialists in their field and most of them heavily influenced by the specialist doctor whom Chekhov most admired, Zakhar'in.

The study of milieu as a source of illness was Zakhar'in's forte: he taught that changing a milieu which was unfavourable to an organism's functional strength was the first step in restoring its equilibrium. This of course led him to emphasise the importance of preventive medicine, and he used to tell his students that the more experienced a doctor became, the more he understood the power of hygiene and the relative weakness of therapy. He stressed that it was only hygiene which could win the struggle with the illnesses of the masses; and it was his concern with prophylactics and public health which did so much to cement the close relationship between the research and teaching at Moscow University and the public medicine of the regional zemstva. Zakhar'in lectured on the therapeutic potential of the environment, stressing particularly climate therapy and the rich natural resources of Russia; and echoes of this interest are quite frequent in Chekhov's letters, as well as in works such as *Uncle Vanya*.

Chekhov's other therapy lecturer, Ostroumov, was influenced by Lamarck as well as by Darwin in his thinking about the role of milieu in the origin of illness. Like Sechenov, Botkin, Timiryazev and many other Russian doctors and scientists, he adopted the Lamarckian idea of hereditary transfer of adaptations derived from living conditions. However, his theory was not fatalistic. With Zakhar'in, he emphasised the possibility of *removing* an hereditary susceptibility to illness through a change of milieu. Predisposition to illness by no means implied inevitability, since external conditions remained the deciding factor.

Again, letters of Chekhov written years later show his continuing allegiance to Ostroumov's ideas: for example, his acceptance of a modified version of Morel's degeneration theory (which claimed that degenerations were deviations from the normal human type, transmissable by heredity and deteriorating\progressively towards extinction). Morel had claimed that the causes of degeneration could be found in alcohol, tobacco and food poisoning, infectious diseases such as malaria, overcrowding in cities, impossible conditions of work, bad education, poverty, and other social factors; and in 1893 we find Chekhov writing to Madame Shavrova that degeneration and neurasthenia (an early stage of the malady according to Morel) can be caused by 'vodka, tobacco, over eating amongst the intelligentsia, an awful upbringing, absence of physical exercise, terrible living conditions in the city, etc.'[131] Chekhov also clearly accepted that illnesses caused by the environment could be inherited: 'there's not a thing in Nature which cannot be harmful and cannot be transmitted by heredity'.[132]

But—and this is the important point—following Ostroumov, he emphasised, not a *fatalistic* heredity as did Morel, Nordau and Lombroso in the West, but the fundamental importance of social and environmental factors which could be changed through better hygiene, better education, and social reform. His brother Mikhail has recorded a conversation between Chekhov and the biologist Wagner,[133] in which the latter was trying to prove that degeneration was incurable. Chekhov strongly opposed this belief, insisting that man's weakness through heredity could always be overcome provided the correct education and a strong moral energy were applied. As we shall see in a later chapter, he wrote *The Duel* to emphasise that even the most degenerate of individuals could be reformed.[134] He associated degeneracy and social atavism (as the opposite of progressive evolution) with contemporary stagnation: Russia, he felt, was still insufficiently influenced by science.

Wherever you find boredom and degeneracy, you are certain also to find sexual perversion, excessive depravity, early impotence and disillusioned youth. In addition you will observe a decline in art, hostility towards science and injustice of every conceivable kind. A society that has lost its belief in God, yet still fears the devil, and at the same time is hypocritical in its mourning for Botkin and its reverence for Zakhar'in. That kind of society has no right to claim it knows what justice is.[135]

Both Chekhov's teachers of therapy then, Zakhar'in and Ostroumov, placed their main stress on prophylactics rather than therapy alone (throughout his literature Chekhov was to be hostile to doctors who were mere therapists[136]). The same was true of Chekhov's lecturer in neuropathology and psychiatry, Kozhevnikov, who followed Sechenov in rejecting a dualistic separation of body and mind for a physiological approach, and was strongly influenced by the emphasis of Botkin and Zakhar'in on external influences behind mental illness. His pupil Korsakov, whose works Chekhov studied, asserted that the care of mental patients should be founded on the provision of a favourable milieu in which to fight the forces that caused the illness.

It is clear from letters, research and works written long after leaving university that Chekhov continued to hold an evolutionary world view. He was in fact strongly influenced by the works of Darwin himself—in 1886 he wrote to Bilibin, 'I'm reading Darwin . . . I love him profoundly'[137]—and based his proposed 'History of Sexual Authority'[138] and his *Sakhalin Island* on Darwinian and Spencerian principles. Both were analyses of the physical and mental evolution of the human organism according to its natural and social environment. It is certainly no surprise that the two most eloquent and insistent of all proponents of Darwinism among Russian scientists, Timiryazev and Mechnikov, were scientists whom Chekhov particularly admired.[139]

In 1892, when the cholera epidemic approached, Chekhov's analysis of the situation was, typically, that of the evolutionist:

In central Russia horses are catching influenza and dying. If one accepts that there is a purpose in everything that happens in Nature, then it's clear that Nature is doing everything she can to eliminate weak organisms which are of no use to her. Famine, cholera, influenza . . . Only the healthy and the strong will remain. It is quite impossible not to believe in a purpose. Our starlings, young and old, suddenly flew away. That puzzled us because migration time was still some way off. Now, however, we learn that clouds of southern dragonflies, mistaken for locusts, recently flew over Moscow. Which raises the question as to how our starlings knew that on a particular day, so far from Melikhovo, there would be a flight of insects. Who told them? It is certainly a great mystery, but it is also a wise mystery. This wisdom, we have to accept, lies behind famine and disease. We and our horses are like the dragonflies, famine and cholera like the starlings . . .[140]

It is an interesting letter because, in addition to the teleological element which suggests the influence of Herbert Spencer, there is also an apparant fatalism which seems to counter everything I have been saying about Chekhov and the Russian therapeutic school. He seems, in fact, to contradict Mechnikov's claim that science can counteract the cruelty of natural selection. Yet it is evident from his work as a doctor fighting the cholera epidemic with the principles of Zakhar'in and Ostroumov that Chekhov was not content with man remaining a dragonfly. And his concern to educate both himself and the public in environmental sciences suggests that a *constituent part of* the *'wise* mystery' was indeed man's potential to know more about it. Unlike Tuzenbakh in *The Three Sisters*, Chekhov was concerned to know *why* the birds flew.

Chekhov's concept of a wise evolution was in fact *purposive*— oriented towards an ideal society. Knowledge was an essential pre-requisite for social action, and action by man he believed, could secure a benign future. In his letter proposing a 'History of Sexual Authority', for example, he wrote of the need for man to help nature create a perfect organism by removing those social factors which hinder its development. At the same time social change would be evolutionary—the product of the actions of individual thinking men—and not revolutionary or dogmatic:

My belief is in individual men. I see salvation in individuals— whether peasants or intellectuals—spread out all over Russia. The power lies with them, even though at the moment they are few in number . . . These are not overbearing people, but the effects of their work are evident. Whatever else, science is on the march, steadily progressing, social awareness is growing stronger, ethical questions are beginning to make people uneasy, and so on, and so on. And all this is happening in spite of the 'crown prosecutors, the engineers, the tutors, in spite of the in-telligentsia en masse and in spite of everything.[141]

We know from an earlier section that among these widely scattered individuals Chekhov would have included the zemstvo doctors (his letter was in fact addressed to one). Their work in even the 'most wretched zemstvo hospital' was pushing forward the purpose of human evolution more than all the intelligentsia's famous ideals, and more too, he believed, than the aims of the new revolutionaries. Here, for example, is Chekhov's typically prag-matic and professional criticism of Savva Morozov, patron of the new Arts Theatre, one of the new, cultured industrialists, and dabbler in revolutionary politics:

> A rich merchant . . . he builds theatres—flirts with revolution— but there's no iodine at the dispensary and the feldscher has drunk all the alcohol in the bottles and treats rheumatism with castor oil. They're all the same—our Russian Rockerfellers.[142]

Revolution, capitalism, 'tooth and claw' survival of the fittest were all, for Chekhov, gross forces unmediated by individual human needs. The touchstone of the evolutionism which Chekhov had been taught was the individual man of many related parts: an organism which, Sechenov announced, 'has acquired a more and more complex organisation with a path of further development mapped out'.[143] There was no place here for suppression of the complex thinking individual, either by the radical 'intelligentsia en masse' or by the cruelty of impersonal natural forces. As Mechnikov put it, 'Amongst lower creatures . . . the individual disappears wholly or almost wholly in the community . . . It is only in men that the individual has definitely acquired consciousness, and for that reason a satisfactory social organisation cannot sacrifice it on the pretext of the common good.'[144]

Optimism in the potential of individual men was the focal centre of the evolutionist vision. And yet the very anthropòcentricity of the ideology itself exposed a tragic fear. In Western versions of Darwinism progress was ensured simply by natural selection working 'solely by and for the good of each being'. But now, by playing down this inevitability, reducing the ultimate role of chance, and extending evolutionary theories to man's own mental endowments, Russian Darwinists opened the way back to the old dilemma. If, as Mechnikov would argue, natural selection had produced a being who could *deliberately* aim for perfection, deliberately after the environment so that new variations might flourish, then the emphasis was no longer on the automatic course of natural history but on *man*, and the gap lay open as before between man's natural potential and what, at worst, he might achieve. Everything would depend on the expert, on his knowledge, his imperfections, and on the social forces which hemmed him in.

It was a problem lying at the heart of some of Chekhov's greatest works (such as *Dreary Story*), which resonated between the conflicting patterns of nature and culture, and made the space for Chekhov's particular drama of hope and tragedy. By isolating man as an unstable variable within the evolutionary process, Russian Darwinists removed the inevitability from the hope of perfection. In its place was a struggle between the forces of evil and light, readily personified as the autocratic state and the scientific spirit. Since illness was considered to be something normal under conditions unfavourable to an organism, the frighteningly isolated struggle for human individuality against terrible external odds was bound to create pathological responses—and these are what Chekhov presents in the Ivanovs, Treplevs and Vanyas of his literature. The subjective individual response to environmental pressure had been a major focus of Zakhar'in's therapeutic school.[145] Chekhov had learned from Ostroumov, for example, that subjective sensations would appear before a clinician could isolate morphological changes in the organs by objective methods. Hence this personal data, in conjunction with a careful study of the patient's home life and milieu, was to play an important part in the day-to-day work of the practising doctor. Doctors who knew him said that Chekhov was always attentive to the individual feelings and mental condition of his patients, and that he attached a lot of importance to the influence of the physician himself, as part of the human environment, on the patient's psychological state.[146] Chekhov himself told Rossolimo that it was extremely important to make medical students understand the importance scientifically of patients' subjective feelings.

When, in the 1890s, Chekhov had hopes of lecturing at Moscow University, his subject was to be subjective pathology and therapy. The lectures were never delivered. But by then Chekhov had adapted the perspective to his literature. The permeating mood, a tension of hope and despair, derived from the world view of a zemstvo doctor: optimistic in the knowledge that man had evolved so far (and had the tools to progress much farther still); desperate at the continuing ubiquity of the forces of repression.

4 The Epic Vision

Having dealt in considerable detail with the genetic aspect of Chekhov's works, I want in this chapter to turn to the more formal structural connotations. These, of course, cannot ever be *purely* formal in a genetic structuralist approach, and nor will one look for causation strictly within the structures themselves, as structural linguists do. As Goldmann points out, 'Significative structures are the result of a *genesis* and cannot be understood or explained independently of this genesis'. We will be examining the formal *relationship* between society and text in a structural way. The determining values which have been described in the last chapters in fact *shape* the forms which will be described here.

A useful way of thinking of this relationship in socio-literary terms was defined by Kenneth Burke who spoke of art forms, like tragedy or comedy, as *strategies* designed to encompass new social situations.[1] Hence art forms are not universal (though, as Goldmann points out, they might *recur* at different times), but dependent for their configuration on contemporaneous social events.

Burke, however, was not a structuralist, and so was less concerned with the formal system of distinctions within a work which makes meaning possible. I defined certain essential features of a structuralist analysis in chapter 2—the exposure of minimal functional distinctions, their syntagmatic and paradigmatic context and relations—and will examine these in relation to Chekhov in the next few chapters. Here I want to demonstrate what I suggested in chapter 2, that, as with Barthes' and Goldmann's analyses of Racine, there are three formal 'spaces', encapsulating two oppositions, in Chekhov's works.

It is easier now to see the genetic basis of these functional distinctions (the degraded world, the epic vision, the false choice) in terms of Chekhov's own interaction with his milieu. This represented a continuous tension, both socially and psychologically, between constructions of the world he 'knew' to be debased (those of the 'bureaucratic-autocratic' élite and, correlatively the brutal-mystical value system of his father[2]), constructions of the world he 'knew' to be authentic, but were constantly threatened from all sides (zemstvo medicine, and its epistemological basis in materialism and evolutionism), and constructions of the world which looked for authenticity in broadening spheres (new literary forms, ideology, sublime 'Art' etc), but found only ambiguity and frustration.

What is significant in literary terms, though, is not simply the homologous relationship between units of the social world and units of the text, but the formal relationship of these 'spaces'. By considering this textual structure we can begin to understand how the text *produces* meaning, and promotes an ideological response, rather than simply reflecting in its content the values of a social group. This is to suggest that a literary work does not simply *mirror* its social context—not even that of the social group or class it expresses—but re-formulates it as an active *textual* strategy. Or, to stand Kenneth Burke on a materialist base, it is to follow Trotsky's insight that the new artistic forms which evolve as a response to new social needs are less a reflection than a 'deflection' of reality—a transformation of the social world into form through the *work* of the artist.

In terms of textual structure, the central location (the 'space' in which the drama is enacted) lies between the degraded world of stagnant Russia which he always portrays and the epic world which the rational-materialist perspective lays open. One could call this location, as Barthes does for Racine, the place of language, in so far that this is the point where all the tension of ambiguity, partial coherence, hope and despair bursts into voice. Except that underlying language there is always the prior determinant of *choice*. He who has no opportunity to choose (usually through lack of an education) is inevitably part of the degraded present and only occupies this space, if at all, to vulgarise or destroy it. He who chooses the 'true' path of reason inhabits this space only as a marginal figure, a complex and endlessly suffering prophet who 'knows' (like Astrov and Vershinin) the way to a better future even while he is 'called away' and crushed by the present. The typical protagonist of the location of choice is the one who chooses to reject the society he knows as debased, yet (like the Marxist's victim of false consciousness) responds with an inauthentic solution that ties him the more securely to the degraded world.

We have then, as in Racine, two oppositions: in this case, between choice and no choice, and between true and inauthentic choice. But the contrast which structures the dramatic context and defines the functional position of the protagonist is not, as in Racine, an opposition of power. In Chekhov it is an opposition of *knowledge*. Ultimately it is an opposition of he who has knowledge and he who has not; and the drama lies in the *resolution* of that simple opposition out of complexity and ambiguity. Hence one of the most significant themes in Chekhov's work is: 'unknowing hero rejects the world and, through the inauthenticity of his acts, is crushed': which, in any one text, becomes a three part chain of elements (hero → defeated/rejection → degraded world) incorporating and clarifying the two oppositions. Paradigmatic alternatives of this suffering protagonist may be young, inexperienced women with a merely 'ascriptive' education, young artists who cannot find authentic forms, young revolutionaries who suppress science beneath dogma, young men who labour for change but with the anachronism of Tolstoyan populism—and so on. In this chapter I want to relate the chain of thematic units in Chekhov to their genetic base; and in the following chapters will look in more substantial terms at the more significant of the paradigmatic alternatives.

* * * * *

Malcolm Bradbury once wrote in the following way of the interdisciplinary possibilities for literary analysis:

> One of the things lettrists, historians and sociologists might try to illuminate in common is the idea of a change in sensibility or consciousness—the kind of change that goes on in men's lives and psychic structures when society itself goes through a period of analysable alteration.[3]

Goldmann's writing, and the work of one or two people influenced by him,[4] has been along these lines, so that we can now begin to see some tentative links between the sociological phenomenon of downward mobility and the literary form of tragedy. We also know, of course, that a 'tragic' interpretation of Chekhov has been quite well established in Western culture since his death. Yet both individually *and* as a member of the medical group, Chekhov was *upwardly* mobile—though this social mobility was hedged in by considerable pressures of both a social and a psychological kind.[5] A simple tragic vision seems, *a priori*, unlikely in view of Chekhov's optimism in the potential of science. We will see when we look later at his works in more detail that the familiar pessimistic interpretation (of the ending of *The Three Sisters*, for example) in fact perverts their central structure; and we will have to look beyond tragedy for Bradbury's connection between changes in consciousness, social structure and literary form.

We will not be helped much by comparable work in the field, because despite Goldmann's plea for case studies (like his *Hidden God*) which might form the basis for a model of literary typologies, almost nothing has appeared. Still, hints in Goldmann and Lukacs, and more general analyses by non-Marxist critics like George Steiner and Sir Maurice Bowra[6] offer *some* consistencies of approach to understanding social genesis in an alternative literary form to the tragic: the epic. It is a convenient point to start.

Lukacs and Goldmann, Steiner and Bowra would seem to agree both that in Homer we find the first and probably only (truly) epic world, and about its constituents. Lukacs defines the epic world according to its 'natural', complete and straightforward unity between man and the world when the 'transcendent was inextricably interwoven with earthly existence'.[7] He is drawing here on Marx's understanding of the sense of equilibrium between man and nature in primitive societies which the commodity production of capitalism necessarily destroys. Goldmann, like Bowra, speaks of a time when man, the world and the gods formed a community; a world, in other words, in which values were 'radically immanent' and entirely anthropocentric.[8] Steiner speaks of a 'consonance between man and the surrounding world', where the barriers between man and object are removed, and men perform as gods (and gods as men) on behalf of central human values and the earth's enduring beauty. The spirit of the epic, Bowra concludes, is 'its attempt to find significance in the achievements of man and to show him in his essential nobility'.[9]

The *transparency* of this measure between man, the world and value is exemplified in the epic imagery: of gods with the lusts of men, of a sensate nature which weeps when the hero dies, and a cycle of seasons which asserts, more powerfully than any individual action, the triumph of humanism. Man is 'the measure and pivot of experience',[10] and what is essential is in this world. 'War and mortality cry havoc in the Homeric and Tolstoyan worlds, but the centre holds; it is the affirmation that life is, of itself, a thing of beauty, that the works and days of men are worth recording, and that no catastrophe—not even the burning of Troy or Moscow—is ultimate'—for the charred towers will be forgotten, and the harvest will come again.[11] The sense of counterpoint between man's detailed acts of heroism and his enduring seasons is close to that at the end of Kurosawa's *Seven Samurai*: when the two surviving heroes survey from high up the peasants they have saved in blood but who, planting once again, have forgotten them. The largesse of human greatness is here rounded by an endurance which surmounts any catastrophe: 'The picture of helmeted warriors scattering before Hector grows dim and now we see the grass bending before the storm'.[12]

Without the 'roundedness' of this primitively transparent connection (of man, the world and value) the whole man becomes divided and his acts accidental. Steiner mentions together Homer and Tolstoi, but it is clear that for him, as for Lukacs, Tolstoi works against the *loss* of that classical heritage. Both agree that Tolstoi's epic sought to *re-integrate* man, and bring him *back* to his natural relationship with the world. Tolstoi's form is thus not a natural epic, but an *epic vision*, since 'It is naturally impossible to preserve among the realities of capitalist society the Homeric intensity of the relations between man and his world'.[13]

The feature of this vision and the quality, for Lukacs and Steiner, of its art, is its ability to move beyond the static naturalism of a Zola, who, they believed, naturalised the degraded objects of his contemporary social world as though they were innate and for ever. Tolstoi's vision gave the otherwise 'accidental' events and objects of the world their significance by relating them to human destinies, thus creating that Hegelian 'totality of objects' through which an entire society is portrayed. It is this quality of presenting reality from a standpoint of enduring human values *outside* the degraded present which defines the epic vision. Lukacs says of Tolstoi: 'He always saw capitalist society as a world of distortion, as a befouling of human reality proper; he therefore always contrasted it with another, natural and hence human reality.'[14]

From this notion of the organic, anthropocentric nature of value, a whole life-aesthetic can follow. In fact from here there can be two kinds of vision of epic wholeness, and two 'organicist' aesthetics: a nostalgia for a pre-mechanistic society, as in Tolstoi, and as in Leavis; and a prediction of a new utopia, as in Revolutionary Romanticism and the 'idealist' aesthetic of Neo-Hegelians like Lukacs.[15]

The crucial factor of each one of these 'epic visions' is the notion of loss and the perspective of gain, the tension of a look of hope situated *within* a degraded world. The epic vision and Goldmann's 'tragic vision' thus have certain common features. They are both deeply concerned with the *rupture* between man, the world and value. And they are both, in Goldmann's terms, 'philosophies of incarnation' in that they 'demand that values should become immanent in the real world'.[16] This in fact distinguishes them from the Absurdist 'Nothing is more real than nothing', and also from the Existentialist's *endless* tension between being and becoming. 'Authenticity', according to both visions, is finite and attainable.

But the epic and tragic visions are also fundamentally different.

(1) Goldmann points to the tendency to *non-historicity* in tragic thought, since there can be no *terrestrial* hope in an absolutely degraded world. But an epic vision, whether of the Marxian kinds we have mentioned, or (and here we return, of course, to Chekhov) the Russian Darwinist kind, *is* historical, since it believes that the degraded world will only be transcended through the actions of men *in history*. Whereas tragic man 'lacks any completely trustworthy theoretical foundation on which to base his certainty that God exists',[17] both Marxists and Russian Darwinists have enjoyed the security of a 'coherent' body of theory which claimed the status of scientific objectivity *and* called man to action on behalf of a world of immanent value.

Chekhov's belief in the unity of science and art involved a confirmed moral commitment. Critics often say that Chekhov refused to judge, which makes it hard to know what he was doing with some of his characters (such as Natasha in *The Three Sisters*) whom he clearly indicts for a crushing evil. The fact is that Chekhov did judge, but always in terms of context. For the positivist it was the *nature* of judgement that differentiated the objective observer from the subjective 'systematiser'. There was no contradiction between the demand for objectivity and judgement. As Nochlin has noted, 'although the Realist refrained from moral comment in his work, his whole attitude toward art implied a moral commitment, to the values of truth, honesty and sincerity. In his very refusal to idealize, elevate or in any way embellish his subject, in his stalwart dedication to objective, impartial description and analysis, the Realist took a moral stand'.[18] As Chekhov wrote in his Notebooks, 'when you show man what he is, then he will be better'.[19]

What distinguished him from other European Realists was his

version of evolutionism: as a follower of Darwin who 'believed in progress',[20] he could not agree with Zola that muck heaps comprised the *whole* landscape. He believed sincerely that things were getting better in Russia because of science, however bleak they might appear at the moment. So there is in his work more concern for continuity, less for temporal fragmentation than in the Naturalist art of Western Europe. Chekhov did not believe that the objective writer must portray unrelieved gloom. Certainly, he must show the muck heaps, *but*, he writes to Leikin, 'The ugly is no more real than the beautiful';[21] and he scolds Shcheglov for his writing which does scant justice to progress.

> I am not all that happy about our times, but one must try to be objective. If life is not so good now, and if the present is unpleasant, then the past was absolutely foul.[22]

This perspective of dour optimism is the one he gives Vershinin in *Three Sisters*: and it is given some sort of continuity by the colonel's ability to see what *is* beautiful in contemporary life. Objectivity, Chekhov insisted to Shcheglov, sometimes demands a hymn of praise:

> Be objective, see the world as a decent man, and write a novel about life in Russia which is not a mere criticism of it, but . . . praising life in Russia, life generally, life which we only get once.[23]

Criticism of life as it was and belief in its evolution towards something better were always and inextricably related throughout his works. He was as severe with writers who *merely* hymned 'life for life's sake' as he was with 'subjective' pessimism. On the one hand he criticises Madame Sazonova, who wants to extract the 'essence' of life out of its social and evolutionary context; on the other he scolds Shcheglov for equating life with the contemporary social mess, and ignoring the future: 'I write of the lack of aims, and you gather that I believe such aims are *necessary*, and that I am eager to seek them out'.[24] But, Chekhov adds, if man ignores further evolution, if he believes higher aims are as little necessary to him as to a cow, then there is nothing left for him to do but 'eat, drink, sleep, and, when he gets sick of that, bash his head open on the edge of a box'.

Chekhov's realism depends on a continuity—his familiar 'long chain' stretching out of the past and into the future—and yet at the same time a dramatic *tension* between 'what is' and 'what ought to be' which, by and large, is absent in the European writers:

> writers whom we consider universal, or even just good, and who carry us away, have one essential characteristic in common: they reach somewhere, they call you there, and you sense, not simply intellectually but with your whole personality, that they have a specific aim and . . . don't invade and inflame your imagination without reason . . . The best writers are realistic and depict life as it is, but because their every line is saturated . . . with a sense of purpose, you touch, as well as life as it is, life as it should be, and this is what is appealing.[25]

So artistic essence is the distillation of the positivistic 'is' and the evolutionist 'ought to be'; accurate observation of the empirical detail is no more than the first stage towards purposeful generalis- ation. Literature must rise above the obsessive, Zolaesque concern for the sordid present *and* above the schematic hunting for 'tendencies', since both these have their origin precisely 'in man's inability to rise above the particular'.[26] To concern oneself dogmatically with this or that style, to involve oneself entirely with faddish and controversial data, is to subordinate objective selection to arbitrary 'tendencies', typicality to topicality, art to journalism. Thus the arbitrary fact attains a specious generality.

The literary device which he believed would compress selected data and generalisation into a literary form was the notion of 'typicality'. Personally, Chekhov wrote, I stick to this rule; 'I portray sick people in only those features which are characteristic and descriptive'.[27] Deviation was only interesting if understood in its significant context—that is, as an essential feature of a society at a particular moment. He was very annoyed when some critics reduced his *Dreary Story*, which analysed the context of the contemporary apathy and pessimism among intellectuals, to no more than an unnatural relationship between the professor and his ward. If he had only a sexual perversion to describe, Chekhov wrote with a puritanism worthy of Lukacs, he would not have written this story. It was the social typicality he was after.

Similarly, he criticised Goncharov's *Oblomov* as no more than a 'trivial, average' character, 'not worth elevating to the position of social type'.[28] There is more than a hint here of Dobrolyubov's brand of didacticism, as there is, again, of Lukacs. But the similarity stems more from the adopted literary form than shared social ideals. As René Wellek has pointed out, though realism claims to be objective, its observation is inevitably from within some reformist and didactic paradigm, whether Marxian, materialist, or whatever. 'Without ever realising the conflict between description and prescription it tries to reconcile the two in the concept of type'.[29] The very *notion* of typicality depends upon a sureness about the way history is moving—made easier if you are a Marxist, or, in Chekhov's case, an evolutionist.

By the same token the logical hiatus between prescription and description will cause problems of interpretation for those who are not in on the secret. In the case of *Ivanov*, the Russian audience could neither understand Chekhov's analytical approach, nor his specifically evolutionary perspective. So Ivanov himself was taken to be a despicable sluggard of the sixties, and the revolutionary Lvov as a worthy, but weakly presented, proponent of Chekhov's values. Yet Chekhov had believed he had created in Ivanov a type who was both representative of his age (as defined by the latest medical theory) and new in literature (which, he felt, up to this point had not been asking the right questions). Previous writers had, he said, created their superfluous men out of their intuition; he, on the other hand, had presented 'the contours correctly'.

The problem was partly a matter of different values, as the continued misinterpretation of Chekhov shows, and partly a matter of artistic form. Chekhov was to spend his career looking for a form which could convey his meaning precisely without resort to the drawn out soliloquys he added to Ivanov's stage part.[30] Meanwhile, he constantly returned to his central notion of typicality in giving advice to other artists and actors. For example, suggestions flowed out to writers as varying in quality as Lydia Avilova, Madame Shavrova and Maxim Gork'ii to describe human misery in the 'cool' objective style, which related the unfortunate to their background more effectively than the alternative of empathy, sighs and tears. Subjectivity of this kind, he wrote, blurs the images and prevents compactness and precision. 'The more objective you are, the stronger the effect'.[31] Sorrow should be placed in its milieu where it would stand out more clearly. On the one hand, the external relations should not be presented so arbitrarily as to reduce explanation (for however successfully the 'central moon' was presented, it could only be understood properly 'if the stars too are understandable'.[32] On the other hand, the uncontrolled temptation to descriptive background detail must be suppressed since this would obscure the typical. He wrote to Avilova, 'You have amassed a whole host of details, the proliferation of which hides the sun from our view';[33] and suggested that although Turgenev's famous descriptions of nature were good, something beyond mere description was needed now.[34]

He also had advice on how the 'central moon' could be portrayed 'typically'. His psychiatric training in Kozhevnikov and Korsakov had taught Chekhov that the observer should be kind to the observed, and throw off his own subjectivity in penetrating the patient's personal feelings. Hence, the author, too, should be 'kind to the fingertips', and, though analysing his subjects objectively, 'must constantly think and speak in their mode and feel with their emotions'.[35] The main innovation Darwinian psychologists had made was in correlating the visible facts of overt behaviour (and the related environmental issues) with subjective moods and feelings. Characteristically Chekhov insisted that an author should avoid subjective generalisations about the psychological state of his characters, but should make this clear from their actions.[36]

> Suffering should be presented as it is expressed in life: not via arms and legs but through tone and expression; and subtly, not through gesticulations. Subtle emotions of the spirit, as experienced by people of education, must be expressed subtly, through external behaviour. You will argue about stage conditions, but no conditions can excuse inaccuracy.[37]

So we have the emotions of an Astrov or a Vanya related to their overt behaviour—a whistle, a lethargic shrug—which in turn is carefully presented in its milieu of 'unhealthy' circumstances. This relationship of subjective sensation, overt behaviour and environmental context is as central to Chekhov's concept of typicality in art as to his medical world view. In a letter to Meierkhol'd, he warns against theatrically overplaying the individually neurotic aspects of his young scientist-hero, who has just come back to his bourgeois family from an intellectual milieu. Echoing Merzheyevskii and his teachers at medical school, Chekhov suggests that the real task of the artist is to present the pathology of a healthy organism trapped in an unhealthy environment:

One must not underline this nervous temperament, because the highly strung, neuropathological nature would hide and misrepresent the much more important loneliness—the loneliness experienced only by a fine, and at the same time healthy (in the fullest sense of the word) organism. Depict a lonely man . . . Do not treat this nervousness as a separate phenomenon. Remember that in our day every cultured man, even the most healthy, is most irritable in his own home and among his own family, because the discord between the present and the past is first of all apparent in the family.[38]

'Objective partisanship'—the combination of description and prescription—is, of course, far more familiar in Marxian writers and critics, from Engels to Brecht. Chekhov's similarity with Brecht in this respect is illuminating. Like Brecht, Chekhov believed that literature should portray the world in its *causal* relationships, to understand it in order to change it. Both dramatists believed that their art should report in a matter-of-fact way, avoiding emotion and subjectivity for their own sake, and avoiding also that complacent illusionism of static types which functions to suppress critical thought in an audience. This is the basis of Chekhov's 'cool' style and of Brecht's 'alienating' devices. Their object was to cast doubt on the 'natural' and 'eternal' character of the existing social world, even while refusing to offer a simple, programmatic solution. The 'solution', in fact, was enshrined in the historical nature of the vision, and therefore in the characterisation. The 'reality' of the Ivanovs and Astrovs was socially conditioned, and social conditions were created by men. Hence theatre should not produce the static types of a set reality, the 'inevitably' neurasthenic Russian Hamlets *reflecting* the current malaise. Characterisation should rather present the reality *produced* by men *in history*, because what is produced by men can be changed by them.

Brecht wrote that in the 'scientific age',

man can no longer be described to man as a mere victim, the object of an unknown but unalterable environment. The world of today can be described to the human beings of today only as a world that can be changed'.[39]

by preventing the spectator from submitting uncritically, empathising, he is forced to exclaim 'I'd never have thought it—

That's not the way—That's extraordinary, hardly believable—
It's got to stop—The sufferings of this man appall me because
they are unnecessary.[40]

And Chekhov, with a similar belief in the power of science, wrote:

All I wanted to say honestly to people was, 'Have a look at
yourselves and see how dreary your lives are!' The important
thing is that people should realise that, for when they do they will
certainly create another and better life for themselves.[41]

It is in this sense of understanding the *inner* truth of reality
through typification (with the rider that once actuality is understood it may be dissolved) that the epic vision *produces* reality.[42]

(2) Apart from the differences in relating to history and human
choice, there is another contrast between the tragic and epic visions.
Whereas both demand absolute values, the tragic vision refuses the
world because all choices within it are equally inauthentic and
inadequate. The demand for 'totality' is irreconcilable with a
'fragmentary', 'compromising' and ambiguous world. On the other
hand since the epic world must arise through human action in this
world, not all choices can be equally inauthentic. So while rejecting
compromise, while rejecting the degraded world (of capitalism, of
tsarism) in its entirety, the epic vision does choose, perhaps in
embryo, the representative features of the world that will replace it.
Whereas, for Goldmann, the tragic vision is totally indifferent to
degrees and approximations and any concept containing the idea of
relativity, the epic vision is crucially concerned with stages of
development and relative truths, with the movement through
quantity to quality. The first Marxist revolution was not to emerge
fully formed out of the head of capitalism in Russia, and nor did
Russian Darwinists expect the scientific society to come out of the
new administrative reforms without degrees of ambiguity, struggle
and false choice. But come, little by little, out of the present society it
must. The call to action, arising out of a degraded world, was
certain to be problematic.

To return to the level of textual structure, we can see that these
constituent differences within world views have significant effects on
the relationship of minimal thematic units. In Goldmann's world of
tragic rejection there is only the tragic hero, a hidden God, and an
incorrigibly brutish society, since if there were a single other person

with whom the hero could converse at the level of essence a
community would have been formed and the tragic universe
overcome. But in the degraded world of the epic vision not all men
are equally inauthentic and brutal. Because of the reappearance of
value, because of the concern for stages of development, man may
choose. And, as part of the 'totality' of the degraded world, he may
choose wrongly. So, as well as the brutish man who makes no choice,
and the man of relative authenticity who, for the moment chooses
rightly, the world also contains the man of inauthentic choice (or
'false consciousness' in the Marxian paradigm) who chooses, but
chooses wrongly. Whereas for the tragic vision there is only the
greatness and final authenticity of the tragic hero and the bestial
certainty of everyone else, for the epic vision the social world
contains at least three types: the brutish 'type' of the degraded
totality, the relatively authentic visionary trapped in the degraded
present, and the *inauthentic* shadow of the absent epic hero.

Syntagmatically, the relationships of the central thematic units
will differ significantly. Goldmann's central plot sequence depends
on a mute opposition between the world, the hero and an absent
God—a three part interaction which depends on the textual
presence of an absent God, and a total, qualitative opposition
between the hero and the rest of the world. Racine's tragedies are
thus characterised by a sequential opposition of hero, world and
value (the absent God); his histories by a collapsing of these minimal
units from a qualitative to a merely quantitative distinction.

Chekhov's structure differs from both these in that there is a
continuous tension *between* quantitative and qualitative oppositions.
The inauthentic hero's choice to reject the world as debased can
never, in the absence for him of value ('true' science), be more than
a quantitative one. Whereas the distinction between the latter and
the epic visionary is, in *essence*, one of quality. The possession of
knowledge is a distinction of quality; yet in *fact* the huge pressures
threatening the epic visionary constantly threaten to collapse even
that quality into quantity. Chekhov's 'open endings' depend on this
enduring potential for fluctuation: for example, the possession by
Astrov in *Uncle Vanya* when *last* we see him of both his scientific maps
(folded carefully, prophets of a better future) *and* vodka (which, the
text makes clear, would destroy him). The tension locates itself in
the central space, of language, of choice, where the two oppositions
are dramatised: the opposition of degraded world and inauthentic
choice—a quantitative distinction helplessly striving for quality;

and the opposition of inauthentic choice and epic vision—a qualitative distinction threatened constantly by quantity.

There can be no positive hero in an alien world. The epic hero is an absent hero, present only as a negating shadow, or in a vision with many partial forms. What is absent in the degraded world is the transparent dialogue between man and the world, 'man as a whole in the whole of society'. What is present is, at best, the divided self—in constant dialogue with an authentic world and with the more powerful degraded world. In the tragedy of rejection, the hero's loneliness springs from the world's inability ever to listen to a voice speaking genuinely of essence; his sufferings from the uninterrupted tension between hope and fear in the face of a hidden God. The suffering of the epic visionary springs from the tension which must be maintained endlessly between the degraded and authentic worlds, yet his loneliness is existential, of this life only. His vision of a new community is uncertain in action, but more structured than a dream.

Life is certainly hard, and for many of us appears pointless, insurmountable . . . But you have to agree that, little by little, it is becoming less onerous and more hopeful. And we can be sure that the day is not too far off when life will brighten up everywhere.

Our own sufferings may bring happiness to those who come after us . . . A time will come when there is a world of peace and happiness, and when that day comes, people will think kindly of us and thank us. No, life is not over for us yet, my dear sisters!

(*The Three Sisters*)

Goldman wrote of Racine that tragic clarity meant awareness of the unchangeable nature of man and the certainty of death.[43]

In contrast, for Chekhov (as for Brecht) 'clarity' meant the communication of an awareness that limits were made by men, and could be changed; 'greatness' lay in endurance, not in death, and in the visionary's refusal either to succumb to the present, or to look for the future community too soon. Death, in Chekhov, is never the 'creative suffering' of tragedy, but merely a hopeless submission to the degraded world. Revolutionary romanticism, on the other hand, he saw as an undisciplined submission to utopia, a facile flooding of the present with the light of a potential future. Neither the 'it will all be the same in a thousand years' of a Ragin (*Ward Number Six*) nor the 'It's almost upon us—I can hear its footsteps' of a Trofimov (*The Cherry Orchard*) could be accepted. Cynical deaths/ naive new beginnings were no more than escapes from the struggle and suffering, from the necessary tension of hope and despair which structures the authentic vision:

> It was almost as though a solution would turn up and a new and beautiful life would begin in just a few more minutes. But deep down they both knew that in fact the end was still a long, long way away, and the hardest and most complicated period was only just beginning
>
> (*Lady with a Little Dog*)

On the one hand, the contemporary presence of value in Chekhov's vision precludes the tragic death. On the other, the inner divisions of the epic visionary preclude the dramatic, concentrated, naked collision, the 'totality of motion', which Lukacs believes to be the aesthetic centre of tragedy. The hero is too ambiguous, too much part of the degraded 'totality of objects'—the brick yards, the schools, the post offices, the vast distances, and the vodka bottles— to attain Lukacs' moment of truth out of collision and the utter dislocation of human affairs. Such conflicts as occur are themselves ambiguous, and never polarised as the dramatic centre of the work. Rather it is the retarding and amplifying elements—what Lukacs calls the epic 'motifs which distance the hero from his goal'[44]—that seem to dominate; and the action is founded frequently on a journey for authenticity, a search and a succession of choices in which the overpowering presence of the present makes failure, wrong choices, a constant refrain. The movement, as in Brecht's epic theatre, is away from individual growth and linear action, and towards a collage of several journeys which generally fail, but in failing clarify and perhaps explain the failure of each other. Each suffering character becomes part of a chorus, recounting, against his milieu, the tale of a whole society. Chekhov's chorus,[45] at least in intention, predicted its function in Brecht: to distance the spectator from the character, directing his attention to the social causal network and sharpening his freedom to calculate. Thus it would mediate and ward off the dramatic concentration of tragedy, and yet also overcome the 'bad infinity' of meaningless social action and a discrete natural world.

For the spectator is never left with the retarding aspects alone. George Steiner has wondered whether 'the motif of a journey towards material or spiritual resurrection and the sense of two worlds' are typical elements of an epic vision;[46] and certainly it is fundamental to an understanding of Chekhov that his two worlds, the one articulating the other, are recognised around and beyond the journeys of rejection. It is because there *are* two worlds—or in Goldmann's terminology, just because God/value is always present—that clear choices are always available which, taken in the right succession, will usher in the epic world. Hence such struggles, though ambiguous, contradictory, sometimes self-defeating and often marginal, will always be significant, clarifying the direction of human failure. If inauthentic choice dominates the stage, it can never be, in this essentially historical vision, a static position or place of withdrawal. According to Chekhov's evolutionary beliefs, the degraded society had a logic of its own. The only real choice, as he shows in his *Sakhalin Island*, is between scientific evolution and social atavism. Just as the epic visionary is linked (despite the bleak possibilities of his personal experience) substantially with the epic world he will never see, so the hero of rejection is linked substantially with the degraded world which he has never really left. The isolation of these two heroes in the space of language and choice clarifies the present loss and the potential gain of a community of man, the world and value.

5 The Epic Vision: Science and Value

The defining opposition of Chekhov's drama is between men who have knowledge and men who have not. 'True' knowledge is the ultimate criterion for valued action. The investiture of an authentic value beyond the individual ego provided a space for 'realism' and the concept of typicality rather than 'naturalism'. It also placed Chekhov within the dominant intellectual tradition of the nineteenth century, defined nicely by John Carroll:

> Copernicus and Darwin undermined man's image of himself as the 'measure of all things'. Newton provided him with a new hope which the Benthamite tradition was to transplant into social theory—that of 'man as the measurer of all things'. Thus the possibility was revealed to man, who had been disinherited from *being* at the centre of the universe, that he might be able to *know* how to work himself back there. Science, at the same time as it destroyed his ontological security, gave him the tools for reapproaching Eden—through eating of the fruit of scientific knowledge he gained the faith that through eating again and again he might be saved.[1]

This was to place between man's monadic being and a mute world a third term: a value, which restored the lost organicism.

Dostoyevskii was, in Carroll's analysis, a seminal thinker of the *alternative, anarcho-individualist* position. Hence we have the curious fact that two Russian writers who were nearly contemporaries expressed two of the most potent *intellectual* orientations of the nineteenth and twentieth centuries. They represented competing statements ('man in an elemental state of conflict with a constraining society and man uniting with man to create an integrated and harmonious community'[2]), the essence of which was the opposition between a subjectivist, psychological orientation (as in

Dostoyevskii) and an objectivist, sociological world view (as in Chekhov).

For Dostoyevskii the soul of each man was unique, a noumenal source fundamentally beyond knowledge or generalisation. His burning opposition to Claude Bernard was based on the belief that the new science was seeking to conceptualise and straightjacket a mystery outside equation. Suppression of contradiction, passion and human responsibility were, as he saw it, the hateful results of positivist science and the technological civilisation which he encountered in Western Europe. Bernard's physiological assault on the deepest recesses of the human psyche threatened to reduce the *ineffable* qualities of man's spirit to banal causality. Before Bernard, Dostoyevskii claimed, science had only sought partial explanations of man's place in the world, and room still remained for the mystery of the noumenal. But now scientists were trapping even those inner places in their equations. $2 \times 2 = 4$ became for Dostoyevskii the signifier of all that was most spurious and one-dimensional about the fanatical search for objective truth; and he presented the irrationalism of the Underground Man as an anarchic defence against not just the existing social order, but against *any* order prior to the individual man, and specifically against the threatening dominance of institutionalised science.

I have noted elsewhere[3] that Suvorin drew on Dostoyevskii's argument in discussing Bourget's *Disciple*, and that Chekhov's answer was to re-affirm materialism and to argue that it was in fact science not the mysterious places which were most threatened in his time. He presented his own equation, which, in its specific reference to Dostoyevskii's obsessions, suggested that he had at least a very clear *negative* reference in contemporary literature: truth, he asserted, was indeed to be found—and not by 'seeking in Dostoyevskii, but by clear knowledge as one knows twice two is four'.

At the centre of the opposition between the anarcho-individualist position and the 'scientific' one (and here Dostoyevskii, but not of course Chekhov, would have included revolutionary socialism) was the emphasis of the latter on establishing an organic and mutually integrated community as the precondition for personal freedom. This was especially true of Russian Darwinism. The influence of Bernard and Herbert Spencer had founded psychology as a biological and evolutionary science *throughout* Europe, so that the idea of the 'adjustment of inner to outer relations' was generally accepted. However, the localised approach to illness of Virchow had been institutionalised in the West to the extent of subverting the practical implications of the organic notion; and in addition, as René Dubos has pointed out in his history of medicine and evolutionary thought, the operational advantages to scientists and doctors of neglecting questions related to the nature of mind and soul has meant that physicians have traditionally acted as if they were still Cartesian dualists, quite irrespective of their philosophical beliefs.[4]

In Russia, though, as Dostoyevskii well knew, stress *was* increasingly being laid on the symbiotic contribution of each organism to the welfare of its neighbour, and mental processes were included in the organic model. As we have seen, the main emphases of Chekhov's medical education were, on the one hand, on understanding mental and somatic illness as cases of misdirected *adaptive* response by neural mechanisms to fluctuating external pressure (as exemplified in theories of degeneracy), and, on the other hand, in the claim that such external conditions could be changed, *via* man's mental endowments, to provide a more stable milieu. This activist approach to the 'higher' processes of human life provided the impetus for the self-same project of social engineering, technology, human improvement and social reform which Dostoyevskii saw as the death-knell of the individual geist: 'I don't accept as the crowning of my dreams a big building for the poor, with apartments leased for a thousand years and a dentist's sign outside the door in case of emergency'.[5] He was certainly right to see in this the death of tragedy, since the worst excesses must now be the result of wilful obstruction or misunderstanding and hence, in principle, be open to human intervention and change.

John Carroll has pointed to a central structural principle of Dostoyevskii's novels: the 'intense absorption with which the central characters, with rare exceptions, pursue their individual salvation'. The unpeeling of an ego unimpaired by conscience or knowledge amounts to a rejection of all organic accretions overlaying the monadic spirit, and is the only point of coherence in the novels: 'no other structurings of reality recover from the demolition into chaos to which they are subjected'.[6]

In contrast to this solipsistic structure, Chekhov works *out* from an apparently solitary milieu—the 'inner action' of his dramas—to a contextual synthesis in the organic relations of social behaviour. His understanding of the intense *reciprocating* community of man, his world and his knowledge, in fact provided him with rules for sets of interchangeable·paradigmatic alternatives, each constituent of which he could use to clarify the oppositions referred to in the previous chapter. The units of man, the world and value (science) have meaning only in relation to each other, in their organic connection. But each could *replace* the others in individual works. Thus, for example, the narrative of rejection and false choice could be told in the context of (i) science, (ii) the social and natural world, (iii) the social communication of men and women. Paradigmatic alternatives for the central role of inauthentic hero could thus be:

(i) scientists immersed in their method to the exclusion of human connection (*Dreary Story*) or Darwinists who elevated natural selection above human action (*The Duel*);

(ii) communicators (e.g. artists) who relate passively with Nature by painting landscapes, and therefore communicate nothing (*The Seagull*), or workers who, in the shadow of Tolstoi, immerse themselves in Nature, and therefore actively produce nothing (*My Life*);

(iii) men who seek to reform their social world (*Nervous Breakdown*) or women their personal world (see chapter 7), but without the knowledge for effective action.

The fatal flaw in each of these false postures relates to the neglect of one term of the synthesis, and hence to the separation of man from himself, from the world, or from science. In other words, it signifies the breach of the postulated community.

I shall examine the constituents of this paradigmatic set in this and the following chapters. The emphasis will be on defining the parameters of substitution, and on their genetic basis in the ideology of Chekhov's social group.[7]

*   *   *   *   *

The inauthentic hero is related to science in a number of stories, but perhaps most powerfully in *Dreary Story* and *The Duel*. I shall concentrate my attention here on *The Duel*,[8] prefacing my remarks with the point demonstrated earlier: that for Chekhov medical science was not separable from human science (though science *was* separable, in its methods, from the materialist philosophies of ideologues and reformers).

In *Dreary Story* Chekhov showed the dangers inherent in separating the scientific method from its proper concern with the whole man; in *The Duel* he demonstrated that the evolutionary vision itself was subject to perversion. Russia, we have seen, was relatively immune to the 'tooth and claw' philosophy of Social Darwinism, but less so to another outgrowth of evolutionary thinking, degeneration theory, which crops up quite frequently in Chekhov's literature.

Degeneration, as I noted earlier, according to the founder of the hypothesis, Morel, was caused by the upsetting of man's natural adaptation to the environment by sudden changes in the external situation. Extending the theory, Max Nordau pointed out that hysteria and degeneration always existed, but only sporadically, and normally had no importance in the life of a whole community. It was the sudden impact of the 'era of discoveries and innovations' which over-fatigued the organism and 'created favourable conditions under which these maladies could gain ground enormously and become a danger to civilisation'.[9]

So for Nordau degeneration in its 'epidemic' form was the product of modernisation, and, crucially, it was thought to be transmissable by heredity. The effect of the various disturbances which set degeneration into motion was to produce a nervous disposition, which in the next generation would become neurosis, in the next psychotic breakdown, and finally idiocy and sterility. The theory was therefore both individually fatalistic and socially hopeful. The degenerate breed would die out and society would be purged.

> Degenerates must succumb therefore. They can neither adapt themselves to the conditions of Nature and civilisation nor maintain themselves in the struggle for existence against the healthy. But the latter will rapidly and easily adapt themselves to the conditions which the new inventions have created for humanity.[10]

The influence of Nietzsche is apparent in Nordau's men of will, as it is in the portrayal of Van Koren in *The Duel*. But much more important from Chekhov's point of view was the systematisation of these ideas within the inner sanctum of *evolutionary* theory, and thence its widespread social acceptance. Degeneracy theory dominated psychiatry for decades, and was extended to the study of genius and criminality by Lombroso, to great artists and thinkers (including Nietzsche himself) and even to entire races by Nordau.

In Russia, as I have stressed, acceptance of the theory did not include its fatalism. Chekhov was taught to be more concerned with healing possibilities for the individual organism predisposed to degeneration, and with its specific (and mutual) relationship with its milieu, than is evident in Nordau.

Significantly, whenever Chekhov makes a character, particularly if he is a man of science, speak on behalf of the fatalistic variant of degeneration theory, he makes him one-sided, fixed in his opinions, a partial, inhuman man unable to serve others or love wholly. The doctor in *Nervous Breakdown*, for example, has forgotten how to feel. He is simply 'polite and frigidly dignified', and able to smile only on one side of his face. Chekhov was probably consciously ironic in this detail, since Lombroso mentioned facial asymmetry and motor anomalies on one side as characteristic of degeneracy: in which case the doctor himself becomes the degenerate! Similarly, in *Black Monk*, Chekhov describes his hero's addiction to the ideas of Nordau and Nietzsche as a case of 'mania grandiosa', one of the later stages of mental degeneration, and was careful to detail the familiar *social* pressures which may have caused it.

In contrast to Chekhov, the doctor in *Nervous Breakdown*, like the hero's student friends, 'objectively' dislikes prostitution, which means in fact that they all ignore it, its context and its victims. When asked whether prostitution is an evil, the doctor agrees and, fatalistically, ignores the issue. He and the other students speak about the women in 'frigid and indifferent' tones, and to the hero suffering neurotically from his experience, the doctor merely offers therapy—bromide and morphia—to ease a sickness that requires social prophylactics. As a proponent of degeneration theory, he simply pacifies his patients with drugs, and leaves things to fate.

Chekhov's opposition to Nordau was thus not over the theory itself, but over the latter's fatalistic and anti-individualistic reading of it. Nordau, ignoring the possibilities of environmental modification, put all his emphasis on the strong will of the healthy and the certain destruction of the weak. In his book *Paradoxes*, which Chekhov mentions reading, Nordau speaks of the man of genius who will counteract the evils of degeneracy. He will be a man of great will and judgment, rather than feeling or artistic sense. 'He is in no way of the sentimental turn. He gives one on that account the impression of being hard and cold. These words, however, indicate nothing else except that he is purely cognitional and not emotional.'[11]

In *The Duel*, Van Koren is, by his own estimation, precisely this man. He is the brutal man of will, totally unsentimental about the harshness of natural selection. He is a ruthless exponent of degeneration theory who bases his feelings in the mind, not in the heart:

Don't you be hypocritical about that force. Don't defy it secretly. . . . . Instead, look it straight in the eye, and submit to its reason and necessity.

'Our love for our fellow men should not be from our hearts, nor from the base of our stomachs. . . . . . It must be from here!' Van Koren tapped his forehead.

Opposing Van Koren in *The Duel* is the neurasthenic Layevskii, who fulfils in every particular Nordau's catalogue of the symptoms of degeneracy: great emotionalism; excessive excitability; feebleness of perception, of will, memory and judgment; inattention and instability. For Nordau the task of the man of intellect and will is to help the healthy in ruthlessly crushing the degenerate breed who endanger civilisation by their example. In *Paradoxes* he speaks of the need to rid society of 'the miserable weakling, whose imbecile brain has not the power to oppose any resistance to his emotions of love',[12] and extends the theory to whole degenerate races which, inexorably, must succumb to the will of Nature in a merciless struggle for existence.[13]

Apart from the racialist extension, every main feature of this philosophy of fatalistic natural selection is evident in Van Koren. Where Nordau speaks of degenerates as 'anti-social vermin',[14] Van Koren talks of a 'diseased, degenerate and feeble breed'. Where Nordau asserts the need to mercilessly crush the degenerate and pitilessly beat to death the 'lusting beast of prey'[15] to protect civilisation, Van Koren affirms the need to remove the lusting erotic maniacs from society:

'Science and our own common sense inform us that mankind is threatened by those who are morally and physically subnormal. In which case we have to fight these freaks. If it's impossible to lift them to the norm, then we've got the ability and power to render them inactive. Frankly, exterminate them.'

Where Nordau predicts the extirpation 'root and branch' of weak by strong, and extols killing as the moral right hand of superior peoples marching inevitably to perfection, Van Koren proclaims the moral validity of killing in accordance with the laws of natural selection, a force superior to man and working for his greater humanity:

'There's no more chance of preventing it than of stopping that cloud drifting in from the sea'.

Like Nordau, he would agree that 'The prospect here disclosed is a gloomy one, but it cannot terrify the man who has become reconciled to the severity of the universal law of life'.[16]

The point is that in Chekhov's judgment the evolutionist Van Koren is not a genuine scientist at all, but an inauthentic one. Layevskii remarks that Van Koren ignores the significant areas of marine biological research in order to make a name for himself. He rejects the thriving scientific centres on the Mediterranenan (which Chekhov himself was very interested in) for the Black Sea, an area extremely poor in marine fauna, simply because he prefers to be 'the leader of a village rather than one of the pack in the city'. Chekhov makes Layevskii's criticism precise to demonstrate that Van Koren lacks the true scientist's humility: he is 'a despot first of all, and only after that a zoologist'.

Chekhov also underwrites Layevskii's description with details of character. We notice that Van Koren is not in the least objective in his treatment of people: like Professor Stepanovich in *Dreary Story*, he never analyses their inner feelings. He does not consider the mental and environmental influences which have made Layevskii and Nadezhda what they are, and prefers to regard them as unchangeable objects, condemned to extinction—and the sooner the better. Even when they reform, he does not relinquish his brutal, necessitarian philosophy: it is simply, he feels, that he has chosen the wrong objects for its exposition. Lacking a genuine objectivity and a concern for the individual organism, Van Koren resorts to grand generalisations and talks, in Chekhov's view, as an ideologue would. As Layevskii points out, all his ideals and actions 'are done, not through love of his neighbour, but on behalf of abstractions such as Man, future societies, or an ideal breed of men. He sees it as his task to improve our breed. And in that respect he sees us as mere serfs— cannon fodder or beasts of burden'. Unable to love one other individual being because of his fatalism and his ideological abstractions, Van Koren succumbs to hatred. When he prepares to kill Layevskii his whole figure, for all his commitment to reason against the passions, is 'entirely bound up with hatred and scorn'. Like Kovrin in *Black Monk*, Van Koren himself suffers from the 'mania grandiosa' of according to himself the task of purifying the human race—and it has made of him a blind beast of Nature.

In a letter to Suvorin, Chekhov wrote:

> I am sick and tired of all this philosophising, and I read fools like Max Nordau with considerable distaste.[17]

In the place of abstract theorising, Chekhov emphasises in his letter his belief in natural science and the materialistic movement. This is what finally distinguishes his evolutionary vision from that of Nordau, who ignored Mechnikov's warning that science must not sanction the law of might in natural selection but should strive to balance its 'cruel or harmful effects'.

The inhumane man of science made his appearance in Chekhov's work before *The Duel*, of course. Critics have often remarked on the continuity of *Ivanov* and *The Duel*, since the play's opposition of the ruthless Dr Lvov and the apathetic neurasthenic Ivanov is reformulated as the central drama of the novella, culminating in an external collision between Van Koren and Layevskii. Deeper continuities than those of characterisation and theme, however, are suggested by the incorporation of Chekhov's 'son of a serf' statement within the text itself in the later work. The years which had passed since the writing of the play seem to have contained an intensification of Chekhov's crisis of literary identity[18]—prefigured in the public reception of *Ivanov* (to which the original 'son of a serf' statement was intimately related), clear in his letters and in his *Dreary Story* (where he contrasted the inauthentic worlds of science and art), and culminating in his journey to Sakhalin. Chekhov was preparing his book on Sakhalin at the same time that he was struggling with *The Duel*, and there is no doubt that he regarded the scientific thesis as more important than the novella. We should remember when analysing *The Duel* that *Sakhalin Island* sought to demonstrate that degeneration of human beings—not simply convicts but intellectuals as well—was the result of appalling social and natural conditions. Now, in *The Duel*, by choosing a locale which he regarded as especially beautiful and favourable to natural life, Chekhov was emphasising the primacy of bad *social* conditions in causing degeneration. The rather emphatic 'scientific' thesis of *The Duel* is certainly connected with Chekhov's personal concerns at this time; and the idle luxury of cards, vodka and women with which Layevskii degrades the beauty of the Caucasus brings to mind another visit which Chekhov made between the Sakhalin expedition and writing *The Duel*—his journey to Monte Carlo where 'the roulette luxuriance reminds one of an opulant water-closet. The atmosphere of this place blights one's feelings for decency and somehow makes the scenery, the sounds from the sea and the moon seem vulgar.'[19]

Out of the social and natural inhospitability of Sakhalin and the purely social decay of the Mediterranean gambling town, Chekhov distilled the Caucasus of *The Duel*, a place of wondrous beauty to the author, but barren and fearful to the effete Layevskii. And since Layevskii yearned instead for the Russian capitals, Chekhov was concerned to show that life in Moscow and Petersburg was essentially the same. Layevskii's trail of false choices and ruined women began there, his personal and social determinants— aristocratic idleness and brutality—were there; and in bringing Nadezhda to the Caucasus, Layevskii unites local values with those of the capitals. Only the locale and the class of Nadezhda's lovers is different.

The social pattern is the same, and this is also clear in the portrayal of the minor characters; the kind but rank-conscious Samoilenko, the ritual-minded Deacon, the piously moral Mar'ya Konstantinova who likes to abstract men and women into inferiors and superiors, the idle bureaucrats steeped in dishonesty, cards and vodka, the brutal police chief Kirilin. Each demonstrates in his turn the all-pervasive value system and power relations of the ascriptive society.

Sakhalin was probably responsible for a difference of characterisation between the novella and *Ivanov*, where Chekhov had taken the case of a man who was initially far from weak to demonstrate the problem of the intelligentsia in the eighties. In *Sakhalin Island* the underlying implication was that even the most degraded could be saved from degeneration by means of the correct social and natural milieu. This was also the main point of his contention with Wagner at the time he wrote *The Duel*. So it can hardly be a coincidence that in Layevskii he chose to portray an extremely weak degenerate who finally, in a beautiful location and with the love of a fundamentally good woman, achieves a new liberation.

The fact that Chekhov chose to portray the collision between Van Koren and Layevskii in terms of false responses to science and art suggests that the dynamic of the story was something much more personal,[20] and ambivalent, than the cool portrayal of a degraded world built out of the minor characters. Both these concerns—with false science and with false art—were very much in his mind at the time, as is clear from his two major articles of 1891; one, 'In Moscow', implied the bankruptcy of Russian literary criticism via a character very similar to Layevskii; the other, 'Conjurors', criticised the fraudulently unscientific zoological station of Professor Bogdanov. There are further biographical pointers in Van Koren himself. Like Chekhov he believes that art and the human sciences 'will prove intellectually suitable when they finally become one with the exact sciences'; but unlike his author he rejects the present and the potential of history for fatalistic dogma, believing that 'The entire world will be covered over with a sheet of ice before that comes to pass'. In fact, Chekhov, after Sakhalin, has little sympathy for Van Koren . By rejecting living people in the present, isolating human thought from the herd and, equally, separating human action from evolutionary hope, Van Koren divides the inner man from his environment, and his mind from Nature. For Chekhov, Van Koren is a false scientist, a systematiser.

The central problem of *The Duel* is the ambivalence of false choice which in its extreme possibilities embraces both destruction—as typified by the duel itself—and the epic vision of hope and suffering which is evident in Layevskii's final conversion. The impossibility of a third stance—of any mediating or stabilising of this opposition—is suggested by Van Koren when he says:

> 'Only men who are honest and men who are cheats are able to find solutions in each situation. Anyone who wishes to be both honest and a cheat at the same time will find no solution.'

He applies this critique of ambivalence to Layevskii, but essentially it applies to the position of all inauthentic heroes.

Layevskii, too, typifies the fatalism of degeneration theory. Whereas Van Koren stands for the inhuman solutions of a Nordau, and therefore for false science, Layevskii represents the social and psychological *functions*—the hopeless, enervating pessimism—of the theory itself, and its utility in perpetuating a degraded world.

Deprived of the will to formulate any coherent identity, Layevskii looks for authenticity via the mediation of some general theory, the search for 'tendencies' which Chekhov rejected:

> 'I find it necessary to generalise about all my actions. I need to discover the explanation and vindication of my absurd existence in another person's theories, in literary types, in the idea, for example, that we men of the nobility are degenerating'.

Like all of Chekhov's inauthentic heroes he rejects the 'banal vulgarity of this life', and seeks to replace it with a succession of quests for something better. Incapable of making life an objective and free enterprise, these characters attach themselves to an adjacent cliché which will quickly pre-empt the need for thought— like Layevskii's model of the superfluous man and his convenient adherence to degeneracy theory. Each one of his 'solutions'— whether involved with saving prostitutes, with art, with the Tolstoyan ideal of labour, or with the 'higher culture' of the capitals—has also been concerned with the division of women between high ideal and base pleasure. So, like Van Koren, Layevskii divides human beings; and each one of his solutions has in fact been a reunion with the traditional Russia he rejects.

His habits incorporate the impedimenta of that society, the 'poshlost' that Chekhov presents through his works. In his drinking, his card playing, idleness, sense of rank, brutality, vulgarity and dirty habits Layevskii himself is part of the 'totality of objects' of a debased society which, through his search, he extends to the Caucasus. The man of intellect but not knowledge sanctions and extends traditional customs, for all his superficial rejection of them; and in the seduction of Nadezhda, in turn, by the intellectual, the brutal official and the merchant the pattern of social evolution is clear. Each inauthentic solution of a false journey carries, as at Sakhalin, the degenerative evolution a stage further.

Near the end, failure itself becomes the source of ideals for Layevskii. As with Masha in *My Life*, the act of journeying itself is the ultimate truth:

> He would jump on a train and leave, and so solve the predicament of his existence. Beyond that he didn't think.

It was, after all, the inevitable decree of his fate.

Van Koren classifies the dishonesty of this stance:

'he smiles bitterly in answer to all my questions and says "I'm a failure, a superfluous man", or, "What can you hope from us, dear chap, the fag-ends of a serf-owning class?" Or, "We're degenerating . . ." . . . . . The reason for his excessive lust and shamelessness is likewise not to be found in himself, but elsewhere, in a vacuum, outside. By this brilliant trick it is not *this* man by himself who is dissolute, neurotic and base, but *we* . . . "We men of the eighties", "We idle and nervous children of serf-owners, we who have been crippled by civilisation! . . ." In fact we are to understand that a man of Layevskii's quality is supreme even in defeat, that his vice, ignorance and slovenliness constitute a law of evolution, purified by inevitability; that the reasons are universal, natural, and that we should burn a candle to Layevskii as destiny's sacrifice, a victim of his era, a product of his heredity, and so on.'

Van Koren is of course being inconsistent in rejecting Layevskii's appeal to fatalistic laws of evolution and heredity while himself rigidly adhering to them in demanding his extermination (and in fact he immediately resorts to degeneration theory after the speech by using Nordau's 'erotomania' concept to categorise Layevskii's preoccupation with women). Layevskii is likewise inconsistent in using the evidence of science, in which he professes not to believe, to clarify the falseness of Van Koren's position. In fact, the 'underground lucidity' of both these men is that of their author. Chekhov makes both of them appeal for identity to the solutions of a false science, and in the light cast by their shrewd perception of each other he presents the audience with an inverted image of something better. The space encapsulated by their dialogue and their duel is that transient point between a human and inhuman evolution.

Like Van Koren, Layevskii contains the potential to destroy. Nordau's metaphor of 'lusting beast of prey' is appropriately applied, since, as Layevskii himself admits, his relationships with people and with nature have always been destructive:

surrounded by living things . . . . . he had done nothing but destroy, ruin, lie and lie . . .

In his cruelty to Nadezhda, particularly in his use of a letter containing news of her husband's death, he is as guilty of ignoring her inner feelings as Van Koren. Both condemn her in their way. Neither, until Layevskii's final conversion, show much awareness of the *social* causes of her fall. For both of them she is a weak—and therefore ordained—victim for exploitation and destruction.

So both men are beasts of prey, and Samoilenko's question to the scientist in fact relates each one to the cruel and humanly unmediated process of natural selection which they proclaim:

'He ruins and kills every other creature that gets in his way . . . crawls into other's burrows, destroys ant hills, breaks open snails . . . . . Tell me, what is the use of this creature? For what purpose was it created?'

Van Koren attributes the creation of this blind beast to the cruel but beneficial process of natural selection, thereby, in effect, justifying the position of both himself and Layevskii, each of whom has crawled into others' burrows: Van Koren with the intent to destroy Layevskii, and Layevskii with the effect of destroying Nadezhda's husband. Van Koren goes on to speak of the merciless struggle when two such blind beasts meet, and the theme of the duel is given its real perspective, untouched by humanity or the human mind:

'It is an interesting fact that when two moles meet each other underground they both start creating a platform, as though by common agreement. The platform is necessary for their fight, and when they have completed it, they begin a terrible struggle, which continues until the weaker of the two falls'.

The duel of cruel predators is one extreme of the inauthentic search.

But the duel to destruction *is* only one of the potential resolutions. As Layevskii and Van Koren mark out the ground of that extreme, the principles of humanity and knowledge through suffering are kept alive by Samoilenko and the Deacon, characters who are themselves too trivial and too bound up with the rank and ideology of an ascriptive society to present dramatic alternatives themselves. Their function is, first of all, to comment on the inhumanity of the forces which drive the action on, and second, to confine them so that the ultimate polarisation (and final choice) may occur: Samoilenko ensures that Layevskii does not escape, the Deacon that he does not die. As he prepares to see them fight, as fascinated by their violence as Mar'ya Konstantinova is by Nadezhda's immorality, the Deacon contrasts the easy and elegant childhood the combattants have had with the harshness, poverty and vulgarity of his own, compares their ensuing ignorance of urgent social problems and tendency to intellectual clichés with his own ant's-eye view of them:

> If they had experienced the poverty which had been his lot since childhood. . . . . How then they would have reached out to each other, how quickly they would have forgiven each other's failings, how they would have valued the good things in each other! After all, the number of people in the world who were even superficially decent was few enough . . . . . Rather than being led by apathy or misunderstandings of various kinds, into seeking out degeneracy, heredity, extinction and other incomprehensible things in each other, wouldn't it be far better to look closer to the ground and focus their bitter anger on the places where whole districts are crushed beneath gross ignorance, covetousness, vice, foul language and cries of pain.

The speech is both a challenge to the inhuman fatalism of Van Koren and Layevskii and a clue to their failure. The life of intellect derived from a luxurious upbringing has deprived them of the social contact which Chekhov knew as a zemstvo worker. Hence the popular focus for progress and change is outside their scope. Yet without their intellectual background nothing is possible either, as the trivialised potential of the Deacon testifies.

Chekhov's own mobility synthesised this contradiction: thesis and antithesis are presented with sympathy, but within a structured perspective which is the author's own. If Van Koren accurately points to the stagnation of lowly people like the Deacon who 'see everything through a fog', the latter clarifies in turn the falsity of the zoologist's life, where great expeditions and a powerful mind are betrayed into submission to Nature through lack of faith in men. So 'everything stays as it was': Van Koren's stagnation is merely at a higher level.

But between the scientific brutality of Van Koren and the befogged and helpless cry for humanity of the Deacon a new perspective opens. Layevskii walks from the duel a new man, open to human love and for the first time appreciative of the world and natural beauty. Layevskii's conversion was as logical and necessary for Chekhov as it has seemed weak and unmotivated to most of his critics. He was anxious to show that even the weakest degenerate could be saved, and having postulated the extreme possibilities of destruction and social concern, he makes Layevskii choose correctly for the first time. The drama is not in the external action of the duel, which Chekhov deliberately makes into an absurd non-event, but in the confrontation of two worlds demarcating the ambivalence of inauthentic choice; or, to put it another way, in the stripping away of false mediators between the only real alternatives of a degenerate or a human evolution.

The problems critics have with Layevskii's conversion tend to be of two kinds: one to do with motivation and the other with verisimilitude. An example of the first kind is presented by Kramer when he complains that the conversion is weak because of the employment of 'exaggeration without any intensity of feeling'. He quotes Eric Bentley's opinion that in drama, 'Intensity of feeling justifies formal exaggeration in art, just as intensity of feeling creates the "exaggerated" forms of childhood fantasies and adult dreams'.[21] It should be noted, in fact, that Layevskii's moment of recognition comes, not at the duel, but after the trauma of finding Nadezhda in bed with Kirilin. His conversion is not the result of a pistol shot, but in the awakening of love and an inner understanding for a woman he has previously treated as a sexual object—a process few critics seem to have found exaggerated in *Lady with a Little Dog*.[22] This is a moment of enclosure (between discovery of Nadezhda's faithlessness and imminent death in the duel, and between the claustrophobia of his study and the storm outside) when Layevskii summons up, recognises and rejects *his* childhood fantasies and adult dreams.

There had never been any need for truth. He hadn't even looked for it. His conscience, dazzled by evil and lies, had stayed asleep or kept quiet. Like an alien being, someone from another world, he had kept himself apart from the daily life of men, had been cold to their sufferings, ideas, religious beliefs, knowledge, aspirations and struggles. He had never offered a kind word to anybody, nor had he written anything that was not trivial and banal. He had done absolutely nothing for others, but he had been prepared to eat their food, drink their wine, take their wives, live on their ideas. And to vindicate this parasitic existence to himself and to others, he had always adopted a superior air, as though he was above them. Lies, lies, lies . . .

Separated from men by his own choice, above the world, and lacking any values of his own, Layevskii can find nothing when his search is forced to stop. He recalls the past, and considers the intense innocence of his childhood. But the image of his mother is frightening. He remembers the cruel parent of a brutal son: seemingly an inevitable evolution in his world. If there is no escape in the past there is none in space either; the false intellectual who looks for salvation in Petersburg 'will never find it. The entire world will be the same for him'.

Finally, he recognises that salvation lies in no external place of escape, but in the inner man, in the search for truth with which the quotation above begins, in rejecting the supression of knowledge with which it ends, in his relations with Nature as he plants trees, and in his relations of love with other human beings. He recognises that there is no future in Samoilenko's naivety, none in the Deacon's inane laughter, none in Van Koren's hatred.

> We have to find salvation in ourselves. If we can't find it there, there's no point in wasting time further. One might as well kill oneself.

The seconds now come to carry him off to the meaningless and inevitable death which his own and Van Koren's fatalism have predicted. But there is another possibility. As he prepares to go, 'he felt that there was somehow something still to be done'; something, of course, of a social nature that he has never done before. He goes to Nadezhda, finds her wrapped helplessly in a rug and looking like an embalmed object—which in effect is what he has made of her. He recognises that 'this wretched, sinful woman was the one person close to him, the one person whom no-one could replace'; and he loves her without mediation for the first time in his life. Women are no longer objects to idealise or degrade: Nadezhda lives at last outside *other* peoples' ideas. Life with Nadezhda now, the text makes clear, will be one of suffering, of hard work and of grinding poverty at the grass roots which the Deacon describes but Layevskii has not known. The suffering, however, is permeated with a new hope, a new will, a 'certain freshness of expression in his face and even in his walk'.

The blind beasts have fought, and as Layevskii watches the scientist leaving on his great expedition, battling through the waves, it is the other potential that he considers:

'That boat is hurled back. It makes two steps forward, and then one back. Yet the oarsmen endure, they row on tirelessly, and are not frightened by the enormous waves. The boat drives on and on . . . . . In seeking the truth men make two steps forward and then one back. Miscalculations, suffering, and the tedium of life throw them back, but the thirst for truth and a stubborn will drive them on and on. And who knows? Maybe one day they will arrive at the real truth . . .'

The perepeteia at the end of *The Duel* is by no means arbitrary. What one could call the subtextual sequence which always underlies Chekhov's dominant associative motif 'inauthentic hero rejects the world and is crushed' (the characterisation of Layevskii before conversion) is here made overt: hero, with a vision of knowledge and suffering, will endure. The final physical and mental divergence of Layevskii and Van Koren replaces the blind duel of natural selection with the *individual* man in search of truth. This sequence, of the epic vision, is of course only the opposite of the first by *convention*—or in other words within Chekhov's *own* construction of reality. Which is also an answer to the verisimilitude debate. The conversion is potentially 'lifelike' within Chekhov's *perceived* concept of reality: he had, after all, his whole medical training to tell him it was so.

6 The Epic Vision: Nature and the World

In recent years structural analysis has given so much fruitful attention to the oppositions between man's social and natural world (Culture/Nature in primitive myth; Garden/Desert in Westerns etc.) that it would be easy to think of these oppositions as somehow immutable. That this is not the case can be seen by a moment's attention to other literatures, other genres that have not yet caught the attention of structuralists. The world of the Greek epics, for example, was anthropocentric. Nature (like the gods) *exemplified* man's actions; and when a hero died, as Bowra notes, the world was so much the poorer that Nature could be seen to weep. In the Western, the natural landscape—John Ford's Monument Valley for example—is visually and experientially masculine, a virile, toughening and puritan counter to the creeping softness of civilisation. In the epic, Nature on the contrary is more feminine in its imagery, penetrated deeply by man's values, thrilling and weeping to his deeds, and embellishing the dialogue of the real protagonists, the men and the gods who are always ruthlessly masculine. The force of the heroes' being, Steiner writes, 'electrifies insensate nature'; the air 'vibrates round their personages' and, analogously with the heroes' women, 'Achilles' horses weep at his impending doom'.[1]

In contrast to the epic, late nineteenth-century literature had come to display a deep crisis in the relationship of man and his world. The most significant change, as Leo Lowenthal sees it, in man's imagery of his environment was nevertheless not a shift from empathy to opposition, but rather an inversion of what constituted object and image. Nature no longer reflected man's humanity. 'Instead he began to find his image *in* Nature. Doubt and despair about personal fulfilment in society, Lowenthal suggests, lay behind this inversion. Now his hope was to 'submit to nature and feel at peace . . . become a "thing", like the tree or the brook, and find more pleasure in this surrender than in a hopeless struggle against man-made forces'.[2]

Chekhov's dominant Nature imagery is not either of these kinds. Nor is it ultimately one of opposition, even though, as we shall see, there is some parallel with the notion of making a desert bloom in his attitude to the 'boundless steppes'. There is, certainly, a crisis in the relationship of Chekhovian man and his world, and there is a *de facto* opposition to Nature. Society is brutish, and when, in terror and despair, man dies, Nature remains insensate. The stars stare down, the steppes stand immense, 'a further thousand years would go by, and they would still be standing as they had always stood, neither mourning the dead nor interested in the living' (*Happiness*). There is also a tendency for socially marginal figures—Ol'ga in *Peasants*, Vera in *At Home*—to look for escape from the burden of social living by submission, in death, to Nature. All of these possibilities—of man improving Nature, of man and Nature in mute opposition, of man submerging himself in Nature—are present in Chekhov's texts, and we need some way of distinguishing structurally between them.

In Chekhov's works there are in fact a number of *inauthentic* ways in which men and women try to restore their contact with Nature— in death, in art (painting landscapes), in unscientific labour (after Tolstoi), in ignorant and terrible myths, in a spontaneous spark of fusion. The feature of all these choices is their *passivity*. In Russia Sechenov, Mechnikov and Timiryazev had emphasised that though as organisms men respond to their environment, their response is not ultimately passive. Man is influenced by his milieu, but his higher sensory development enables him to choose to modify particular habitats out of the possibilities open to him. Man does more than lose himself in Nature, and Nature does more than reflect his heroic action. Rather, it will respond to his choices. In place of a mute opposition, there can be dialogue, in which man perfects Nature for the sake of his own development.

This world view was unlikely to produce a Hardy or a Tolstoi, for whom the advance of civilisation could only divide man and destroy his harmony with Nature. Significantly, Dr Astrov in *Uncle Vanya* does not complain of spreading *civilisation* when he points to the loss of natural beauty. He accuses the stagnation of a *given* social world:

Overall, the story is one of gradual but certain decay which will clearly be completed within ten to fifteen years . . . . . if we had new roads and railways, workshops, factories and schools in place of these devestated forests; then our people would be more healthy, better educated and more prosperous. But in fact there's nothing of the kind here! We are still faced with the same swamps and mosquitoes, lack of roads, frightful poverty, typhoid, diptheria and fires. It is a tale of degeneration resulting from a crushing struggle for existence, but one caused by lack of effort, ignorance and total irresponsibility: just as when a man who is sick, hungry, and cold reaches out from his instincts to save the poor remnants of his life and protect his children, grabbing at anything which will end his hunger and give him warmth, and in doing it destroys everything, quite mindless of the future . . . Almost everything has been destroyed, and nothing has been put in its place.

Astrov, in his roles as forester and zemstvo doctor, brings together the potential of natural beauty and technology in opposition to a degraded, unscientific world of inaction and decay. As a doctor who is trained to be aware of the significance of the environment, he can visualise a world where Nature is in harmony with man. But as a doctor labouring in a given society he can also see a world of degenerative adjustment, where man, unaided by his mind, finds the struggle for existence against him, where his psychological and physiological adaptation to nutritional scarcity, cold, insecurity and helplessness bring on behaviour patterns actually unfavourable to future health and social growth.

Man's contact with Nature is thus clarified by a choice which articulates the only available worlds: of progressive and degenerative evolution. The epic visionary relates the evolution of man to Nature through knowledge and technology. The degraded world does nothing to turn the 'disharmonies into harmonies', ignores Nature itself, or its laws, and Nature in turn is alien to man and master of his fate. Unable to communicate with Nature, man is crushed by it. At best he has illusions, but in fact Nature is not a place of escape. For those denied choice—convicts at Sakhalin, peasants on the steppes—it is a world of wonder, oppression and fear. In *Happiness* the size of the steppes weighs down the thoughts of shepherds and sheep with 'tedium and oppression . . . . . smothering them with apathy'. In *The Steppe* there is a woman's song without words which 'seems to call for someone's forgiveness that the heat and drought have stolen her youth and her beauty, and turned her life into something terribly harsh, sad and mournful'.

The crosses covering dead souls lost in the steppes signify both the brutality of a social world which murdered them and man's sad isolation in Nature. The two things—a backward society and man's misunderstanding of the natural world—are related. But for Chekhov's peasants and wayfarers all these things are the subject of fear and incomprehension. Like all primitives, these men try to make a mysterious environment meaningful through myths: wonderful and terrible tales of murder and revenge (*The Steppe*), a hidden, golden treasure of happiness beneath the steppes (*Happiness*), legends of time past when trees grew, rivers flowed, game flew, and the gentry were real cavaliers (*The Pipe*).

In *Dreams* a penal convict stumbles through cold and fog which, like the walls of his social world, 'seem to keep you in the same place, whatever distance you walk'. He has a vision of a purified world, free land where he will have a home, corn and a garden, and where he will plough and sow, keep cattle, a cat, ikons, and bring up his children. His vision affects even the policemen who guard him:

In the silence of autumn, when the frozen, sullen mist rising off the ground throws a lead weight on your heart, when it rears up like the walls of a prison in front of your eyes, reminding a man of the limits to his freedom, the images of wide and swiftly flowing rivers lined with high, wild, luxuriant banks, of impenetrable woods, of the endless steppes, come like precious thoughts . . . . . Peasants then visualised a life of freedom they had never known.

But the brutality and subservience of a bureaucratic order quickly reasserts itself. A policeman callously tells the peasant he will die on the journey. The peasant shrinks in fear and guilt. His vision is replaced by one that is harsher and more prosaic: long delays in the hearing of his case, terrible prisons, freezing winters, death in the cold and sullen mist which still surrounds him.

All these myths which relate man to Nature are escapist dreams. And Nature in turn remains insensate and cold. In *Woe* the shiftless old turner has resorted to drink rather than myths to alleviate his life, but the same cold fate awaits him. The harshness of the social and natural world has in fact always informed his actions—his drunken apathy, the years of brutal beatings which have turned his once attractive wife into an old hag; and the same harshness determines the resolution of his life as he drives his sick wife to the

hospital. At this moment of recognition, the turner looks round and
pities his dying wife, regretting the 'forty years that have dissolved
like a mist'. The old man, active at last, confronts in this final
journey the cruel world he has tried to escape for so long.

> This lazy, drunken wastrel all at once found himself busy,
> deceived, as though he was in conflict with Nature itself.

A terrible snowstorm beats him and he loses his way. Finally,
wishing he could live life over again, and live it kindly, he succumbs
to the cold.

In *Happiness* a young shepherd watches an old man dreaming of
joy, which for him is a golden treasure beneath the steppes. He
wonders what the use of earthly happiness would be in any case to
this old fellow who might die any day; and pondering over the
absurd illusion of human happiness, he is oppressed by an
inexplicable animal panic. Without a perspective on life, time
passes irrevocably for these ignorant men, until the final rigours
come and they are faced with the triviality of their lives in the face of
eternity:

> The endless steppe had a morose and death-like look. There was
> an atmosphere of timelessness and complete indifference to man
> in its stillness and its silence.

Depriving Nature of meaning, man's life, in its pointless con-
tingency, is meaningless too.

> The crows woke up and flew one after another above the earth.
> There was no meaning to be gained from the lazy flight of these
> long-living birds, nor from the morning which comes round
> punctually every twenty-four hours, nor from the endless stretch
> of the steppes.

In *The Three Sisters* the flight of birds is a central motif.
Tuzenbakh says that the meaning of their flight will never be
known. But for Vershinin man's entire future depends on his
determination to know what everything means. The quest 'just to
know' is his legacy to the sisters. Similarly, in *The Crow*, when the
narrator tells the bird that he is a fool for learning nothing in the
space of his long life, the latter replies that wisdom does not come

from age but from education and science. Moreover, crows do not have wars and brutalities like men, or content themselves with building schools for modern languages, or surround themselves with flunkeys, sycophants and hypocrites. Then, with this thumb-nail sketch of the ascriptive society, he flies away, leaving life as barren and insignificant as before.

The stars which have been staring down from the sky for thousands of years, the unfathomable sky itself and the mists around you are utterly unconcerned with man's brief existence and weigh you down with their muteness, even when you confront them face to face and seek out their meaning. Then you begin to think of the loneliness which waits for all of us at the grave, and the meaninglessness of life drives you to horror and despair.

(*The Steppe*)

Mute to each other, man and Nature must nonetheless *physically* relate. Without knowledge or communication man adjusts to his milieu by retrogression, as Chekhov describes at Sakhalin and Astrov in *Uncle Vanya*. Like the hero of his story *Home*, Chekhov believed that 'The living organism has the capacity to adapt itself quickly, and becomes accustomed and habituated to any kind of context'. If man could not place himself at the centre of a purposeful evolution, he must adapt in more atavistic ways. So Vera in *At Home* sees the steppe in isolation and finds it beautiful; but encountering it in a degenerative relationship with her debased family, is crushed by it. The stagnation of the family and the steppe become indistinguishable in her imagery:

the endless plain was so huge and empty that it frightened her. This silent, green monster seemed as if it would eat up her existence and leave no trace . . . . . there stood her hateful bed, and if she looked out of the windows all she could see were leafless branches, dirty snow, hateful jackdaws, pigs that were destined for Grandpa's tummy . . . . . but what was she to do? . . . . . What if she took on her aunt, pushed her aside and rendered her harmless? What if she prevented grandpa thrashing around with his stick? What good would that do? It would be like getting rid of one single snake or a mouse out there on the great plains. The huge size of it, the endless winters, the monotony and

boredom made you lose hope. There didn't seem to be any way
out. What was the point of raising a finger when nothing was any
use?'

Chekhov's inauthentic heroes try to answer Vera's question in a
variety of ways:
     (a) Sometimes, as in *Miss N's Story*, it is through a life of passive
expectation followed by memories and regrets. In youth, Miss N.
and her lover relate happily with Nature in a scene of Tolstoyan
intensity. They ride excitedly through the rain and lightning; the
excitement of the weather communicates itself to them; they talk
nonsense; they are carried away by the 'quick, impetuous motion',
the wind, the sound and the sense of the rain pounding on lawn and
roofs, the sensuous smell of the hay, the shadow in the barn beneath
the rain and clouds, the crash of the thunder and the flashes of
lightning; in a moment of poetic inspiration they declare their love.
     But the social hierarchy of the town divides them; and their lack
of will and vocation is paralysing:

> The bright days and balmy nights flittered by. Nightingales sang;
> the air was perfumed by the newly mown hay. But this precious,
> wonderful memory passed away, for me as for all men, leaving no
> trace, uncherished, dissolving like a cloud.

Now they weep for the potential of a lost love. Their society is
divisive, and their spontaneous relation with Nature was without
action or understanding. Miss N. can only remember the beauty of
the summer trees and the springtime of her youth as lost causes.
Before them is another world, which is empty and desolate:

> In front of me I see an empty perspective, without feature. Not
> one living person inhabits this deserted waste. And over yonder,
> on the horizon, everything is black and fearful.

     (b) Sometimes the answer, as with the peasants, takes the form of
myths—journeys into illusion, into past history, or perhaps the
picaresque series of journeys in endlessly changing locations (now in
the mind and ideological, next in travelling and new places): 'the
People', 'sublime art', 'ideal love', 'to Moscow'. Thus the hero of *On
the Road* has chased his ideal through inner and outer space and
time—adventure in America, science, Nihilism, Populism,

Slavophilism, Ukrainophilism, socialism, non-resistance to evil, and finally, the 'all-forgiving love of women'. Each one has been topical for a while, a 'tendency' adopted without a thought for the significant world around him. Like Professor Stepanovich he has meanwhile ignored the 'inner milieu' of those who love him, and his 'reckless acts' have driven his wife to decline and death. We last see him still on his road, dragging his daughter by the hand to extend it after him. He battles on against the forces of Nature, 'seeking with his eyes for something through the clouds of snow', and always forgetting that the 'something' lies closer at hand.

(c) Sometimes the answer is just a fragmentary, momentary melancholy rejection. So, in *Beauties*, as men see a girl's fresh beauty juxtaposed with the dirt, ugliness and decay of their own lives, they are 'filled with a great wish to say something honest, sincere and beautiful—as beautiful as she was herself'. Instead they, and the natural world around them, are filled with a sense of loss and sadness. Between the two worlds fleeting beauty must be harnessed or decay, so that it 'seemed as though only a brusque breeze need blow . . . . . or a few drops of rain fall for this tender body to bend and its transient beauty to fly away like pollen from a flower'. Always at the end of myth, memory and dream Vera's question remains unanswered. The beauty fades, the snow beats down, the desolate waste beckons—and daily life gets harder.

Yet there was, in Chekhov's view, an authentic answer. The steppes, could be subjected to science, technological labour, systematic farming, the planting of trees. In describing the steppes Chekhov once said:

> I was pained to see these wide open spaces—which you'd have thought had all the conditions for a richly civilised life—positively smothered in ignorance.[3]

When Ilya Mechnikov first visited the steppes he felt, like Vera and Chekhov's peasants, 'the power of the natural forces' and understood 'the fatalism of the poor inhabitants of the land'.[4] But like Chekhov he quickly realised that one could live in this land, love it, and, by planting trees, bring the soil to life. Astrov (*Uncle Vanya*), the zemstvo doctor who plants trees, says:

> when I walk near the woods that the peasants own, the same woods I saved from the axe, or when I hear the young saplings

rustling which I planted with my own hands, I remember that the climate is to some extent dependent on me too, and that if man is happy in a thousand years from now, I will be ever so slightly responsible for it.

His words reiterate Chekhov's when he planted a tree in his garden at Yalta:

> Before I came here all this was waste land and ravines, all covered with stones and thistles. Then I came here and turned this wilderness into a cultivated, beautiful place. Do you know that in three or four hundred years all the earth will become a flourishing garden. And life will then be exceedingly easy and comfortable.[5]

Chekhov's message is explicit: the mutual adaptation of man and Nature will alleviate the harshness of the struggle for existence *and* improve society.

Vershinin in *The Three Sisters* enters a stagnant society with the most rigorous of climates, but his optimism embraces it:

> Just imagine you put aside the life you've lived up to now, like a rough draft, and started a new one, a fair copy. If that were to happen I believe that you'd be most careful not to resurrect your old life. At the very least you would try to create a new environment for yourself—rooms like these, for example, with flowers and a lot of light.

> I'd have thought that you have a genuinely healthy climate here, a true Russian climate. Woods, river . . . birch trees as well . . . . . It's a fine place to live.

Like Chekhov, Vershinin believes that the whole earth can become a flourishing garden. But at the same time he notes the reason for people's stagnant lives: ignorance and irrationality—'the station is fifteen miles from the town, and nobody knows why!' In *My Life* Chekhov draws the causal connections of this same irrationality—a station miles from town—from a dense social malaise. In the drama the detail stands metonymically for the social fabric the sisters dream to escape.

Lopakhin in *The Cherry Orchard* has the same complaint with society. Behind the pretty face of the orchard there is social decay.

Unlike Astrov, Lopakhin brings an axe to his trees, but it would be a mistake to accept the 'philistine kulak' or 'real estate dealer' interpretations which are so well established in the Soviet Union and the West. The orchard itself is in decay, and Lopakhin sees it as surely as Astrov recognises decay behind the facade of the beautiful Yelena. Lopakhin cuts the trees down, but afterwards there will be Chekhov's cultivated gardens and a 'new, living world'.

These men of understanding who recognise and act on the potential of authentic beauty are Chekhov's epic visionaries. Their difference from the landscape painters, 'sweat of the brow' Tolstoyans, dreamers and myth-makers of his works comes out in his description of the Wood Demon:

> As a result of his labour there was one more tree on the earth! It was the start of his own distinctive creativity. He fulfils his ideal, not on canvas or paper, but in the earth, not with paint which is lifeless, but with living organisms.[6]

The man of science and the true artist are not passive in the face of Nature. For Chekhov, theirs is an expressive behaviour with an ideal; and the environment—social or natural—is the means to self-actualisation.

Again, the values here are those of the scientific community. Timiryazev spoke of perfection as the process of history which involved an active understanding of Nature. The method, he wrote in *The Life of the Plant* 'must not be that of passive observer, but rather that of active experimenter'.[7] Nature, Mechnikov taught, provided the beauty of the wild flower by natural evolution. Man improved upon it with the beauty of the cultivated rose, and so scientific botany harmonised with Nature's plans.[8] Similarly, scientific medicine was strengthening the beneficient cells in man's organism, transforming 'the wild intestinal flora into a cultivated flora'.[9]

By analogy, the immensity and wild beauty of Russia, like Mechnikov's wild inner flora, offered enormous possibilities. On the one hand, Russia's 'little man', as Chekhov described him, overburdened with ignorance, poverty and soulless bureaucracy, got lost in the vastness of Nature 'without the strength to explore his way'.[10] But on the other hand, the scope of the possible adaptation could make man the equal in creativity to epic gods.

Lopakhin has this vision. We have been given, he says, huge

forests, immense plains, expansive horizons: 'then surely we should be akin to giants, living in a land such as this'. The artist in *House with a Mezzanine* spells out man's available choices:

> We're higher beings. If we could only actually realise the full capacity of human genius and live only for higher purposes, we would finally become akin to gods.

Then he adds,

> But it won't happen. Man will degenerate and every hint of genius will vanish.

If man is not to degenerate, his genius must somehow break through the meaningless passage of time, 'the eternal sequence of days,' which bends and breaks Sof'ya Petrovna in *Misfortune* and ultimately all of Chekhov's inauthentic characters. The answer comes from Mechnikov—or Chekhov's crow. The source of wisdom is not in endless days and boundless steppes, but in subjecting time and space to meaning. Education and science will give man an historical perspective and harness his milieu. Time will become, then, the rationalist's chain of truth and beauty, passing purposefully through history, dispelling the Student's fears that 'the very same ignorance and frustration, desolate wastes, darkness, sense of brutalisation—each of these terrors had always existed, still existed, and would always exist, so that even a thousand years from now man's life would still be no better'. Vershinin has a practical reply:

> In ancient times mankind was constantly waging war. His whole existence was given to campaigns, advances, retreats, victories . . . But that is all over now. In its place we have an enormous vacuum calling to be filled. Mankind is fervently looking for something to fill that vacuum, and it will of course find something in the end . . . . . If we could only educate those who work and at the same time make our intellectuals more industrious.

The future depends, Chekhov once wrote, on intellectuals who can think *and* work; and unlike Mechnikov who left Russia for Paris because he felt oppressed 'from above, below and from all sides', zemstvo doctors were men of Vershinin's model, labouring backbreakingly against the same pressures, but at the same time bringing science and the imagery of social reform to the Russian countryside.

One day, sitting high on a mountain overlooking the awful prison settlement of Sakhalin, Chekhov looked further out—to the sea, the ravines and mountains; and experienced a sense of melancholy at the absurd gap between Nature and the deeds of men. It was an illustration of what he had written in his embryonic 'History of Sexual Authority' some years before, when he began to compare 'Nature . . . which, as you know, is aiming at the perfect organism' and the absurdity of human institutions which prevented it. Eight years after his Sakhalin visit he wrote *Lady with a Little Dog*, and in it Gurov also sits on a mountain above a degraded community. He, too, experiences melancholy as he watches the timeless action of the sea and compares the potential of Nature with what man has achieved:

> In this continuity, and in this utter indifference to the life or death of any one of us perhaps there lay latent the promise of our salvation—in this endless movement of life on earth, the continuing evolution towards perfection. As he sat beside a young woman who looked so lovely in the dawn light, and was made calmer by the enchanting sight of all this fantastic scenery—the sea, the mountains, the clouds, the deep sky—Gurov thought that after all everything in the world really was beautiful. Everything, that is, other than our own thoughts and deeds when we forget the higher aims of our existence and our pride in being human beings.

His sense of hope for man in the continuity of Nature seems remarkably like that of the pastoral epic, until one notices the juxtaposed validation of *man's* higher aims, and recalls the contrasting narrative sequences which stretch out on either side of his thoughts: on the one side a degraded past, on the other, in love and Anna's personal beauty, the glimmer of a better future.

Nature in fact seems to exist in Chekhov to tell this tale, and articulate these polarities. In earlier stories the feeling of melancholy is sometimes ascribed to Nature itself, as in *Sleepyhead* where crows and magpies weep for Chekhov's little men who carry loads too great for them and fall by the wayside, like peasant Ivanovs; or when the steppe calls mournfully of its 'Waste, Waste' as it looks hopelessly for a poet and a man of understanding:

> Then in the buzzing of insects, the strange figures and tumuli, in the blue sky, the light from the moon, in the flight of nocturnal birds, in everything you see and everything you hear, can be sensed a great beauty, youth, revival of strength and fervent thirst for life. One's being responds to this beautiful and austere Nature. One wants to fly over the steppe with these nocturnal birds. Yet, in the awesome beauty and expansive joy, one is aware of tension and sorrow. It is as though the steppe understands that she is beautiful, that her treasures and creativity are lost in the universe, that her qualities are commemorated by no man. And in the midst of her joyful tones one can detect the melancholy and hopeless call for 'A poet! A poet!'

There *was* then a treasure beneath the steppes: a potential of man himself. In *The Steppe* the sense of Nature's mourning over dead and brutalised souls is no more than a subtext, a lyric of the night at the margins of the stifling, degraded day. In *The Cherry Orchard*, on the other hand, Trofimov's own fearful and wonderful tale of the dead and exploited souls shrieking out from the trees of the orchard is more central to the drama, and is opposed by Lopakhin's active reason. But whether central and dramatic, as in the plays, or as a lyrical subtext as it generally is in the stories, the potential of the natural world is invariably present as a locus for man's alternative evolutionary possibilities. Here, for example, is a passage from one of Chekhov's bleakest works, *Peasants*:

> A fragile wooden footbridge crossed the river, and just beneath it, in the transparent, limpid water shoals of fat chub swam. The green bushes which reflected in the water were sparkling with dew, and there was a hint of warmth and joy in the air. It was such a beautiful morning! And how beautiful life on earth might be if it were not for poverty; poverty that ground you down so far that you could not escape. A single glance at the village brought all of yesterday's events starkly to mind, and in a second the atmosphere of joyful pleasure vanished.

At the end of William Morris' *A Dream of John Ball* the Narrator has a dream of a countryside which is beautiful, clean and free. But, as John Goode remarks, it is an illusory dream, a withdrawal from reality, and the Narrator must 'turn back to the city . . . back into his own alienation', negating the present with surly irony as the hooters call.[11] Ol'ga's vision of Nature in *Peasants* is certainly not merely illusory, though it is undercut ironically by its mystified association with religion. The natural world responds to man's actions according to the nature (qualitative or quantitative) of *his* rejection of society. Nature is the place where man may act out his future; and yet the village calls Ol'ga as insistently as the city calls Morris' narrator. For both, the historical negation of the present must come actively in the world of men and women.

7 The Epic Vision: Woman and Man

Russian Darwinism had a dream of organic man: of thought, feeling and technology. Against this it saw an ascriptive value system, which made man a creature of ideology, dividing his responses as appropriate to his official point in the hierarchy. Mobility and change within this hierarchy were not a matter of achievement and rationality, but of changing places within an essentially unchanging structure. In Chekhov's *Anna on the Neck*, for example, his heroine draws on just one aspect of her self, her sexuality, to rise from the lowest rungs of society to the highest. With the privilege of marginality, Anna throws light on an entire society as she rises, and demonstrates that the hierarchy is in fact a unity. Every rank cringes slavishly to the one above, and each higher rank ruthlessly enhances its position by brutality to those below. The entire structure of this apparently timeless society is elucidated at the moment when Anna's bureaucrat husband, who had previously suppressed her cruelly, cringes in her presence, and is suppressed brutally in his turn.

Her success is not accidental. We learn that her mother (herself once a governess and imitator of her superiors) has brought Anna up according to an ascriptive pattern of education for 'young ladies'. She has taught her to speak French, to dance well, and to dress in the latest fashion. She has counselled her to put on an appearance of status, to adopt affected mannerisms and to attract men with her 'feminine' vanity, 'half-closing her eyes, lisping, striking elegant poses, in raptures if necessary, or perhaps just looking enigmatic and sad'. From first to last Anna knows no values other than deference to rank and affectation.

For Russian Darwinists the solution for this apparently unending conservative pattern was not to be revolution, which was thought to be 'ideological' too, and therefore equally fragmenting. The rationalist-reformist tradition turned on a familiar solution: *relations of information and rational communication* would end the ideological disintegration of Anna. If only, Chekhov said, people *knew* more about how degraded their lives were, they would certainly act to create something better. What was needed was universalism, not particularism, information and awareness, not hierarchy and dogma. A critical evolutionary sociology would analyse societal irrationalities, and freely relating individuals (who were attuned to knowledge and ideas of service) would emerge from an appropriate educational design.

De-mystification, to use a more contemporary term, would be carried then through the *communication* of individuals, and not by revolutionary praxis. Individuals are in fact more or less 'authentic' in Chekhov in proportion to their ability to communicate:

(i) His inauthentic heroes are invariably ambivalent. Lacking the evolutionist vision, at best they drive the action of a debased society forward, like Anna; or like Misail in *My Life* who also has been denied a rational education and grows to find a life which is uncultured, ignorant and dirty:

> The town had no park, no theatre, no decent orchestra. The libraries of the town and the clubs were only frequented by Jewish boys. Journals and new books lay around unopened for months. The rich and educated slept in hermetic, stifling rooms on beds that were crawling with bugs. Their children were shoved off to foul and filthy holes which they were pleased to call nurseries. The servants, even the senior and respected ones, slept on rags on the kitchen floor. . . . . . The food was unpalatable, the water unhealthy.

It is Misail's own father's architecture which embodies this whole repulsive system. It is its 'style', ruling human relations within the family and throughout the town. His building plans begin where men of rank foregather—the reception hall and the drawing room—and the rest is added on in an irrational, 'vague, constricting and very confused' manner. These are houses of oppression where brutal men mould their children, with facades that wear 'a hard-hearted and forbidding expression', and ceilings so low that no-one can stand up or grow. Misail rejects it all, and tries a number of escapist alternatives, including a Tolstoyan reprise in Nature. But, lacking science, his life is determined fundamentally by his father's style, and he ends up back in town building houses too, as isolated, stern and forbidding as the rest of them.

Chekhov's Misails typically escape their crushing ceilings for a while. Across the plays and stories they number a substantial deviant community, each member of which rejects the only world he knows but has no permanent and authentic world to replace it. At the moment of recognition, each one becomes lonely, because the searching community is self-centred and transient; anomic, because there is no identity beyond the one rejected; and often frightened of a frozen future or a death which articulates how meaningless the journey has been.

These inauthentic characters can communicate only at the level of rejection (of society, of each other), never (to use Goldmann's term) at the level of essence: hence the familiar Chekhovian dialogue of oppositions, each one solipsistic, but with a subversive lucidity. Such is the relationship of Yelena/Vanya (*Uncle Vanya*), Lida/the Artist (*House with a Mezzanine*), early Layevskii/Van Koren (*The Duel*), Katya/Professor Stepanovich (*Dreary Story*), Ivanov/Lvov (*Ivanov*), Yekaterina/Ionych (*Ionych*), Orlov/the Narrator (*Anonymous Story*), Sof'ya/the Nun (*Big Volodya and Little Volodya*), Misail/the Doctor (*My Life*), Tuzenbakh/Solenyi (*The Three Sisters*), Nadya/Sasha (*The Betrothed*), Ragin/Gromov (*Ward Number Six*). Communication among these people functions to stir an often-forming consciousness of despair and rejection, but never with an authentic alternative. In *Uncle Vanya*, for instance, Yelena recognises the malice which degraded Vanya, and he recognises the banal 'love' which wastes Yelena, but neither helps the other positively because they themselves are divided. Similarly, in *House with a Mezzanine*, the artist recognises the inauthenticity of Lida's unscientific, unprofessional and merely therapeutic attempts to help the peasants when only societal change would achieve anything lasting or fundamental; she, on the other hand, recognises the emptiness of a shiftless generaliser who rejects doctors, medical centres, schools and libraries altogether because they are reformist, and yet does nothing himself at all. In *Ward Number Six*, Gromov points to the inauthenticity of Ragin's escapist philosophy, but his own neurasthenia is scarcely any alternative. Again, in *The Betrothed*, Sasha's urge to Nadya to leave her oppressive ceilings is authentically conceived, but his own revolutionary solution is somehow sick and shabby: Nadya goes beyond him—to education.

(ii) Chekhov's epic visionaries also, of course, live in an over-burdening world, and for all their visions, are constantly being 'called away' by its tedium. The presence of value in the world does open the way to authentic communication: Vershinin's individual vision passes on to three sisters, and they in turn may pass it on, we are told, to greater and greater numbers; Astrov may communicate with a future and better society by planting trees and ending the degenerative evolution of his own milieu. But it is all so local, and the task is so great. In the succession of choices on which their perspective depends, they may at any time choose wrongly, as when Astrov turns to drink and then solves complex problems with the ruthless one-dimensionality and fatalism of a Van Koren. The epic visionaries are limited men, split personalities, and the best that can be said of them is that their future is open. Chekhov, as we have seen, is careful to give us alternative futures for Astrov, with his vodka and his carefully folded maps. On the one hand he is now free of the woman who, he admits, was destroying his trees and his vision. But on the other hand, what hope has he for imparting his values widely when he is unable to communicate them even to the woman he loves, and has nothing more to say to Sonya, the woman who loves him and has adopted his vision? Where *can* authenticity lie if it is absent from the most intimate relations of men and women of good will? Women, we will find, are at the heart of the problem of communication in Chekhov. Their mediation in the question of choice is a recurring structural device.

*   *   *   *   *

In his outlined 'History of Sexual Authority' (1883),[1] Chekhov proposed an analysis of the 'woman problem' on Russian Darwinist lines. Beginning with the Darwinian adherence to the laws of natural selection ('Nature will not tolerate inequality'), Chekhov traces an evolution towards complete equality of the sexes from cells (where there is equality), through insects and birds which use muscular activity during pregnancy (where there is inequality for reasons of essential adjustment) and mammalia (where authority is weaker), to the perfect organism 'higher' than existing man where all will be equal. Extending considerably the teleological implications in Darwin, Chekhov insists that Nature 'is aiming at a perfect organism' and that 'the perfect organism creates'. However, he points out, it is clear that in the present world there is inequality: man is higher than woman, women do not create. Hence the conclusion that society hinders Nature in its quest for equality. The task then is to realign the laws of society with those of Nature, to help Nature help man perfect himself.[2]

Using the Darwinian method of examining variations within and between species, and seeing why some species are more fitted to survive than others, he intends to look at variations within authority patterns by means of zoology, anthropology, general history and the history of knowledge (the history of women in universities) to examine the way in which these variations co-vary with other factors (e.g. types of illness, types of social organisation, etc.). His hypothesis is that where social organisation re-enforces equality, authority patterns are not so clear, as for example among peasants where one finds a similar upbringing and similar labour patterns for men and women. Hence his conclusion is that the education of middle and upper class women in Russia interferes with Nature's plans for equality.

It is clear that Chekhov retained this unfatalistic view of Russian women and the evolution of sexual interaction, because twelve years later he considered the same problems in one of his stories, *Ariadne* (1895). Just as in 'History of Sexual Authority' he says that pregnancy alone cannot be blamed for the inequality of women since Nature will either shorten the period of pregnancy or create some other method, so in *Ariadne* when Shamokhin is explaining the inequality of women, he says:

> We've simply got to stop looking to physiology, pregnancy and childbirth to support our argument, because in the first place a woman doesn't have a baby every month, secondly not all women have babies, and thirdly your average peasant woman works out in the fields right up to the day of her confinement and is none the worse for it.

In *Ariadne* too, the conclusion is that female inequality is caused by a reactionary society, not by Nature. The same contrast between peasant women and women from other classes is presented:

> woman keeps up with man only in the villages. There she thinks and feels like a man, and enters the evolutionary struggle for progress as fervently as he does.[3]

In both 'History of Sexual Authority' and *Ariadne* it is education which is the key issue—the Russian type of education for women hinders natural evolution: a good education would help Nature in the perfection of the species. In *Ariadne* Chekhov develops at some length his views as to what the right education should be. The need, as he sees it, is to do away with the ascriptive type of education which fits women for their place in society, training them to be superficially attractive to the male of the species who responds in turn by dividing women—idealising them spiritually and degrading them physically. The education that replaces it should be oriented to achievement and rationality, and based on that natural fusion of science and art on which the future of civilisation depends. As in 'History of Sexual Authority' Chekhov singles out for criticism those reformers, emancipators etc. who continue to speak of the male/female war and not about whole people in honest communication.

In his 'History of Sexual Authority' Chekhov refers to the 'excellent essay' by Herbert Spencer on the subject of education in modern society. It is hardly surprising that Chekhov should have been drawn to the theories of a man who extended evolutionism to the question of human perfectibility, and was so influential in Russian scientific circles. In the particular articles Chekhov is referring to,[4] Spencer speaks of the need for education as a social science based on the natural sciences. A correct understanding of the laws of natural development is a necessary prerequisite for any rigorous science of man. Referring to education Spencer makes the point:

> If . . . you insist on premature or undue growth of any one part, [Nature] will, with more or less protest, concede the point; but that she may do your extra work, she must leave some of her more important work undone. Let it never be forgotten that the amount of vital energy which the body at any moment possesses is limited; and being limited it is impossible to get from it more than a fixed quantity of results.[5]

Here we have Chekhov's belief, expressed in 'History of Sexual Authority', that too much energy expended in either one of bodily or mental exertion will diminish capacity in the other. More importantly, here too is the idea that Nature must not be hindered by man, but should be aided by the right kind of social conduct. The 'right' education is, of course, a key to better social conduct.

Spencer insists, like Chekhov, that any scientific study must be based on the method of Claude Bernard. Since social science and education must also employ the scientific method, certain subjects are innately more appropriate than others in the education of children. Whereas scientific studies are based on objective observation, experiment and comparative research, other studies such as foreign languages and badly taught history are based on 'accidental' and unorganisable facts. Spencer's analysis of the difference in quality of contemporary language teaching and a scientific education is particularly interesting because Chekhov, as we will see, makes a similar distinction in his literature between the 'ascriptive' education of girls in languages and the need for a scientific education in its place.

For Spencer, the scientific method teaches objectivity by tracing organic relations (i.e. 'knowledge of the way surrounding phenomena depend on each other'). Language learning, on the other hand, tends, by emphasising memory, to increase respect for authority, for the teacher, for grammar books, etc., so that the pupil's 'constant attitude of mind is that of submission to dogmatic teaching . . . a tendency to accept without enquiry whatever is established'. But science 'in its constant appeal to individual reason, to individual striving for objective proof, creates independence of character. The prime essential of the successful scientific method is sufficient self-renunciation to achieve an honest receptivity and a willingness to abandon all preconceived notions, however cherished, if they are found to contradict the truth'.[6]

It is, of course, precisely this individualism signified by 'honest receptivity' that Chekhov's inauthentic characters most lack. Their failure of individualism is most apparent in their seduction by any fashionable 'tendency' which comes along, their inability to think independently, and their solipsism which negates any receptivity to the 'inner milieu' of those about them. It is interesting, too, that among the school-teachers he portrays, some of the most absurd, conformist and 'authority'-conscious are precisely the teachers of 'dead' languages (for example, the ultimate conformist in *Man in a Case*, and also Kulygin in *The Three Sisters*). There is certainly no doubt that successive Ministers of National Education in Russia agreed with Spencer's connection of languages with social conformity, since they applauded the teaching of Greek, and on the other hand nervously equated the natural sciences with an independence of mind that was dangerous in teachers or their charges.

The question of what passed for valid communication between

one man (or woman) and another was developed by both Spencer and Chekhov from this basic attachment to the scientific method. Objectivity of method promoted the 'honest receptivity' to the inner feelings of others which Chekhov was himself noted for as a doctor and which was the basis of his individualism. Both men opposed any social system in which, in Spencer's words, there is 'a restless craving to impress our individualities upon others, and in some way subordinate them'.[7] Spencer wrote:

> Society is made up of individuals; all that is done in society is done by the combined actions of individuals; and therefore in individual actions alone can be found the solutions of individual phenomena.[8]

Chekhov wrote:

> My belief is in individual men. I see salvation in the diffusion of individuals all over Russia.[9]

Elsewhere he connected this individualism to its important basis in the rational human mind:

> The power and salvation of a people lies in its intelligentsia, in the intellectuals who think honestly, feel and can work.[10]

This is a tribute to separate individualities who, unlike many of Chekhov's intellectuals (Stepanovich, Ragin etc.), eschew a spurious solipsism for recognition of the way surrounding phenomena depend on each other: these are men of knowledge, love and technology. It is also a call for a social system which allows self-discipline and independence of spirit, and educates men in accordance with natural needs. Spencer points out that 'strong will and untiring activity due to abundant animal vigour go far to compensate even great defects of education',[11] but insists, like Chekhov, that man will only attain a perfect equilibrium if a scientific education aids individual will. This is the reasoning behind Chekhov's insistence to Wagner that education and will together could counteract degeneration; and an important aim of his works was to provide such an education where any other was lacking.[12] The conservative function of women's education in Russia is a latent, but constant, motif in his works.

From the structural role of these motifs in his works, from his other writings, and from his acceptance of Spencer's ideas we can infer the following things about Chekhov's attitude to women in Russian society. In the first place, women's education fits them for their place in a debased social world. Instead of the sciences and arts they are taught piano-playing and languages. Separated from an objective relationship with men by the ascriptive patterning of 'femininity' women are hindered in their proper evolution towards equality. Moreover, society divides women into something higher and more pure than reality or something lower and more bestial. Women, in turn, divide man as between husband and lover, idealist and cavalier. Hence women, socialised by society, are themselves a mechanism of human fragmentation, and an example of the process of retrogressive evolution. This conception underlies Shamokhin's educational philosophy in *Ariadne*:

> Make every girl understand from her earliest days that a man is not first of all a cavalier or a potential husband, but a human being like herself, her equal in everything. Teach her to think logically, to evaluate, and don't make her believe that because her brain weighs less than a man's that she can ignore science, the arts, and major questions of civilised life. A young boy apprentice to a bootmaker or decorator has also a smaller brain than an adult, but he involves himself in the laws of evolution nonetheless. He works and he suffers.

Shamokhin, like Chekhov at Sakhalin, goes on to recognise the chain reaction which can follow an inappropriate upbringing:

> This educational backwardness of women is a serious threat to civilisation, for in her regression she will drag man after her and prevent his progress.

Educated, but without judgment and understanding, seeking relations of love, but unable to communicate objectively, women are critical links in the dialogue of solipsism and false choice in Chekhov's works. Like all his inauthentic characters, women reject the only world they know, but search for authenticity in simplistic, borrowed or ascribed stances—'love', 'art', 'the People', 'to Moscow'. Lacking independence and the individualism to recognise the complexity of life, they project a simplistic and pure authenticity in a world where there cannot be one, repeatedly seek sublime truths in abstract visions, and, inevitably, fail.

Thus Anna, in *Lady with a Little Dog*, yearns for a new life of honesty and purity:

> I told myself that there had to be a different kind of life. I wanted to live. To live, to live.

Anna has burned with curiosity for this life, married an official to find it, and discovered he is a flunkey. Again she burns for a new life, until she is seduced by a 'rather coarse' and arrogant man whom she takes to be 'fine, wonderful, high-minded'. In the very act of being seduced, she aspires still for a 'pure and honest life'. The pattern is exactly the same in *Lights*: Kisochka marries a flunkey, is then seduced by a coarse egoist whom she sees as a 'fine, enlightened and very educated man'; and in this man, who deserts her, she exalts 'love . . . . . to the realms of ecstasy, heartbreak, and a total revolution in my life'. Nadezhda in *A Visit to Friends* burns with the dream of a husband and naively combines this vision with an equally simplistic notion of service to the people:

> Without understanding a thing about it, she was carried away with the idea of work and independence. She was concocting schemes for the future: that was quite transparent from the expression on her face. The prospect of working and serving others seemed quite beautiful to her, and poetic.

Yekaterina in *Ionych* first dedicates herself to music, since 'a human being has to reach out to some great and shining goal', and then falls in love with the money-grubbing Ionych, seeing him as 'a man so ideal, so perfect'. Zinaida in *Anonymous Story*, to escape the vulgarity of her family life, becomes the mistress of yet another brutal egoist, believing him to be 'a great and precious person'. When disillusioned, she rejects love altogether and finds that 'life's meaning is contained in one thing only—fighting'. But she never does fight; instead she dies by suicide, betrayed by a false revolutionary. Nina in *The Seagull* passes through two stages of idealised love related to idealised art. Katya in *Dreary Story* also escapes into idealised art and love. Both are seduced and betrayed. Anya in *The Cherry Orchard* combines a naive love with an idealised desire to serve the people. Nadya in *The Betrothed* does the same, and at the moment of elopement with her faded revolutionary lover, 'gazed fixedly at him, her saucer eyes brimful of love, as though enchanted, and she waited for him to tell her something significant, something of infinite meaning'. She waits in vain.

In each case the narrative sequence is the same. A girl rejects the boredom and vulgarity of the only world she knows, falls with infinite naivety and brimming eyes into some false ideal, and finds it as degraded as the society she rejected. Spencer's 'familiarity with rational relations' is conspicuously absent. On each occasion the visionary ideal lacks objectivity, the ability to judge people and situations; and in its 'poetry' lacks stability and coherence. The ultimate of this type is Ol'ga in *The Darling* who takes up as many ideals as she takes up husbands, quickly forgetting each ideal as soon as it is superseded. In her Chekhov demonstrates that any ideal, whether the most noble or the most trivial, when based on ignorance and subjectivity, belongs to the society of ascribed values.

This pattern of abstract and degraded interaction in Chekhov is close to the one described by René Girard in his book, *Deceit, Desire and the Novel* where he discusses the role of 'transfigured love' in the search for 'metaphysical transcendence'. Girard writes:

> Men who cannot look freedom in the face are exposed to anguish. They look for a banner on which they can fix their eyes.[13]

God is absent, and 'to escape the feeling of particularity they imitate *another's* desires, they choose substitute Gods because they are not able to give up infinity'.[14] Girard shows that for these 'vaniteux' the real qualities of the loved one are abstracted through the concentration on a mediating 'value' or 'object', and genuine love, which is based on 'esteem . . . a perfect agreement among reason, will and sensibility'[15] is lost. The feature of transfigured love is that in gaining its object, the latter *loses* all value since it was only desired in simulation of the mediator. However:

> Disappointment does not prove the absurdity of *all* metaphysical desires, but only that of this particular desire which has just led to disillusionment . . . This power he confers elsewhere, on the second object, on a new desire.[16]

So 'the hero goes through his existence from desire to desire, as one crosses a stream, jumping from one slippery stone to another'. In the face of inevitable disappointment 'two possibilities present themselves. The disillusioned hero can let his former mediator point out another object for him, or he can change mediators'.[17] These are in fact the two possibilities available to Chekhov's inauthentic heroes—and here we are concerned not only with his women, but with all the characters of false choice which create a paradigm: the Layevskiis, the Misails, the hero of *On the Road*, and all the others who move from one 'tendency' to another. In the first case, they move from lover to lover, as in *The Darling, Lights* etc. In the second case they can move from one mediator to another, such as from love to revolution—the path of Zinaida in *Anonymous Story*.

However, we need to pin down this relational pattern more precisely to authors and world views than Girard does. Sometimes he seems to imply a deterministic sense of evolution himself, as he traces the process of transfigured desire closer and deeper into the psyche. It is interesting that he ends his account with Dostoyevskii, since John Carroll has recently pointed out that the anarcho-psychological tradition which Dostoyevskii belonged to *chose* the posture of transfigured love as a positive value. 'In the end', Nietzsche wrote, 'one loves one's desire and not what is desired'. As Carroll puts it, 'one man never loves another immediately . . . He uses the other as a complementary electrode: he needs him in order to express and realize himself, in order to experience his *own* passions.'[18] Chekhov's position, as I suggested earlier, was directly opposed to this solipsism, and looked to the expression of individualism through organic connection. Inability to communicate was a matter of history and choice—for Chekhov a false choice—not a matter of ontology. Hence his texts always present an alternative.

First of all through characterisation: Chekhov's epic visionaries, in particular, zemstvo doctors like Astrov and scientific army officers like Vershinin who, for all the ambivalence of their personal biography, communicate genuinely and for the first time. Their function is to begin the chain of reactions which will finally turn quantity into quality, and which Vershinin predicts in *The Three Sisters*. These are the rare moments of dramatic emphasis when radical change does take place, and the mediation of the epic vision replaces that of the degraded world: hence the well-known 'moment of concentration' when Masha moves from Kulygin to Vershinin ('Takes off her hat: "I'm staying for lunch"') which signifies more than a change of men and more than a *mere* change of mediator, but a change of quality.

More frequently the perspective is contained in the subtext. Tolstoi correctly diagnosed this in *The Darling*, remarking that when writing the story Chekhov had in mind the image of a 'new woman: . . . of a woman mentally developed, learned, working independently for the good of society as well as, if not better than men'.[19] The fact that Tolstoi strongly disapproved of this absent heroine (and instead chose to celebrate the textual one, Ol'ga) did nothing to hinder her reincarnation time and again in Chekhov's works. She speaks, in effect, from the shadow of the motivating detail which Chekhov chose to surround his women; in particular the unscientific education at the hands of tutor, boarding school or conservatoire which *determined* the repetition of events, lovers and mediators we have described. Thus in *Dreary Story* Katya passes straight from boarding school into an idealised art world, and the professor complains of the educational backwardness of modern women who, because of their wretched learning are 'as weepy and insensitive today' as women were in the Middle Ages. Woman's cruelty is also a theme of *Ariadne*, and again is directly related to her backward education. Zinaida in *Anonymous Story* and Anna in *Lady with a Little Dog* both 'escape' by marrying a falsely idealised man directly on leaving boarding school.

The young Yelena in *Uncle Vanya*, straight from the music academy, married 'for love' the futile Serebryakov, who seemed 'an intellectual, a famous man. It wasn't genuine love. It was quite empty, but at the time I believed it was real enough'. The young Masha in *The Three Sisters*, educated in several foreign languages at boarding school, married at eighteen, and straight from school, the absurd schoolmaster, Kulygin: 'At the time he seemed so awfully learned, terribly clever and important. I'm afraid things look very different now'. Misyus in *House with a Mezzanine* falls in love with the artist's landscapes (as does Nina in *The Seagull*) after an unbalanced education by a tutor, in which she overtaxed her mind with trivial reading, studied nothing serious, and did no physical or practical work at all.

There is a detail that is systematically absent. All these dejected, searching women lack science, and nearly all lack any training for a practical profession. Yelena with her musical education is unable to teach or nurse the peasants: 'I've no idea how to, and I'm not interested anyway'. Vera (*At Home*), with her three languages from boarding school, realises she is totally unequipped to face the harsh working conditions of doctors and teachers of peasants. Languages, music and poetry are common in a girl's education; science is always absent. So that Sof'ya in *Big Volodya and Little Volodya*, struggling to find something beyond the purely physical sexuality and the mechanical religion which compose the polarities of her dreary life, begs her seducer, at the very moment of seduction, to tell her something which will give her faith, to tell her 'of higher aims . . . . . of science'.

As they travel and search these women carry their inability to communicate to the world of men. When genuine love breaks through, even the greatest obstacles are swept aside—the advanced degeneration of Layevskii (*The Duel*), a lifetime of vulgar egoism and seductions in Gurov (*Lady with a Little Dog*). But more often women, denying men in like manner the direct and objective relations which society has denied to *them*, cripple man's potential or are the harbingers of death. Her beauty hiding her emptiness of feelings, woman becomes a siren or a predator, destroying achievement and creativity. Yelena (*Uncle Vanya*) lures Astrov away from his medicine and trees; Ariadne is a cruel predator who destroys organised agriculture; Ol'ga (*The Grasshopper*) destroys a potentially great scientist; Yekaterina (*Ionych*) is intimately concerned with the moral decay of a zemstvo doctor. The failure of communication is specific: these women destroy love—and therefore objectivity, individualism, sensitivity and active ideals as well.

On the other hand love will negate false mediators (even if it is unreturned) provided that a genuine vision of art or science is somehow available. Then solitary women of will—Nina in *The Seagull*, Masha, Irina and Ol'ga in *The Three Sisters*, Sonya in *Uncle Vanya*—exchange their search for an epic vision. In each case they love genuinely as they throw off false ideals—Nina grows beyond the conception of art as fame and popular success, the sisters grow beyond the 'To Moscow' dream, Sonya outgrows the narrow devotion to her father as a supposedly great art critic—and aspiration for what Chekhov conceives as real art, real knowledge, real science replaces inauthenticity. Judgment comes with the realisation that any reduction of the tensions of this life means defeat; objectivity with the dogged yet desperately tenuous refusal of all simplistic solutions. Thus at the end of *Lady with a Little Dog*, Gurov and Anna subjectively yearn for a nearby and non-contradictory solution in this world; but their love gives them the

strength and judgment to maintain the tension of hope *and* despair
of the epic vision:

> Both knew that in fact the end was still a long, long way away,
> and the hardest and most complicated period was only just
> beginning.

Layevskii, as we have seen in *The Duel*, has a similar vision of the
suffering, the obstacles and the contradictions of the essential
journey, but it is nonetheless a journey of meaning and hope:

> Miscalculations, suffering and the tedium of life throw them
> back, but the thirst for truth and a stubborn will drive them on
> and on.

The journey from quantity into quality will last many generations of living and dying, in the course of which the wo/man of will
and suffering, but not her vision, may be forgotten. Existentially the
achievements are hope, the rejection of illusion and compromise,
the loneliness of knowledge—and the chance to communicate with
a society which, though it forget her, is the product of her vision.
This is Vershinin's message in *The Three Sisters*:

> At the moment there are just three people of your intellectual
> qualities in the entire town, but future generations will produce
> more people like you. They will continue to produce more and
> more people of the same kind until a time will finally be reached
> when everything will be done exactly the way you would have
> wished it. People will then live lives according to your model.
> And after that, even you may be out of date and a new and better
> breed will come along and replace you.

So the three sisters, educated in languages but converted by
Vershinin to a new vision, will be followed by greater numbers of
their own kind, and then, finally, by a new quality. The evolutionary message is taken up by Ol'ga as a vision of communication
through death:

> The years will pass. We will have passed on too, and no-one will
> remember us. . . . . . Yet our own sufferings may mean happi-
> ness for those who come after us . . . One day peace and

happiness will cover this whole earth, and then, at last we will be thought of kindly and thanked.

Astrov's message in *Uncle Vanya* is essentially the same:

> Those who live one or two hundred years after us and despise us for our ignorant and vulgar lives—maybe they'll find a way to be happy . . . And as for us . . . there's only one hope for people like you and me . . . The hope that when we are at last lying at rest in our graves we may see visions—maybe even happy ones.

This is the doctor who plants trees despising the Astrov who drinks himself into the brutally simplistic solutions of Van Koren, trying to see a time beyond the grave when his trees have grown into a qualitatively new society. Then, as Sonya says, 'we will see all earthly ills and all our sufferings swept aside by a grace which will cover the whole world.'

According to his vocation man will find purpose in life, as the knowledge to endure relates the meaning of life. At the end of *The Seagull* Nina says:

> What matters is nothing to do with one's fame or one's fascination, nor with all the other things I once dreamed of. What does matter is having the knowledge to endure, how to suffer and yet have faith.

Early in the play, the young Nina had conceived of art in terms of a public chained to the chariot wheel of her personal success. By the end she realises that art has more to do with struggle, travelling interminably in third-class railway carriages with peasants and associating with vulgar merchants. It is not, however, trivialised by that experience any more than Chekhov's vision as a doctor at Melikhovo, or as a medical researcher en route for Sakhalin was reduced by similar experiences. Nina, it is clear, has a faith—like her author. But not 'faith without science'. Nina has become 'objective' and, tearing herself from the constricting 'seagull' identity imposed by others, has become an individual. Typically, this is signified by the change in her personal relationships. The young Nina had loved Trigorin as she had loved the notion of art: for the sake of notoriety and fame. Trigorin deceives her. She sees through him, and yet loves him still. With the mediation of fame and celebrity stripped away, she loves now, we are to believe, the inner man. She sees Trigorin in his entire weakness but, unlike the object of transfigured love, he still has value for her after consummation. Nina is strong enough to live in freedom. Her *hopeful* acceptance of a life of suffering marks the end of metaphysical desire. It is this objective ability to see inwards, into people, while finding the social world more tarnished than her youthful naivety expected, which marks the greatest moment of authenticity available, and links Nina with Masha, Irina and Ol'ga, Astrov and Sonya, Gurov and Anna, Layevskii and Nadezhda, for all of whom

> a new life of suffering and clarity was beginning that was incompatible with personal happiness or repose.
>
> (*The Teacher of Literature*)

8 The Three Sisters

Action in Chekhov takes place explicitly in the debased present. Whatever the location of the drama, whether in a provincial town far from Moscow, such as Perm where *The Three Sisters* is set, or on an estate nearer the capitals as in the other plays, the society of Chekhov's works is unified (while yet hierarchical) in that the mass of its members, from peasants to the élite, seem unaware of any fundamental values other than those based on subservience to status and rank. In *My Life*, for instance, the provincial town of Misail's family lives entirely according to ascriptive values. It is a society in which everyone, from the half-witted butcher Prokofii to the governor general, orders his actions to the supreme value, 'Each class must know its place'. The hegemony of this value system is apparent in the fact that not only does every class accept it, but believes in it too. Thus it is not simply Misail's father who deplores the fact that his son has not yet achieved a 'recognised social position'; he is insulted by shopkeepers and workmen for the same reason. Prokofii tells Misail approvingly that 'We've got rules for governors, rules for clergy, rules for officers, rules for doctors—each class has got its own rules'; and the governor admonishes him because of 'the perfect incompatibility of your behaviour with the lofty position of noble which you are privileged to have . . . . . I require you, in consequence . . . . . to redeem your behaviour and take upon yourself the responsibilities sacred to your position'. Even the disparity of their speech—Prokofii's is vulgar, the governor's absurdly pretentious—unites them in opposition to the simple 'cool' style Chekhov believed in.

The cultural accretions of the hegemonic values are described in detail—the bribery, dishonesty, lies, superstition, rudeness, dirt, the absence of science, art or rationality. With the fawning due to higher ranks goes the symptomatic brutality to inferiors, so that nobles beat their children with sticks and refer to working people as 'serfs' and 'insects', petty officials threaten to punch workmen in the face for asking for their wages, and even the 'most insignificant clerk' treats workers 'like animals, with crude and vulgar insults'. If one is unlucky enough to be in the lowest station of all, one can always torture the animals. From the highest rank to the lowest the brutality is based on ignorance. In *The Three Sisters* we hear that the station, for no logical reason, has been built miles from town. In *My Life* the irrationality of provincial society is spelled out more clearly: here shopkeepers prefer to be treated during a cholera epidemic by a simpleton butcher rather than by doctors; men who gamble fortunes away at cards beg unsuccessfully for lesser loans to build a decent water supply; and the station is built miles out of town because the authorities refuse to pay the engineers extra money, not able to calculate that a linking road will cost more than the bribes.

Yet, for all this weight of banality and ignorance, evolution does take place. In both *The Three Sisters* and *My Life* we are presented with a degenerative change, in which one social élite is replaced by another that is more brutish. The sisters, tender as flowers, are displaced by the bourgeoise Natasha, likened by her own husband to a blind beast, and symbolically representing, like Van Koren's blind mole, the destruction of an entire world: trees, town and the existing social community.

At the same time, however, there is a residual core which does *not* change, so that we can talk of a degenerative evolution in which essential features of the social order remain the same. The emphasis on hierarchical authority and ritualised role performance is unchanged: servants were treated better by the sisters, but they underpin their class just the same, and officiate at parties where it is regretted that less men of rank appear than before. The flattery and brutality of social relations is simply more implicit, among the traditional rulers, and less vulgar (until Andrei forgets himself under pressure).

The sisters are the best representatives of this fading élite; the declining nobility in *My Life* are among its worst. But they share a common element of ineptitude in the face of natural potential and social challenge. The point about setting *The Three Sisters* in a bleak northern town is not, as some critics have suggested, to enable a description of stagnation; Chekhov achieves that in all his works, wherever they are set. Rather it is to indicate the potential for growth in the harshest milieu: the size of the task (as in the case of Layevskii in *The Duel*) is representative of the burden, but also the potential of changing an entire social order. As Vershinin points out, a wonderful place could emerge out of this landscape; but the sisters can only respond with dreams of escape. The grass is greener in Moscow, the buds there are already in blossom. The sisters reject their own milieu; then Natasha accentuates their logic by trivialising or destroying it. In *My Life* the down-at-heel nobility, like the sisters, have a passive relationship with their environment. As in *The Cherry Orchard*, the nobility's contact with Nature is one of neglect and decay: 'an old garden allowed to run wild—and infested with weeds and untended bushes . . . . . cherry trees, plum trees and apple trees, growing rank and rotten with canker'. The 'corpse-like old lady has an appearance fitting to this neglect. But when she does come to life it is in the world of ascriptive values, preserved alike by nobles and petit-bourgeoisie. The apparent inevitability of their decay (the son typically accounts for his misfortune according to fatalistic degeneration theory), the continuing adherence to rank and social graces, the fawning to new superiors like Dolzhikov which has replaced the overlordship of serfs—all this binds a degraded society in a determined timelessness. As Misail notes in *My Life*, serfdom no longer exists, but new forms of exploiting the weak evolve along with the new capitalism, and in the end everything remains what it had been at the time of the Tatar invasion.

This theme of the unending violence and stagnation of history, and of each evolving generation being crushed by the one before, is a central one in *My Life* and *The Three Sisters*. The reactions of Misail and Andrei are identical. In *My Life*, Misail asks his uncomprehending father:

> Why, in all these houses you have spent your time building during the last thirty years, has there not been even one person I could learn how to live from, how not to feel guilty? . . . . . Your houses are fearful breeding holes which mean death for mothers and daughters. They torture the children . . . . . You have to lose yourself in cards, vodka and scandal, you have to fawn, be a hypocrite or else ritually draw up designs year in year out not to notice all the torments festering in these houses. Our town has existed now for several hundred years. But in all that time it hasn't produced one significant man for our nation—not even one. You've stifled everything in embryo that had a spark of life and vitality.

In *The Three Sisters*, the despairing Andrei says to the deaf and uncomprehending Ferapont:

> This town has lasted for two hundred years. It contains a hundred thousand people, but not a single one who rises above the others! It has never had a scholar, an artist, or a saint—or anyone else with that special something that makes people notice or want fervently to imitate him. Here all they do is eat, drink and sleep until they die. Then others replace them, and eat, drink and sleep in their turn. And, to add a bit of spice to their lives and avoid complete boredom, they go in for their revolting gossip and vodka, their gambling and their litigation. Wives deceive husbands; husbands lie to wives and pretend they can't see what's going on. And meanwhile the children are crushed beneath this mountain of vulgarity. Any hint of potential they may have had in them is extinguished, and they, too, become wretched, dead-and-alive creatures, indistinguishable from each other, and just like their parents.

The towns, it is clear, are essentially the same—and the pattern is the same: human potential lies with the children, and stagnation comes from their parents and from their physical environment. Without a single human being who is worthy of emulation, the children grow up in that familiar dichotomous world of Chekhov, where grinding daily trivia is overlaid with the rhythms of dream and escape. In *The Three Sisters*, as befits the social milieu of a general's family, the form of escape is in the gay whirl of balls, parties and, when these decline with the general's death, the dream of moving to where such 'culture' is eternal, Moscow. Yet it is, as both Misail and Andrei point out, a dichotomous world only on the surface. The procedures of escape are in fact projections of the stagnant society itself, hypocrisies which obscure vision and make the real seem accidental.

In *The Three Sisters* the problem of human beings worthy of emulation is central. But in the play 'totality of objects' is replaced by action. The houses which typify the 'style' of the provincial town in *My Life* are replaced by the ruthless movement of Natasha. Circling with her candle she physically embodies this style: the cramping, destructive, dispossessive values of a world whose objects—the school, the brickyard, the post office, Protopopov, the Headmaster, the Council Office—are confined to the intervals between acts (Irina's various jobs, Ol'ga's teaching, Masha's marriage etc.) What is presented on the stage is the full range of reponses to the question of choice subsumed in the progression from escapist vision to the harsh reality of social action, within the Prozorov family.

The sisters embody different qualities, different stages, of the typical Chekhov heroine—from 'transfigured desire' of love, work, the people; through the pattern of dreary marriage and seduction; to the mental and physical stagnation of life without a vocation. Ol'ga, the oldest and worn down by hard work as a teacher, preaches duty and wears a uniform. She would have liked a husband but never got one, does not want to become a headmistress (since this will tie her to the town) but becomes one all the same. Appropriately her desire to return to Moscow is one of wishful memory. Masha wears black; signifying the death of hope and of the naive boarding school love which made her marry a man she believed to be of great intellect, but turned out to be one of Count Tolstoi's ultra-conservative and authority conscious teachers of classics. Irina, in white, is the youngest, and as innocent in her dreams of the future as all those white-garbed generations of *The Cherry Orchard*. Unlike Masha, she has not yet been disillusioned in love, and yearns for it like a schoolgirl. Nor has she faced the rigours of real work when the play opens, unlike Ol'ga. For all her claims to be an adult, Irina's responses are those of a child; she is stirred by childhood memories, and delights in the toys which the young soldiers give her. Her level of sophistication in ideals is that of the early Nina in *The Seagull* and Anya in *The Cherry Orchard*—a simplistic response of abstract love, work, and manual service to the people in the face of the complex problems that confront them all. Irina tells Tuzenbakh that she yearns for work as 'one longs for a drink on a hot day'; and one is reminded of Chekhov's remark: 'When one longs for a drink, it seems as though one could drink a whole ocean—that is faith; but when one begins to drink, one can only drink altogether two glasses—that is science'. It is an appropriate comment on Irina's idealism. As the play develops and the dreams of hard work are extinguished by the practice, she despairs and prepares to subsume the difficulties of both her sisters. She will immerse herself in the bleak life of the school like Ol'ga and be married to a man she does not love like Masha. The sequence from dreams to hopeless reality of the three sisters will be complete. Thus compositely the sisters form one type, the youngest threatening to repeat the process of those who are older. They symbolise the pattern of *generational* sequence without hope or change of a degraded world.

All these girls were educated in languages for the ascriptive society, and because of this training in delicacy are unable to face the rigours of the brutal life they reject. Yet while shrinking from it, they are slowly coarsened as their quest for a new life brings only irritation and frustration. They all respond to the question of choice with the simplistic stance, 'To Moscow'—life will be better when they move to the very heart of the ascriptive society:

> Ol'ga: Every day of the four years I've worked at the school I've had just one desire, and that has got stronger and stronger. . .
> Irina: If we could just return to Moscow! If we could only conclude the life we lead here, sell the house and return to Moscow.
> Ol'ga: Yes Moscow! Just as soon as we can.
>
> Masha: I believe I wouldn't even notice the weather if I lived in Moscow.

It is a cry that becomes the more compulsive as the fragile world of the party is replaced by the stages of dispossession and destruction of the ensuing Acts; but it is empty nevertheless. Vershinin is, characteristically, to have the alienating function of saying, 'you won't even notice its Moscow when you are back there again'.

The 'To Moscow' cry speaks—among the affairs, gossip, gambling and vodka of which Andrei complains, Chebutykin's endless reading of popular newspapers, Tuzenbakh's constant talk of work, Solenyi's Lermontov image and preoccupation with scent, Fedotik's photographs and childish presents—as part of the chorus of reality-avoiding rituals which define the true status of this party world prior to the entry of Vershinin and Natasha. One inauthentic response comments on another. Thus Ol'ga's first expression of longing for Moscow has as counterpoint from the back of the stage Chebutykin's 'The devil you do!' and Tuzenbakh's 'Ridiculous, I agree'. The conversations are separate, but they propose to the audience a composite meaning. Similarly Chebutykin's newspaper reading elicits Balzac in Berdichev in mock counterpoint to his dear Irina's thoughts of Moscow; and Solenyi's scent and violent thoughts are a constant response to Tuzenbakh's dreams, and a dark hint of their demise. Sometimes the effect is consciously funny—as in Chebutykin's 'I'm not going to work' in response to Tuzenbakh's heroic 'I'm going to labour, and in twenty-five or thirty years time each man and woman will have begun to work— every single one'; sometimes ominous and predictive, such as Solenyi's ensuing response that in twenty-five years time Tuzenbakh will be long dead with Solenyi's bullet inside him. But each effect functions to 'alienate' and to elicit the grim reality beneath party rituals. In this sense Chebutykin, Solenyi and Tuzenbakh have an important function in making the inauthenticity of the sisters more general, giving it perspective in preparation for the action to come.

Thus Chebutykin, the doctor who has not read a book since leaving university and long forgotten all his medicine, not only places in perspective Andrei, the would-be professor whom time also passes by, but the whole sequence of time without change of the world of the three sisters. His medical knowledge is now inseparable from his ritual of reading newspapers—it is there that he finds trivial remedies for trivial complaints, and there that he comes closest to the raging smallpox epidemics. His relationship with Irina represents his attempt, like Madame Ranevskaya's in *The Cherry Orchard*, at a nostalgic fixing of time, an attachment to the past through the innocence of the girl in white who is so like her mother.

Chebutykin has no relationship with progressive time, with science or art, and when confronted with the inevitable demands of change—a woman needing medical treatment, Natasha's affair with Protopopov, Irina's decision to leave his world—his only response is to deny the significance of time (symbolised in the breaking of the mother's clock) and affirm that life is meaningless. In his futility Chebutykin has no world to replace the one that discomforts him, and he retreats into a denial of reality. For if nothing exists, then what difference does anything make? This 'what's the difference' becomes a motif not only justifying his inaction and enclosing his despair, but commenting also on the accidental and fragmentary nature of all around him. In reducing time and purpose to nothing he does no more than speak the logic of all their lives.

Maurice Valency is right when he says of Chekhov and this play that 'Vershinin speaks for his faith; Chebutykin for his doubt',[1] but not quite in the way he suggests. Chebutykin speaks for Chekhov's doubt because his is the stagnant reality beneath the sisters' dreams, and their Moscow is as empty of hope as his den beneath the ballroom floor. He is the obverse of the one honest man, 'a scholar, an artist, a saint', so needed by the towns of Misail and Andrei. But the doubt is not ontological. There was certainly room in Chekhov's society for the Chebutykins, but not in his soul as Valency suggests. The same might be said of Solenyi, for if Chebutykin is the passive representative of the meaningless and accidental passage of time, Solenyi is its activist. He, too, is a lonely and intelligent man who overcompensates for his shyness by being offensive and strange in company. He longs to be understood, but, rejected and isolated, he retreats into his Lermontov image which, as he well knows, seeks authenticity in meaningless action: 'As though in storms there lay his peace.' But the Lermontov mask is no more authentic than the Hamlet one, or any other fixed personality-type in Chekhov. Solenyi's 'peace', like Chebutykin's, kills; Tuzenbakh's life is cut short, and the false ritual of each man demonstrates his inability to provide a refuge from death and decay.

Tuzenbakh, a kind and generous man who is highly sensitive to his exploiting position as an aristocrat, has been subject to amazingly contrary interpretation. Thus Soviet critics, seizing his famous words 'a monstrous storm is coming to liven things up!', find that his realism consists of predicting the Revolution; Styan, on the other hand, considers him a realist precisely because he *denies* the ultimate value of change.[2] The simple fact is that Tuzenbakh is entirely inconsistent and embraces contrary positions on more than one occasion. And he is inconsistent because he is irrational—he rejects the scientific vision. As such, he too generalises the party world of the three sisters, standing, in his proposed marriage to Irina, for the ultimate circularity of their development. In Chekhov's terms, Tuzenbakh is not a realist at all. He does not believe in a new order of life based on the diffusion of knowledge, believes that life will always be the same, that the evolution of Nature is a mystery and will always remain so.

I believe that life won't change. Life will go on being hard, mysterious and full of joy.

Life doesn't evolve. It always stays the same. It sticks by its own laws which neither interest us nor can be understood by us. Just consider the birds migrating in autumn—cranes for example—which fly on and on. It makes no difference what kind of ideas they've got in their heads, whether they are significant ones or trivial. They just go on flying, without any idea where or why.

The contrast between Tuzenbakh's emphasis on the unending mystery of Nature and Vershinin's concern to understand it parallels the distinction Saltykov-Shchedrin made between 'idealists' and 'materialists'. The latter took upon themselves 'the task of explaining the relationship of man to Nature, . . . and of eradicating the conditions unfavourable to social progress'; whereas the 'idealists', like Tuzenbakh, were content to see man as permanently dependent on the mysterious forces of Nature. Rejection of the Russian Darwinist vision is explicit in Tuzenbakh. Characteristically his conception of work is Tolstoyan—labour without science; and as a corollary, his vision is subjective, abstract and simplistic—related entirely to his rapturous love for the naive Irina. His responses imitate hers, and his failure suggests the inauthenticity of her choices, as much as Chebutykin's failure to choose underscores Andrei's. The real significance of Tuzenbakh's 're-volutionary' speech about the need to work is its absolute dependence on Irina. It comes as a refrain of love—in response to Irina's own abstract speech about the need to work by the sweat of the brow to offset the idle depravity of her social position. It is not the content of his speech that is significant, but the nature of the response itself. Irina repents her social idleness, so does he; she talks naively of physical labour as the simple solution to their problems, so does he. Tuzenbakh's inconsistent optimism is a function of his love for Irina, and he admits it himself:

I desire life so fervently. I yearn to work and struggle. And every bit of this yearning is somehow associated with my love for you, Irina. Life appears beautiful to me for the simple reason that you are beautiful too.

Deprived of Irina his vision is empty:

As I contemplate you now, I can't help thinking of that day so long ago—your Name Day—when you told us of the delights of labour . . . You were so joyous, so high-spirited that day . . . And how happy my future life seemed to appear! But where has it all gone . . . . . Oh, if only I could lay down my life for you!

Tuzenbakh does give his life for his love, but in a trivial, arbitrary way which has nothing to do with social progress. He is shot in a duel by a man who belongs to the Romantic past. Like that other prophet of revolutionary change Trofimov, Tuzenbakh cannot avoid anachronism. Before he dies, Tuzenbakh shows quite how subjective his love was. Like the 'revolutionary' artist's love in *House with a Mezzanine*, it never really goes beyond the two of them:

> I'll spirit you away tomorrow. We'll labour. We'll get rich. And my dreams will live again!

Chebutykin, Solenyi and Tuzenbakh are already at the party when the play opens. In fact they have been part of the sisters' world for a long time. Together they form a community where nobody develops, and decisions and hopes of the moment are unfulfilled after years. But in Chekhov the escapist stance which rejects this world yet remains in limbo can never be a permanent alternative. Into this milieu, in the first Act, come two new characters, Natasha and Vershinin, and they dramatise it by posing directly the question of choice. The world of the party is stripped away by the impact of these two characters who offer as genuine solutions the two—and only two—worlds of ascription and science, the degraded world and the epic vision.

Natasha, the socially climbing petite-bourgeoise who destroys the party world and the dreams of the sisters, is a complete representative of the degraded world. Like the heroine of *Anna on the Neck*, her mobility embraces a whole order of subservience and brutality. From being a young girl who weeps on being told of the vulgarity of her dress by Ol'ga, she becomes the mistress of the house, driving the sisters from their rooms on behalf of her babies and from their house on behalf of her powerful lover. As mistress of the house *she* now represents its culture: her harsh treatment of the servants seems the very opposite of the sisters' ineffective tenderness, her self-conscious French and society manners a parody of their ascriptive culture, and her final insult to Irina for vulgar dress no more than crude revenge. In fact her dominance of servants, her insult and her French are really reproductions of the old order, but with a new and more vulgar basis.

Natasha cuts down the trees which are part of Vershinin's vision. She turns the would-be man of learning Andrei into a pathetic figure who pushes about in prams babies that may not be his, and whose new summit of achievement, a position on the town council, depends on the influence of Natasha's lover. Potapenko's influence can be felt everywhere—behind the destruction of Andrei, behind the appointment Ol'ga did not want, behind the dispossession of the sisters. This is the 'style' of the towns of Misail and Andrei which deprives the inhabitants of humanity. And its mediator, Natasha herself, is a worthy representative of it; as Andrei finally admits, she is 'a kind of self-centred, blind, nasty animal—not at all like a human being'.

Opposed to the brutish evolution of Natasha is the intellect and vision of Vershinin. He is a representative of the new army which was radically professionalised after the failures of the Crimean War. Garthoff points out that from the reforms of Milyutin until 1914

> the continuing trend of the officer corps was evolution from the partial and sometimes part-time service of a segment of the nobility towards a professionally and technically qualified group drawn from all classes. This trend was in part a reflection of the general social change produced by growing industrialisation, urbanisation, educational progress, and other factors. But in part it was also a response to the definite needs of the modern army. As war and armaments became more technologically advanced, it was necessary to have officers with corresponding technical qualifications.[3]

Since, according to the reforms, non-nobles became personal nobles automatically on reaching officer status, Garthoff can speak of a new and increasing merger of technical specialists with the military career segment of the nobility. *Within* the army it was the artillery and engineer corps sections which, demanding more technological expertise, were more open to the social mobility of the new type of officer than the infantry and cavalry. Tuzenbakh and Vershinin are artillery officers, and apparently represent the old and the new style of officer respectively. Tuzenbakh, an hereditary noble, had all the comforts and style of an aristocratic education and has been to the élitist Military Academy, whereas Vershinin did not go to the Academy, and, like Lopakhin in *The Cherry Orchard* (who is also upwardly mobile), is uncomfortably aware of the gaps in his learning and his ignorance about books. The difference in educational style is reflected in their visions: Tuzenbakh's is that of a repentent nobleman, Vershinin's is the scientific vision of the new technologist.

Chekhov was very insistent that the new qualities of the army—its greater education and culture—should be emphasised instead of its old preoccupation with the rituals of rank. Stanislavskii points out that Chekhov was well disposed to the army, 'which according to him was carrying out a cultural mission by going to outlandish parts of the country and taking with it . . . knowledge, art, happiness and joy.' He was worried that his officers would be 'turned into the usual heel-clickers, with jingling spurs. He wanted us to play simple, charming, decent people, dressed in worn, untheatrical uniforms, without any theatrical military mannerisms. . . . "The services have changed . . . They've become more cultured . . . and many of them are beginning to understand that their peacetime job is to carry culture with them into out-of-the-way spots."[4] The new officers then, along with zemstvo doctors, were examples of those unheralded individuals of knowledge on whom, Chekhov wrote to Orlov, the future depended.

All the army officers do in fact come over as human beings. It is not, however, the apathetic Chebutykin, nor the ritualist Solenyi, nor the repentent nobleman, Tuzenbakh (who rejects the civilising task of the army for manual labour in a brickworks!) that stand for the knowledge, education and hard work in the provinces of the new army. It is Vershinin who promotes the spirit of science and discovery—in opposition to all transient 'tendencies':

It's strange to realise that people just can't predict the things that will be thought important and significant later on, and the things that people will disregard as trivial nonsense. After all, weren't Copernicus' discoveries—and Columbus' too for that matter—thought of as useless and insignificant at the outset, whereas the mumbo-jumbo of any crazy charlatan was thought of as a sign of divine wisdom? It could well be the case that in the future our lives will be seen as odd, difficult, ignorant and none too hygienic—perhaps even sinful.

Against Tuzenbakh's notion that society may have reached its highest state, and that the future will be no different from the present, Vershinin asserts the belief that knowledge and education will bring a better life—but the change will be evolutionary, not revolutionary:

> I believe that every part of this earth is on the way to gradual change. Indeed we can see it evolving right in front of our eyes. In two or three hundred years from now—or perhaps a thousand years, the time scale is not so important—men's lives will be of a different order. They will be happy. We won't be able to share in that future life, but we are helping in its inception with our present lives. We work . . . and we suffer, too, in order to establish that life.

To Tuzenbakh's 'revolutionary' and simplistic 'The time has come', Vershinin opposes a vision of hope and suffering based on knowledge and education. To the sisters' pessimism about their stagnant lives and their useless education, Vershinin replies with a prediction of evolution:

> It seems to me that there is nowhere on earth, however harsh and depressing, where intellect and education are not of some use. Let's consider for a moment the fact that there are, among the hundred thousand ignorant and uncultivated souls of this town, just three people like yourselves. Naturally there is little hope of you triumphing personally over the mountain of ignorance that hems you in. As you live longer, you will find yourselves compromising bit by bit until you are indistinguishable from the rest of the hundred thousand. You'll be sucked in by the vulgarity of life. But you won't vanish without trace—you'll leave your mark on it. After your deaths, six people like you may turn up, then twelve, and so on. Finally the majority of the crowd will have got like you. So, life will evolve to something that is wonderful and beautiful on this earth within the next two or three hundred years. We yearn for that kind of life. We dream about it. And we get ready for it—since everyone must know more than his father and his grandfather did.

Vershinin's vision of an evolution in which all the children become indistinguishable is subtly different from Andrei's: there is the matter of knowledge, and of leaving one's mark. In answer to Andrei's appeal for just one person worthy of emulation, Vershinin suggests three who are only partially so; but it is a progressive vision, in which three becomes six, and quantity becomes quality as each child becomes a better being than its parents.

So whereas Tuzenbakh threatens to complete the circularity of development of the sisters, Vershinin offers a vision of evolutionary change as each generation becomes outmoded in turn by 'a new and better breed'. Like Shamokhin in *Ariadne*, Vershinin regrets the 'false' polarisation of mind and matter:

> We Russians can achieve such high intellect. Why, in that case are we content with such squalid days.

And like Dr Astrov, he recognises the beauty of Nature, the illogicality of social existence, and the need to end this separation in a new environment.

But like Astrov, too, Vershinin is certainly no positive hero. He talks too much (a quality, though, that Chekhov apparently often attributed to himself when expounding his dearest beliefs[5]) and, like Andrei, he has married carelessly—twice—while young, which has brought premature age both to himself and his present wife. Vershinin's experiences have made of him a limited, guilty man, and like Astrov he is always being dragged back from his vision by a patient, in this case his wife who tries to commit suicide from time to time.

When he speaks to the sisters of 'compromising bit by bit' but also leaving their mark, it is, of course, his life as well as theirs that he is defining. His experiences do not break him. He remains kind and sensitive to the end. He does not desert the wife who persecutes him, as Tuzenbakh would have him do; nor does he use Masha and then abandon her, as is the pattern with so many of Chekhov's seducers. He leaves his heart with her and his hopes with them all, as he moves on to bring culture and hope to another out-of-the-way spot. Vershinin carries Chekhov's recognition that progress has already been made, his belief in the intelligentsia who 'think honestly, feel and can work', and his realisation that the path is long and contradictory. Those who make 'two steps forward and one step back' will die and be forgotten—'Yes, we'll be forgotten. That's in store for us and we can't change it'—but from their work a new quality will evolve.

Vershinin's function in the narrative is exemplary in terms of his own predictions: he leaves his mark, the sisters accept his vision, and, as he disappears from their world, one becomes three. For if

Vershinin is not a positive hero, nor is he the pompous ass which many critics suppose; and to interpret him as such is to seriously misinterpret the structure of the play. In his film production of *The Three Sisters*, Laurence Olivier has Vershinin throw away his most important lines as the patter of a cheap seducer. Consequently the final sequence of the suffering but *optimistic* sisters has no possible connection with the play's development (and Olivier solves the problem ludicrously by relating their vision to the martial strains of the Russian Revolution on the soundtrack). Styan's analysis, which he claims to be based on the text and stage method alone, is more serious. But he also misses the fact that Vershinin is the mechanism of change in the play and therefore, more logical than Olivier, denies that there *is* change. Rejecting Magarshack's 'simplistic' interpretation that the play ends optimistically, he concludes that Chekhov was not himself so simple-minded as to think that these social problems could *ever* be solved. Styan's 'absurdist' position reveals itself, for all his claims to confine himself strictly to the text, when he interprets the flight of birds (which, as we have seen, has precise connotations in the opposition of Tuzenbakh and Vershinin) as signifying the 'infinite time and space which dwarfs us all'.[6]

Styan not only deprives Vershinin of coherence (his vision of a natural, and better, environment in Act 2 is completely lost on Styan, who says that Vershinin 'immediately loses interest in what he is saying and turns to admire the flowers in the room'[7]), but completely destroys the structure of the play as well. The crucial dual impact and polarising function of Vershinin and Natasha in and from Act 1 is lost, since for Styan 'Colonel Vershinin's introduction into the play is mildly cataclysmal, but falsely so. The Colonel makes an impressive entry—he likes to make his presence felt. He is all blandishment and striking pronouncements. But as time goes on, they sound more and more the repetitive, empty phrases of a somewhat hollow man, and the processes of the play steadily belittle his romantic figure,'[8] until he leaves the little community 'rather worse off than better'. Inevitably then, Act 2, far from showing the stirrings of a dual reality after the illusions of Act 1, is no more than a crushing anti-climax in which 'the mood of torpor and nostalgia all but halts the action'.[9]

Against this rather typical 'mood' reading of Chekhov, a positive interpretation of Vershinin reveals the following structure. Natasha and Vershinin arrive in Act 1 when the inauthentic ritual and escapism of the sisters, Chebutykin, Solenyi and Tuzenbakh has already been well established. From this moment they begin to polarise action and choice. Natasha captures Andrei who from now on does not 'understand anything' or do anything. Vershinin has a decisive effect on Masha who, on hearing his speech about the possibilities of progressive evolution, dramatically abandons her boredom, her decision to leave the party, and her hat with 'I'm staying for lunch.' It is her first decisive action of the play, and contrasts with Irina's dreamy sighs over the glamour of this new visitor.

By the beginning of Act 2 the scene has shrunk. The flowers and light Vershinin noted in Act 1 have become darkness and the threatening movement of Natasha about the house as she puts out candles and abuses the servants. Beyond her, and hidden, Bobik, tyrannical from the cot, and the missives of Protopopov promise further impoverishment, as the Prozorov's possessions—wives, rooms, house, dreams—are menaced. Andrei is already disillusioned with the wife who dominates him, and has turned to a different procedure of escape, gambling, under Chebutykin's influence. He dreams now, not of Moscow university, but of restaurants, and the triviality of it all is parodied by Ferapont's nonsense about Moscow and pancakes. Andrei's conversation with Ferapont echoes that of Konstantin and Sorin in *The Seagull*—these arbitrary and separate lives, the one dream-like, the other full of daily trivia, are part of the same order. The relationship of Vershinin and Masha has also developed, and contrasts with the destructive one of Natasha and Andrei, as well as the static relationship of Irina and Tuzenbakh. Vershinin has found in Masha the one person with whom he can communicate, and already loves her deeply. Masha's bored whistling has been replaced by a quiet laughter as she responds to him; and when Tuzenbakh rejects his belief in progress, Masha's response shows that she has taken up Vershinin's faith in knowledge of man and Nature:

I believe human beings must have faith, or at least search for it, otherwise existence would be quite pointless. How can you pass your days, and yet not know why the cranes fly, why children are born, or why there are stars up there in the sky! Either you must know why you live or else nothing makes any difference—and life is like so much uncultivated grass!

Masha has already rejected both the mystical optimism of Tuzenbakh and, explicitly, the pessimistic 'what's the difference' of the 'false' man of science, Chebutykin. But the path is long and problematical; Vershinin is called away and Masha, angry and upset, is abusive. For those whose dreams began this play, reality is already beginning to show through. In Act 1 Natasha joined the party; now she prevents it, and goes to Protopopov. Their progeny will increase, and Irina's 'To Moscow', surrounded in Act 1 by her dreams, is now accompanied by a lullaby to Bobik, the next inheritor.

In Act 3 all the responses and relationships are clarified against the consuming background of the fire. The scene has shrunk still further, to the shared bedroom of Ol'ga and Irina.[10] It is not only the Prozorov family that gathers in this claustrophobic place, but all the party-goers of Act 1. Life is closing in on them all, and they all respond as they can—Kulygin with advice on rank and order, Chebutykin with drink and 'what's the difference', Solenyi with threats, Tuzenbakh with dreams. It is in this Act that Natasha completes her brutal domination of the household, a course of destruction which consumes this and every other provincial town. Andrei, after an attempt to assert and justify his position, collapses at the feet of his sisters. It is a fall for a would-be man of learning which is as explicit in his overemphasis on rank to Ferapont as in his sister's comments:

Since he started up with that woman he's lost the originality he once had. Not so long ago he was looking to be a professor; but yesterday he was crowing about getting onto the Council. Imagine!—he's a member and Protopopov is the chairman!

In the midst of a scene of universal despair and exhaustion, set against the distant, vague and muffled sound of the fire bell, only Vershinin and Masha develop to balance the destructive activity of Natasha. In contrast to the weary apathy of the others who, as he says, seem all to have gone to sleep, Vershinin is bursting with exuberance, and tells how when he saw his little girls standing alone and defenceless in a doorway during the fire, he wondered whether there was any difference from the days of fire and pillage of marauding armies. But for him there is a difference; it is all part of a process to a better future and an improved breed of men. Full of energy and enthusiasm, Vershinin says, 'I feel a terrific will to

live'—it is to be his legacy to the three sisters who will repeat his
words an Act later, and is in marked contrast to Tuzenbakh's weary
attempt to convince himself that his dream of manual labour is not
mere talking in his sleep. Similarly, the lively love duet between
Vershinin and Masha contrasts with the hopeless resignation of
Irina's decision to marry Tuzenbakh and be a dutiful wife. Irina's
'To Moscow' is now to the sound of conflagration. Vershinin and
Masha are lovers, and the double theme of adultery continues the
polarity of action. Natasha's adultery with Protopopov underlines
the destruction of Andrei, who is dominated at home by one and at
work by the other. Masha's adultery with Vershinin is a relationship
at once lively and tragic, for Vershinin has been posted. Their
happiness together will be short, and their road hard and full of
suffering.

In the final Act, the scene change immediately introduces the real
worlds underlying the party dreams of Act 1: all the Acts have
moved towards this moment of perspective. The house is in the
possession of Natasha, and she besports herself inside with Bobik and
Protopopov. Thus the enclosed social milieu belongs visibly to the
degraded world which only the illusions of the first Act obscured.
Outside the house are the dispossessed, the Prozorovs, essentially as
homeless as the tramps who come for alms. Beyond the Prozorovs, a
vision of Nature beckons—as Styan says, '"a long avenue of fir
trees" leading to a "view of the river" and thence on to a wood on
the far side of it, take the eye out and away'.[11] Into that distance will
march Vershinin and the soldiers, bringing a little bit of culture to
another provincial place; and with them leave the birds whose
journey has been a motif of this play. Their flight has meant white
dreams to Irina, old age and rejection to Chebutykin, the mystery of
life to Tuzenbakh, the rational relationship of man and the natural
world to Vershinin and Masha. As always, the vision of natural
potential confronts the stagnant and enclosed order of the social
world to the sound of melancholy, the sound of harp and violin
somewhere in the town. Illusions are gone. Masha watches her dear
birds fly from her, and weeps with the boredom of the first Act as
Kulygin tells her, 'We'll take up our lives again—just as before'.
Ol'ga is now the headmistress she never wanted to be. Irina prepares
for a loveless marriage. Andrei, about to be driven from his room by
the proliferation of Natasha's babies, is a submissive figure of ritual,
pushing a baby's pram backwards and forwards across the stage.
His calling to account is complete, and like Chebutykin, he despairs

of a society which he chose not to reject. Andrei has a vision of a better life:

> What a terrific feeling of elation I get when I think about the future! . . . . . How I look forward to a day when I will be free, and my children will be free—free from lethargy and drink, free from the endless wallowing in goose and cabbage, and from the following recuperative naps, free from all the degrading sponge-ing and flattery!

Andrei's vision of a new society is complemented by Tuzenbakh's final vision of a different Nature—as he recognises in the inquisitive look of Nature man's real potential for the first time:

> You know, I feel quite euphoric. I seem to be looking at those firs and maples and birches as though I'd never properly seen them before. And they seem to be looking at me with an inquiring, expectant look, as though waiting for something. How beautiful the trees are! And how beautiful our lives should be in a place with trees like that.

But Andrei returns to his pram and cringing subservience to his wife; and Tuzenbakh goes to his death, recognising that his share in future life will be as a dead tree among the living, a sincere but anachronistic moral force, like the Tolstoyan creed he had em-braced. As Natasha asserts brutal control over all those around her, and, further extending her milieu, prepares to cut down the trees, living and dead, of Vershinin and Tuzenbakh, only the former's vision of work, hope and knowledge remains alive. His call for *educated* industry is a final answer to Tuzenbakh.

> Yes, our lives are hard, and the whole affair may seem hopeless for many of us—a dead end. But you've got to admit that it is slowly getting a little lighter. And it is quite evident that the days are not too far off when the light will be everywhere . . . . . Oh, if only that could happen soon! . . . If we only could educate those who labour, and make our educated people work . . .

It is crucial to the understanding of the play's finale to recognise that when the sisters finally speak to the cheerful strains of the military band, they speak as one with the words of Vershinin and with his affirmation of life. The unity of repetition which Tuzenbakh threatened has been avoided, and a new unity of hope and suffering has replaced it. The sisters, Masha insists, will remain alone to begin their lives anew:

> We must go on living . . . we have to keep on living . . .

And in the first version of the play she added that the meaning of the birds' flight would one day be known. Irina now calls for knowledge as well as work:

> One day we will understand why these things happen. People will know the reason for all this suffering . . . Then all mysteries will be understood . . . Until that day, we must go on living—and working! . . .

Irina carries on Tuzenbakh's ideals of work and service to the people. But her vision of life when everything is known and all mysteries are resolved belongs to Vershinin. Ol'ga picks up Vershinin's belief that though they themselves will be forgotten, their spirit will survive as more and more people find authenticity: and 'Perhaps if we can last for a while longer, we will come to know the reason for our living and our suffering.' She now has the same 'will to live' we heard from Vershinin in Act 3.

The sisters are certainly not, as Styan asserts, asking the same questions as at the beginning; and if the mood of hope and suffering is more complex than Magarshack's 'gay affirmation of life', it is at least nearer to this than to Styan's 'sterile' cycle. The new kind of army which brings knowledge and art has completed its mission: the sisters have changed, and seek the knowledge that distinguishes Vershinin's vision from Tuzenbakh's. The army goes off, and while Ol'ga repeats the message of hope and suffering they have learnt— 'Just to know! Just to know!'—the ritualised figures of the degraded world are evident too. Kulygin as always smiles happily, Chebutykin as always reads his newspapers and mutters 'what's the difference', Andrei pushes his pram backwards and forwards. The ending is left open, as the epic vision must be. But now the escapism and inauthenticity of the opening scenes have been stripped away, and the real polarity of degraded world and epic vision revealed as Natasha and Vershinin have moved on to the stage and then left it on opposite sides.

There is, then, no cyclical movement in *The Three Sisters*, and it is misguided to suggest a return in Act 4 to the mood of Act 1. In fact the movement and theme is similar to Chekhov's recent story, *On Official Duty*, where the dancing and culture of three sisters in a country house is also initially seen as an oasis in the middle of social banality, and a pale reflection of life in the capitals. But at the end of the story its hero recognises that these worlds which appear separate are in fact 'parts of the same organism', and that the dreams of elegance and the brutish world are dependent on each other—a theme which is taken up in the play through the relationship of Andrei and Ferapont, and also in the meeting of the 'homeless' sisters with the penniless vagrants. Andrei and Ferapont, like the neurasthenic and the constable in the story, 'go on and on and on' in their suffering; but there is hope in the fact that a new generation suffers over things its parents ignored. The children of parents who despised work, children who were educated for their place in the old world, suffer at their inability to labour for a new one. But then some of them suffer *and* labour; and beyond these children we see yet another generation: the children of Natasha proliferating and renewing the old world more basely; and the children of Vershinin, embodying all his guilt, his hopes and his fears. Speaking for a new life of understanding, the sisters stand to break the cycle which produces children crushed in potential 'just like their parents'. Each generation will go beyond the last, suffering for its convictions but, like Nina in *The Seagull*, firm in its vocation.

In his speech to the First Session of the Russian Medico-Psychological Association in Moscow in 1887, Merzheyevskii described the disenchantment of those intellectuals immersed in 'uncongenial climatic and social conditions' where their 'yearnings after higher aims find no sympathy'. On the one hand, he describes their degeneration into 'utter physical and moral debility . . . proneness to nervous irritability, to excitability brought on by the slightest external impressions, and . . . excessive weakness to undergo protracted labour or discipline'. On the other hand, he poses his evolutionary solution. The cultivation of higher aims through the development of knowledge, the study of science and art, and the free expression of feelings and faith will (by improving the 'psychic tone' of each generation) become the basis for 'a future and better life on earth which every generation is preparing by its own work and ordeals'.[12]

It is precisely this polarity that Vershinin and Natasha have dramatised in the Prozorov family. When we last see Andrei he is nervously excitable, 'just about ready to threaten the audience with his fists'[13]—but also ready to return to the inaction and moral collapse we saw in his previous appearance. When we last see the three sisters they are decisively preparing for a new generation through their work and ordeals. Merzheyevskii insisted in his speech and Chekhov in his play that these two poles of response were ultimately the only ones available.

9 The Cherry Orchard

The Cherry Orchard is unusual among Chekhov's dramas in that the central focus is not the problem of choice among the intelligentsia. Whereas *The Seagull, Uncle Vanya* and *The Three Sisters* are all related to fundamental questions of identity for their author as a professional doctor and writer—the problem of art, the problem of science, the problem of education and upbringing—*The Cherry Orchard* is a play about social mobility and change. In particular, the play examines a moment in time when large-scale industrialisation had made possible a proletarian solution in addition to the evolutionist-technological vision of his earlier literature. The estates on which the action of the earlier dramas takes place are of course historically typical, in so far that the specific problems and the conflicting responses are typical of the situation of intellectuals in a modernising autocracy. But they appear timeless, and the epic vision becomes a commitment of method, a matter of endurance, a programme for living in which a better future lies in the hands of each individual.

In *The Cherry Orchard* the estate is no longer timeless. It is threatened by a new order of modernisation which enables a peasant to become master of the estate which owned his family as serfs; and threatened, too, by other, more violent, aspects of industrial growth. The cherry orchard is confronted with the modern capitalist and the modern revolutionary. The question of choice, and with it the crisis of identity, while remaining individual is subsumed within broader social movements.

Each character typifies a social position in his response to the orchard. Trofimov sees in the trees dead souls; Lopakhin sees in them the opportunity for technology and growth; Madame Ranevskaya thinks only of style, elegance and the white figures of the past; Varya, a girl raised above her station by the kindly condescension of a status-conscious society, thinks only of saving that order through petty cheeseparing and recourse to religion, its official ideology. To say, however, that Chekhov poses the question of individual choice within the framework of social movements is not to interpret his play in the light of a straightforward class struggle. Chekhov is favouring neither an aristocratic, nor a bourgeois, nor a proletarian solution.

By choosing the decay of a landed estate (and the complete inability of the old landowners to come to terms with the problem of farming without serfs) for his theme, Chekhov was not only selecting a problem about which he had written more than once, and of which he had a close personal experience, but also a typical contradiction of a society which tried to modernise yet, in terms of social stratification, stay the same. The *situation* in *The Cherry Orchard* is the moment when the autonomous world of tradition has been breached by the serf reforms and the will to modernise; when in Firs' words, 'everything is muddled', and action must be rational and decisive, yet within mores and institutions which remain ascriptive. The reactions of each landowner to the problem of debt differ at the personal level—Ranevskaya escapes to Paris, Gayev into dreams of liberal gentry and superfluous men, Simeonov-Pishchik into money-grubbing and a hand-to-mouth existence from day to day while he waits for something to turn up. But *socially* their reactions are qualitatively the same. They are simply incapable of adapting to the demands of a new rationality; Pishchik is as incapable of entrepreneurial activity when profitable minerals are discovered on his land, as Madame Ranevskaya is of profiting from the spread of new urban wealth to the country. Essentially they are people preoccupied with the old style of life, servants in livery, large tips to the waiters, casual philanthropy and amateur medical treatment for the poor—people who act from day to day, move from place to place, but really stay the same.

Yet the *contradictions* of the modernising autocracy have deprived these people of sureness of response. There is in *The Cherry Orchard* none of the rhythmic Arcadian symbolism of the English conservative tradition when *it* was threatened by the 'mob' beneath; nor yet a negative perspective, of angst, as the hero fights against frightful odds and fails. Neither allegory nor angst are possible moods for an author who stands outside a social group in decline, and views that decline with intellectual approval mixed with personal sympathy for those he knew and respected. Rather, the mood is elegiac, compounded of an intensely human crisis of identity at the personal level and a distancing, comic inconsistency of interaction.

In their isolation the landowners are marginal and anomic figures. Ranevskaya, the aristocratic woman who married beneath her station, travels from place to place seeking purpose in locations and in a lover who cheats her. Faced with the sale of the orchard she retreats into her past when everything was elegant and certain. Gayev also retreats into the past, given an extra and pompous dignity by his references to learning and social service. But his relationship to reason and the Enlightenment is empty; it goes no further than justifying the continued existence of the unproductive orchard on the grounds that it was mentioned in the Encyclopaedia. For all his escape into a pathetic flow of words, his refrain, 'I'll be silent, I'll be silent', is that of a man lost. Anya is aroused by the revolutionary ideals of Trofimov, but the vision of a new life of this naive girl is strangely mixed with the intention of planting another orchard and living happily ever after with her mother as they read to each other in the long evenings. Varya is divided between a desperate attempt to save the old order, to which she would somehow or other attach Lopakhin, and a desire to escape into the nun-like existence of Ol'ga in *Big Volodya and Little Volodya*. Increasing mobility within this crumbling, self-conscious structure simply intensifies social marginality which, in the absence of a confident and coherent symbolic system becomes spiritual anomie as each individual faces alone the meaninglessness of his existence.

But there is little tragedy. Spiritual isolation is signified by a comic failure of communication when characters are *collectively* faced with the reality of change. So when Lopakhin first suggests the need to cut down the cherry orchard and let the land for summer villas, the reaction among the landowners is a comic and trivial dialogue of escape. Firs speaks of an old recipe for drying cherries; Ranevskaya asks for the recipe, but it is lost. Pishchik then asks whether they ate frogs in Paris, and Ranevskaya says she ate crocodiles, which Pishchik greets with great wonder. Lopakhin tries again with his plan. Gayev replies 'what idiocy!' and after a brief exchange between Varya and Ranevskaya which reveals both the former's workaday ritual and the latter's asylum in Paris, Gayev launches into his famous oration to the old and venerable bookcase which has been the source of his family's devotion to the people for so long. Silenced by Lopakhin's irony, he retreats into his billiards talk, and almost immediately the remaining landowner, Pishchik, reveals his extraordinary unconcern for the realities of life (and medical science!) by swallowing all of Ranevskaya's pills. Each individual responds quite typically to Lopakhin's suggestion; and each response reveals inner isolation. Yet the interaction, revealed as a collective style of life, is comic and absurd. The private worlds of Ranevskaya, Gayev, Varya and Pishchik, sad and lyrical though they may be, are a focus of irrationality, and thus, situationally, of the absurd.

It is within this overtly comic and nostalgic mood (which is nevertheless serious and sometimes fearful) that Chekhov is able to portray the genuine human values which are *overcome* in his works. As in *The Seagull*, the typical time perspective associated with the ascriptive society is a tension between time that passes meaninglessly, often absurdly, and the desire to make time stand still. The tension is rendered in *mood* by the relationship between broad comedy and nostalgia in the play; and *scenically* by beginning and ending the play in the same location, yet a location grievously altered.[1]

Act 1 introduces the problem of the cherry orchard in a location of compulsive nostalgia: the nursery of generations of cherry orchard owners, each one (as in *The Three Sisters*, but in a more genteel setting) growing in the image of his parents. For Lopakhin active decisions about the future of the orchard are urgent, 'time flies by'; but for the landowners, accustomed to a different time scale, there can be no meaning in its passing. It is better not to consider the matter; something will turn up—an act of God, or of rich grandmamma; Anya may marry a wealthy man, or money may be won on a lottery ticket. Meanwhile resort to nostalgia can convince that nothing has changed:

> Oh, my childhood—my dear, innocent childhood! I once used to sleep in this nursery. I looked out from here at the orchard. Each morning that I awoke happiness awoke with me, and then the orchard was exactly as it is now. White all over—it hasn't changed a bit.

Objects which relate them to their youth are plentiful in the nursery: toys, little tables, aged bookcases, faithful retainers. And when the thought arises, 'strange though it may appear', that action must be taken to save it all, they can look into the eternal orchard and see the ghost of their mother walking. Faced by the visible passage of time, the dying and ageing servants, the balding Trofimov, the compulsion to nostalgia is even greater. For

Ranevskaya, who throughout the play is torn most acutely by the tension between time passing and time past, Trofimov can only bring to mind the memory of her dead son—which is, in itself, a sign of an uncertain future. Nostalgia is then incorporated within a wider but equally escapist mood—fatalistic guilt in which everything, the passing of time, the sale of the orchard, the death of her child, are the punishment for her past and an act of God. Varya takes up the theme of dependence on God's mercy, while Anya, whom Ranevskaya loves with all the resonances of nostalgia, lives anew the innocent naivety of her mother's early days. Thus the dialogue between the flower-like innocence of youth and a trust in God for its passing, which continually tears Madame Ranevskaya, is acted out by her 'daughters'. As the close-knit family prepares to sleep with its memories and pious hopes, these two girls, these two values, see the Act to its close. Everything is in decay, but the scene is tranquil. 'From far away' the sound of a shepherd's pipe is heard, an echo of Chekhov's story *The Pipe*, where an old shepherd plays nostalgically, complaining that Fate, God, the Emancipation, have destroyed the real gentry (when half were generals), and destroyed with them the fertility of Nature. The mournful sound responds to the nursery's proper tone, relating it to the orchard just outside— but to the cherry trees' timeless and beautiful past (when, as Firs too would say, the place was full of generals) and not to their present decay. It is a sound which evokes the enclosed nostalgia of the nursery, embalms the dialogue of fragile innocence and fatalistic experience, and speaks of man's inability to comprehend the world beyond the nursery walls.

Act 2 confronts us with a dramatic scene change. The nostalgic claustrophobia of the nursery is gone, and the world beyond assumes its contemporary form. In sharp contrast to the enclosed space of Act 1, the author insisted on a boundless view of Nature, 'a sense of distance unusual on the stage'.[2] In this place beyond the nursery, time is clearly not without significance. Man has related with Nature, and technology has spread; for beyond the poplars there are telegraph poles, and a town is to be seen on the far horizon. The drama is purely visual, in the scene change itself. The vision of Nature and technology stands in quiet testimony to the meaningless enclosure of time and purpose in the previous Act. The sound of the shepherd's pipe belonged to the nostalgia of the nursery. The world of change, however, is no more than a *mute* backcloth[3] to the antics of both masters and servants.

When the sound of change does come out of this vast environment, these people will not recognise it, because they do not understand its sequence or its laws. For Gayev the railways are useful merely to take him to town, where he can converse with the waiters about the Decadents, and then to bring him back in time for a game of billiards. For Ranevskaya the sequence of life's change, from innocent upbringing, through marriage to a drunken spendthrift, to the arms of the usual lover, and from the death of her son, through desertion in Paris, to attempted suicide, is explicable only in religious terms—sin, and appeal to the mercy of God. Meanwhile she squanders money just the same, pours her love and her hopes on Anya and Varya, and prefers to ignore the issue of the orchard for 'what we were talking about yesterday'. The lives of these 'improvident, unbusinesslike and strange people' has simply not been patterned to ordered change, and when something new occurs passive fatalism is the only available response.

Time for them has always been cyclical—the filtering of generations through the nursery—and when instead it manifestly destroys, their reactions are confused and fearful. Madame Ranevskaya clings helplessly to Lopakhin (the agent of change whose message she cannot heed or even understand) because 'I keep imagining that something awful is about to happen . . . like the house collapsing on us'. A tramp comes by, and, like the peasants on the steppes, they are filled with wonder and fear by the sounds and strange figures of the expanse beyond them. And also like the peasants who cling to their protective fire, they retreat to their own enclosed world where, in Act 3, we find them once more, amidst the brightly lit chandeliers and luxurious fittings, whirling to the dance and drowning the outside world with the brash sounds of the ball.

Act 2 has opposed a world of purposeful change to the encapsulated time of Act 1; and the response of the landowners is, typically, not so much to reject as to flee from it as something disturbingly incomprehensible. Pishchik's dance calls, which, like the lotto calls in *The Seagull*, assert a timeless repetition, are more familiar and more comforting. Yet time does move on; it is the day of the auction, and the social poverty of the ball itself is an insistent comment on change. Madame Ranevskaya waits helplessly for this final judgment on her past, Varya continues to call on God, and Anya dances, a butterfly heedless of time. Meanwhile Sharlotta, engaged as always in tricks, produces something from nothing, thus parodying by sleight of hand the full scope of the landowners' vision.

For Ranevskaya it is a time of pitiful decline and, with the entry of the new owner, collapse. This woman, once brought up with the tenderness of a flower like Anya, has no knowledge or inner resources with which to face the crisis; and when to Trofimov's claim to be above love, she answers 'I suppose I am below love', there is an echo once again of the ascriptive division of the Russian woman between the idealist and the seducer. Her only recourse, in fact, has to be external, back to her seducer. Though she knows she will be 'going to the dregs', she cannot bear to hear Trofimov speak in spiteful categories about her lover—it is the kind of callous 'truth' with which the revolutionary, like Lvov in *Ivanov*, destroys.

In Act 4 the family location has shrunk back to its real temporal and spatial proportions, the enclosed nostalgia of the nursery. But the nursery is bare. All the objects of nostalgia in which Gayev and Ranevskaya could hide from their fate have been stripped away. Time has actually passed, and the absurdity of it all for these people is emphasised by Pishchik's unexpected and quite undeserved fortune, and his final 'Don't worry, all things finish in their time'. Gayev will take a job in a bank, which will certainly prove to be a fiasco. Ranevskaya will return to Paris, keep her lover on the limited sum grandmamma sent for the estate, and then will be a pauper. Even her last wish comes to nothing: the sick Firs is not taken to hospital but is left in the deserted house; and Varya will never be married to Lopakhin.[4]

In a most moving scene, alone on a bare stage, illusions spent, Gayev and Ranevskaya weep quietly together, unheard by Trofimov and Anya whose illusions are just beginning; and whose naively hopeful calls begin the whole process of empty dreams again in a new form. Finally Firs, alone and near to death, speaks Chekhov's deep sympathy for those caught in this process of meaningless time:

Life's over as though I'd never lived.

The summary of life by an abandoned servant is entirely appropriate, for in this play without the foregrounding of the usual love triangles, servants perform an important structural role. In plays which considered the mediating role of art, education etc. such as *The Seagull*, Chekhov was able to portray the relationship of authentic and false choices as relations of love, and so give them dramatic immediacy. *The Cherry Orchard* demanded a rather different thematic organisation since here he was dealing with a whole order in decline, in which he knew people as deserving of sympathy as Trigorin and Treplev, yet who collectively created the world of Arkadina. In a play which demonstrates the humanity of these people, yet also displays the harsh social network on which the humanity rests the close analysis of the world of the servants is not coincidental.

Each of the landowning group finds a reflection here. Thus Firs, like Gayev, is always looking into the historical past; Yasha, like Ranevskaya, seeks escape to Paris; Dunyasha, like Anya, escapes into dreams; Sharlotta, like Varya of doubtful birth, drowns her unhappiness in ritual too (Varya in keys and dried peas and Sharlotta in tricks); and Yepikhodov, as submissive to fate and to women as Pishchik, like him stumbles from one chance occurrence to another. Moreover, the servants' style of *interaction* reflects that of their masters. At the beginning of Act 2, their response to the natural and technological world beyond them is prologue and paradigm for the landowners' mixture of spiritual isolation and comic interaction. Thus Sharlotta, abandoning her tricks for a moment, says thoughtfully,

> . . . Where I'm from or who I am I don't know . . . I don't know anything . . . I'm longing for someone I could talk to, but there is no-one. I have no-one.

The desire for direct relations and the weariness with rank of a governess who performs tricks on command is identical with the loneliness of Chekhov's *Bishop*: her words are his:

> I've got nobody to talk to. I'm alone, quite alone. I have no-one and . . . and who I am, or what I am alive for, no-one knows.

The theme is taken up by the clerk Yepikhodov:

> I don't really seem to know the direction I want to go, or what I'm really after—that is to say, should I live or should I shoot myself, as it were.

(In an earlier version of the play which, according to Stanislavskii, Chekhov rather unwillingly altered, Firs too was incorporated in the anomic theme).

These lonely cries are enmeshed in a trivial and comic interaction in which Yepikhodov courts Dunyasha while she courts Yasha, who shows off to everybody, Sharlotta munches a cucumber, and Yepikhodov waves a gun about, explaining the fact that cockroaches get into his kvass by fatalistic laws of history. However, the structural importance of the servants is not simply as a comic parody of their masters (who, after all, do that for themselves). It is not the pretension of the masters that is laid bare by the servants, as, say, in a play by Molière, but their humanity—which is genuine, but at a cost. The servants have an 'alienating' function in the Brechtian sense, a 'making strange' of familiar scenes (there was certainly nothing new about dramatising the decline of a landed class)— thereby, supposedly, channelling the audience's patterns of response away from emotional identification with a group which, *intellectually*, Chekhov disapproved.

Hence Firs' nostalgic aspiration for a time when the 'peasants knew their place and the gentry knew their place'—when in fact peasants were flogged, generals danced at the balls and there was no proper medical treatment for the servants—puts into historical focus Gayev's effusive:

> you have promoted within us the ideals of public service and social consciousness.

Similarly, the social climbing Yasha, who is prepared to dally with Dunyasha (but not publicly because of his status) and who is ashamed of his peasant mother, not only reproduces at a lower social level the avarice and vulgarity of Ranevskaya's lover, but comments on the whole framework of ascriptive love relations—on Ranevskaya, who like Dunyasha, is 'below love', on her sin of marrying 'beneath her', and even on the attempted match of Varya and Lopakhin which would have fitted social convention so well. Dunyasha, 'like a flower', and with her preoccupation with make-up and mirrors, reflects not only the 'spring blossom' Anya, but her mother's giddy and lost innocence too, and beyond that all the other cherry orchard ladies, dressed in white, educated to dazzle socially with the latest hair-style and Paris fashion. Sharlotta, whose spiritual isolation is less protected by the layers of nostalgia of her betters, parodies with her baby noises in the final Act Ranevskaya's only remaining resource: personal and familial resurrection in Anya—so a moving and human moment is shown to be an empty response to the pressure of choice.[5] One can only pity Ranevskaya, but her actions have deprived Sharlotta and Varya of meaning too. And when in Act 2 Yepikhodov, with his back to the expansive technology beyond him, assigns to unchangeable historical laws the trivial events of his life, he too goes beyond comedy, lighting up not only Gayev's equally futile attitude to technology and his 'you'll still die in the end, whatever you do' response to Trofimov's ideals, but also the whole immobile crowd of these cherry orchard people who find change 'so vulgar'. Even the tramp, emerging as if out of the sound of the breaking string, has an alienating function: Varya is frightened of this man who speaks of the suffering people she has been raised above; Ranevskaya gives him money, and her kindly generosity is given perspective as the typically static philanthropy which, Chekhov once wrote to Koni, 'in Russia has such an arbitrary quality'.[6] A man wanders ill, he is given money and wanders out again—and behind him there is the growth of a rational technology.

A whole order is tied together with this immobile procedure; and the same reforms which created zemstvo medicine are here seen as the 'troubles'. Moreover, the order in decline may itself 'leave its mark'. Everyone is involved in ritualised actions:

(a) the class in decline—Ranevskaya always giving money away, Gayev potting the red and eating sweets, Pishchik borrowing money and saying 'extraordinary thing';

(b) the lower classes who aspire to rise—Dunyasha always powdering her nose, Yasha always giving himself airs and saying 'what stupidity';

(c) and even those who have risen—Varya always cheeseparing and spying on the lovers, and Lopakhin constantly being deferent and waving his arms about. Thus the new order of social mobility is threatened with inclusion as the traditional world adapts and renews itself.

It is clear in the values of the younger servants, in the deference that Anya and Varya expect from them, and particularly in Lopakhin's consciousness of hierarchy, that the real human crisis does not lie in the historical decline of a particular group. It lies in the division of human personality by ascriptive values which existed in Firs' golden past, continue in the present, and threaten to be incorporated in the merchant values of the future (as Chekhov had shown in earlier works, such as *The Mask* and *My Life*). The *social* crisis of the landowning class, and their particular anomie, is thus not the central one of the play. The social crisis rather clarifies the loss of wholeness by tearing away the comfortable ideology which hid it hitherto. Just as in *Dreary Story* and *Bishop* Chekhov used the impact of physical decline to reveal the meaningless passage of time, so in *The Cherry Orchard* he uses the impact of social decline to reveal the same thing. The question of identity and the problem of meaning extends beyond this class to the process of modernisation itself. As Lopakhin says, 'what hordes of people there are in Russia, my friend, who have no aim in life at all!'

Against the passive and hierarchical world of the landowners, Chekhov sets two forms of modernisation, embodied in two major characters, the revolutionary Trofimov, and the merchant (and former peasant) Lopakhin. It is their activist dialogue which carries Chekhov's vision. Trofimov in fact articulates a number of Chekhov's cherished beliefs—in the importance of science and art, education, and an intelligentsia which works:

> Mankind is constantly marching forward, constantly perfecting itself. Everything which we can't understand at the moment will one day be comprehensible. But to reach this point we have to give everything to our work, and we have to help those people who are seeking after truth. Here in Russia, hardly anyone has begun to work as yet. The great majority of intellectuals that I know don't search for anything, don't do anything and as yet are incapable of working. . . . . . They merely chatter on about science and don't know a lot about art either.

Yet for all his talk about love for the people, unremitting toil and science, Trofimov is conspicuously unable to love, work or be scientific. Despite the obvious tenderness of the inner man, Trofimov does his best to drive out sentiment. He claims that his relationship with Anya is above love:

> . . . . . we are above love. The whole object and meaning of our life is to rid ourselves of everything that is petty and illusory in life, everything that hinders our happiness and freedom.

Like Shamokhin in *Ariadne*, he abstracts love, denying feeling. Nor does he work; he is the 'eternal student' who not only is criticised by the other characters for doing nothing, but himself admits that he will probably be a student for the rest of his life. And, as we saw in chapter 1, in his eagerness to generalise, he also denies the achievements of contemporary science. His famous speech about the frightful condition of workers draws too much on revolutionary abstraction to be accurate. In denying the great advances made in zemstvo medicine (of which Chekhov was so very proud) Trofimov is opposing the evolutionary vision.

Like all of Chekhov's revolutionaries Trofimov has become, despite his undeniably sympathetic qualities, a 'walking tendency', with a simplistic ideological vision that makes him prone to categorise quite brutally all those about him. Thus his attitude to the orchard is not scientific but revolutionary—the landowners must atone for the dead souls who cry from the trees about years of persecution. Significantly, he tries to categorise Lopakhin according to a determinist Marxian formula—the *necessary* evil of a bourgeois period in Russia:

> My opinion of you, my dear Lopakhin, is simply this: you're a rich man, and soon you'll be a millionaire. Now, as part of the natural process by which one kind of matter is converted into another, you are a necessary evil—just as Nature needs beasts of prey which devour everything in their path.

It is interesting that Trofimov speaks a language of fatalistic Darwinism reminiscent of Van Koren to disguise the Marxist content from the censor; but it is not untypical, since for Chekhov both these value systems were part of the same 'inauthentic' paradigm.

Trofimov's vision of the future is as boldly uncontradictory as his evaluation of the complex Lopakhin. Having told Anya that they are above love, he continues, 'Onwards! We must march irresistibly together to that brilliant star shining there in the distance! Onwards, my friends! Let us not lag!'; and again 'It's upon us! Happiness is drawing closer and closer. I can almost hear its footsteps!' The speeches are as rhetorical as the vision is simplistic, and the whole thing is put into perspective by Chekhov in making Anya translate this new life into planting a new orchard with her mother, and in making Trofimov himself ludicrous and laughable. Like the revolutionary Dr Lvov in *Ivanov*, Trofimov is a prig, and Chekhov is eager to make him appear absurd, with a beard that won't grow and a premature impotence. He is, in Madame Ranevskaya's words, 'an absurd prude, a freak', and is so upset by her suggestion to take a lover that he falls downstairs. Also, like Chekhov's other revolutionary creation at this time, Sasha in *The Betrothed*, Trofimov is dirty and down-at-heel. In every way he lacks beauty and wholeness, and despite his statement that man should not be proud since physically very imperfect, he claims to take a pride in being a 'moth-eaten gent'. He claims too, like Gusev, to be strong, and above the need for other men—yet he trails along on the coat-tails of the landowners.

Between on the one hand the student who deeply loves his mistress and her daughter, and on the other the revolutionary who believes that landowners have to atone for their oppression, there is an ambivalence of identity which deprives Trofimov of action, and so immerses him in the familiar rhythm of comic trivia and personal crisis with all the other characters of immobility. He is as irresolute as the family he clings to—and like them (and like Sasha again) this revolutionary is strangely anachronistic. At the end of Act 2, Trofimov tells Anya:

> Your mother, you yourself, your uncle don't understand that you are living in debt, at the expense of others. You live off people whom you don't even allow into the house. We are at least two hundred years behind the times.

But at the end of Act 3, Lopakhin puts Trofimov out of date:

> Oh, if only my father and grandfather could rise up from their graves and see what's happened here . . . . . I have bought the very estate on which my father and grandfather were serfs, where they weren't even allowed into the kitchen.

In Chekhov's view it is the rational and beauty-loving merchant that makes the revolutionary anachronistic, and not the other way around.

In a play of ritualised action and withdrawal, it is Lopakhin alone who is mobile—both socially and dramatically. Undoubtedly there are elements of the old-fashioned, subservient Russian merchant about him, as well as elements of the more independent new capitalist who had just begun to appear in Russia. He is acutely conscious of his peasant origins and of the eternal hierarchy of the old order. At the same time he shows an equally acute understanding of change, and the profits to be gained from it. But he is certainly not the ruthless capitalist that Trofimov describes, nor even the type of grasping merchant Chekhov portrayed in earlier works—which is what contemporaries seemed to expect him to be. In his letters Chekhov insists that Lopakhin is not this type of merchant:

> You have to remember that he is not a merchant in the crude sense of the word.[7]

Quite unlike the shiftless Trofimov, it is around Lopakhin that the action moves. Chekhov's letters suggest that he structured his whole play round his development:

> Yes, Lopakhin is a merchant. But he is a good man in the fullest sense; and his presence must suggest considerable dignity and intelligence. There should be no trickery or pettiness attached to him. I thought that you would make a great success of Lopakhin's role, which is the central one of the play. If you decide to play Gayev, get Vishnevskii to play the part of Lopakhin—he won't succeed in being an artistic Lopakhin, but he'll avoid being a petty one. Luzhskii would play the ruthless foreigner and Leonidov would make a kulak out of him.[8]

Chekhov's letter to Stanislavskii rejects the Western 'capitalist' *and* the Russian 'kulak' interpretation of the merchant, and calls for him to be artistic, intelligent, and thoroughly human, thereby countering those Soviet and Western interpretations which prefer to see Lopakhin as a brutal destroyer of beauty. (The Western 'aesthetic' analysis is as misconceived as the Soviet class one—typical of the former is Magarshack's: 'The cherry orchard indeed is a purely aesthetic symbol which its owners with the traditions of the old culture behind them fully understood . . . to Lopakhin it is only an excellent site for "development".' In fact it is Lopakhin and not the owners who understands this decaying orchard.[9])

Chekhov was equally adamant about the centrality of Lopakhin's part to Nemirovich-Danchenko:

> If [Stanislavskii] decides to play Lopakhin and succeeds in the part, the play will be a success. But if Lopakhin is made trivial, played by a trivial actor, both the role and the play are certain to fail.[10]

To emphasise the artistic sensitivity and humanity of Lopakhin, Chekhov added some words to the final version of the play, in which he makes even Trofimov recognise his qualities:

> Your fingers are fine and gentle, like an artist's, and you are refined and sensitive at heart.

And to the actor Leonidov, Chekhov insisted that Lopakhin should 'look like a cross between a merchant and a professor of medicine at Moscow University'.[11]

We are given in the letters the image of a man of intelligence, sensitivity and humanity, with features of both the artist and the scientist about him; and this is the image which Chekhov draws with great care in the play itself. Lopakhin loves beauty, but recognises the brutal reality of the world of serfdom which fashioned the values of the cherry orchard people; he regrets his poor education, but as a man of intelligence recognises the emptiness behind Trofimov's supposedly scientific conversation. Like Chekhov, Lopakhin was the grandson of a serf, and too near the people to romanticise them in an abstract or nostalgic manner. Like Chekhov, he was brutally beaten by his shopkeeper father as a child. And like Chekhov, the career of this man with artist's hands and the appearance of a professor of medicine is much concerned with squeezing the serf out of his soul—in terms not just of social mobility, but spiritual mobility as well. His tipsy but joyous cry from the heart in Act 3 is one of liberation, but his search for identity does *not* end with a merchant's possession of real estate. Lopakhin has a creative vision, of a new life evolving as the unproductive orchard is replaced by gardens where people grow things. In place of the decayed old order and their orchard where beauty hides stagnation, 'our grandchildren and our great-grandchildren will one day see a new living world springing up here' —as always in Chekhov, the reference to the future children, and to the particular time-scale, is significant.

So it is Lopakhin, not Trofimov, who finds meaning in work, and who responds 'scientifically' to the problem of the cherry orchard. It is Lopakhin who has the evolutionary and epic vision of a world of limitless potential peopled by giants. It is Lopakhin alone who, awkward and out of place with his gauche gestures in the claustrophobia of the nursery, does not turn his back on the sweeping horizons and growing technology of Act 2. Yet, unlike Trofimov, his visions are never left as vast generalities. While

Trofimov talks arrogantly and abstractly of his place in the vanguard of progress in Act 4, Lopakhin's practical policy of replacing the infertile orchard goes methodically ahead:

> Trofimov: Mankind is on the march to the ultimate truth, the most supreme happiness that can be achieved on earth—and I am in the vanguard!
> Lopakhin: Will you get there?
> Trofimov:I will . . . Either I'll get there or I'll light the way for others!
> (The sound of an axe striking a tree is to be heard in the distance)
> Lopakhin: Well, my friend, goodbye. It's time we went. We torment each other, and meanwhile life goes on just the same. When I work long hours without a break I think a bit more clearly, and then I seem to know the reason for living.[11]

Trofimov's pause contrasts with the relentless sound of the axe, and his generalities with Lopakhin's enduring work. Thus in Act 2, in response to Trofimov's speech about the need of the intelligentsia to work on behalf of science and art, which concludes with the inaccurate generalisation about workers' conditions, Lopakhin answers pragmatically:

> Now, I want to tell you that I am always up by five every morning. I work from morning till night. I invariably have my own and other people's money around me, and I get plenty of opportunity to see what kind of people they are. You only have to begin work to find out how few honest, decent people there are around.

Trofimov's speech begins with the exhortation to work by a man who never does, and concludes with a false generalisation; Lopakhin responds with a speech about real work in the present and concludes with the vision of a land fit for giants. It is the pragmatist *as well as* the visionary we need to remember. Lopakhin does not oppose Trofimov's appeal to science—indeed he subsumes it in his following words and actions. But he does oppose the abstractions Trofimov is committed to.[12]

Despite the inconsistencies and occasional naivety of a peasant who has become a landowner, Lopakhin has no simplistic solutions.

He recognises the human suffering as well as the hope that accompanies progress, and at the moment of his triumph weeps genuinely for the woman he had desperately tried to help. His maturity is of a dialetical kind: he wants to save the old class by changing it; he wants to preserve its human values while removing their social basis. The values of the old order should not be killed, as Trofimov would have it, but subsumed, incorporated within a new, growing humanity—just as Trofimov's vision of science is incorporated. Ranevskaya and Trofimov, master and revolutionary, are given value—or more precisely, both synthesised and rejected—by Lopakhin. But the way is hard, and unlike the revolutionary, Lopakhin cannot hear the footsteps of the new life:

> How I wish we could get past this stage. If we could just change this unhappy and arbitrary life soon.

Lopakhin can *feel* Ranevskaya's tragedy, and knows, like Gurov at the end of *Lady with a Little Dog*, that the way ahead is not simple.

Against Ranevskaya's suffering there is hope, and against Trofimov's hope, suffering: it is in this context that the sound of the breaking string can be understood. A detailed reading of the text surrounding its first appearance reveals a typical pattern. Ranevskaya wants to avoid the question of the cherry orchard by reverting to the talk of the past. Trofimov talks of the future of man and science—punctuated by Gayev's fatalistic pessimism, by Ranevskaya's eagerness to find some meaning in him, and by Lopakhin's irony over his pseudo-science. There follows Trofimov's speech about Russian intellectuals and the condition of the workers, then Lopakhin's practical refutation of it and his vision of a land fit for giants. Ranevskaya immediately trivialises Lopakhin's vision with her own fears:

> Why on earth do you want giants? They're fine enough in fairy tales but they terrify me anywhere else.

The juxtaposition of her banality and Lopakhin's sense of potential induces a feeling of melancholy, emphasised by the guitar of 'twenty-two misfortunes', Ranevskaya's pensive 'There goes Yepikhodov' (repeated by Anya) and the going down of the sun. There follows Gayev's typically fatalistic acceptance of the separation of Nature and man:

(quietly, as if reciting): Oh, Nature, glorious Nature! You shine with your eternal light, so beautiful and yet so impervious to our fate.

Anya and Varya as usual beg him not to talk so pompously, and Trofimov emphasises the escapism of Gayev's vision with 'You'd better double off the red back into the middle pocket'. Gayev relapses into his other refrain, 'I'll be silent. I'll be silent'.[13] There follows a pensive silence, broken only by the subdued muttering of Firs. Suddenly, out of the dark vastness of Nature itself comes a cry of melancholy—as in *The Steppe*; there it was a bird calling for understanding, here it is the sound of a breaking string from the technological world these nursery people have ignored.

The reactions are typical and significant. Lopakhin explains the sound rationally and practically—it comes from the mine. Gayev continues his thoughts about Nature, and thinks it was some bird, perhaps a heron. Trofimov converts this into a bird presaging ominous and great events, the owl. Ranevskaya is frightened and almost immediately gives more money away, as though buying off something incomprehensible. Varya is also frightened, but worries about her mistress' improvidence. Firs dreams of the golden days before the great 'troubles'. Gayev shakes and wants to escape from implacable Nature to his billiard room, just as Trofimov had suggested. So the sound of the breaking string, like the cherry orchard which began this conversation of evasion, distinguishes the alternatives of action in a world where 'everything's muddled'. Afterwards the landowners, as always, escape, Lopakhin turns to the practical question of the cherry orchard, and Trofimov stays with Anya to talk of revolution.

The second sound of the breaking string also takes place in the silences around the muttering Firs; and is directly stimulated by the contradictions, the hope and suffering (of Anya/Trofimov against Ranevskaya/Gayev; more personally of Lopakhin against Varya), which dramatise the question of the cherry orchard. The sad sound of the axe punctuates Firs' statement of the tragedy of human potential:

Life's over as though I'd never lived. . . . . You've got no strength left, you old fool. Nothing's left, nothing.

As this last, decayed man falls motionless, the sound of the breaking string coming out of the wide sky again speaks the elegy of man separated from value. The betrayed potential of the cherry orchard people is evident in this isolated old servant in the abandoned nursery where he is the only object of nostalgia left. The shepherd's pipe calling to the youthful Anya and Varya in the enclosed nursery of Act 1, which is an ambivalent call of potential and stagnation, is not answered. But the ambivalence is clarified. The true value of the nursery is now clear; for nostalgia there is emptiness, for naive youth there is abandoned old age. And outside, in the final moment of the play, there is the sound of Lopakhin's axe. Real value, real time, like Lopakhin's more successful actions, lie beyond the nursery, and that is the dramatic point of the play.

*   *   *   *   *

Chekhov created the part of Lopakhin at a time when industrialisation and advancing technology were at last beginning to bring social maturation and mobility to areas of life wider than the intelligentsia, but had not yet made Russia into a fully capitalist country of the Western type. He was totally committed to the spread of technology and, as Kuprin records, placed great hopes in it. Between the mercenary promises of capitalism, which had never been popular with Russian intellectuals, and the stagnation of a traditional society, Chekhov believed in the possibility of another solution: zemstvo doctor Astrov's 'roads and railways . . . . . workshops, factories and schools' which would make the people 'more healthy, better educated and more prosperous'. This specially Russian solution, set against that of the old order on one side and revolution on the other, was also the difficult path of the Pirogovists at this time—the period up to the Revolution of 1905 when a few Trofimovs tried to pull the Society in one direction and the state pulled in the other. And it was also, as a matter of interest, the solution presented by the wider body of professional sociologists, to which Chekhov was linked through its most productive member, M. M. Kovalevskii. These positivists and evolutionists, Vucinich writes, 'made sociology part of an essentially democratic ideology, which opposed both the stationary view of society built into the tsarist ideology and the revolutionary view of society advanced by Nihilist and Marxist ideology'.[14]

One is reminded of Chekhov's belief that the future lay with individuals, whether intellectual or peasant; and reminded too, with the peasant Lopakhin in mind, of the entry in Chekhov's Notebook that so much depended on the merchant and the teacher.[15] Lopakhin is a representative of Chekhov's alternative path, and it is not surprising that the Russian audience could not fit him into its preconceived conceptions of the grasping kulak, nor that Chekhov insisted that Lopakhin would not be understood in the capitalist West. He was right. Lopakhin *has* been misunderstood here, and with it has gone a tiresome misreading of the play (Magarshack is typical with his 'warning against the Lopakhins of this world, a warning that can be understood everywhere since the menace of the speculative builder has been felt not only in Russia'[16]). The emphasis of this book has in general been away from the 'universality of art' notion implicit in the Magarshack quotation, and towards a reading that has been historically specific. The next stage, omitted here for lack of space, would be to locate the personal—Chekhov: *this* writer, *this* doctor—in the historical. Hence my conclusion refers back to this book and indicates the scope of another: at the social level *The Cherry Orchard* clarifies the potential responses of stagnation, revolution and scientific evolution to the contradictions of the modernising autocracy; at the personal level, it dramatises the struggle of a man of artistic and scientific sensitivity to squeeze the serf mentality of Russia and of his childhood out of his soul.[17] The struggle for development was both Russia's and Chekhov's own.

Notes

NOTES TO CHAPTER 1

1. See letters to Maria Chekhova, Aleksandr Chekhov, A. S. Suvorin, A. N. Pleshcheyev, Madame Kiseleva, N. A. Leikin, and to Chekhov's mother between April and October 1890. The best collection of Chekhov's letters is in *Polnoe sobranie sochinenii i pisem A. P. Chekhova* (Moscow, 1944–51) Quotations from Chekhov's works and letters will be taken from here, except where stated.
2. Anton Chekhov, *The Island: a Journey to Sakhalin*, trans. by Lubia and Michael Terpak with an introduction by Robert Payne (N.Y.: Washington Square Press, 1967) pp. 41–2.
3. Chekhov to Suvorin, 2 Jan. 1894.
4. Chekhov to Suvorin, 9 Mar. 1890.
5. Chekhov to Shcheglov, 22 Mar. 1890.
6. Maurice Valency, *The Breaking String: The Plays of Anton Chekhov* (N.Y.: O.U.P., 1966) p. 53.
7. Thomas Winner, *Chekhov and his Prose* (N.Y.: Holt, Rinehart and Winston, 1966).
8. Valency, p. 185.
9. Ibid., p. 184.
10. Ibid., p. 199.
11. Anton Chekhov, *Uncle Vanya*, Act 1.
12. See letters to Maria Chekhova, Ivan Chekhov and Madame Kiseleva, March 1891.
13. *The Island*, p. 82.
14. Valency, p. 194.
15. The term is Chekhov's, used frequently in criticising the gloomy tradition in the production of his works.
16. Valency, p. 125.
17. Morel had claimed in his *Traité de dégénérescences* (published in the 1850s) that degenerations were deviations from the normal human type, transmissable by heredity and deteriorating progressively towards extinction. The fatalism of the theory had enormous impact in Europe, influencing writers, philosophers and scientists, such as Zola, Nordau and Lombroso.
18. I. P. Merzheyevskii (Mierzejevsky), 'Mental and Nervous Diseases in Russia', trans. in *The Asylum Journal of Mental Science* (1888) p. 136.
19. Chekhov to Suvorin, 30 Dec. 1888.
20. Chekhov to A. Chekhov, Oct. 1887.
21. Chekhov to Pleshcheyev, 2 Jan. 1889.
22. Chekhov to Suvorin, 7 Jan. 1889.

23. Valency, pp. 196–7.
24. Ibid., p. 125.
25. Ibid., p. 280.
26. The zemstva were representative assemblies set up at provincial and district levels to fill the gap which the ending of gentry control over the serfs had left between the village and the central government.
27. E. Osipov (Ossipow), I. Popov (Popow) and P. Kurkin (Kourkine), *La Médicine du Zemstvo en Russie* (Moscow, 1900) p. 247.
28. J. L. Styan, *Chekhov in Performance. A Commentary on the Major Plays* (Cambridge U.P., 1971) p. 234.
29. Ibid., p. 219.
30. Ibid., p. 151.
31. Valency, p. 194.
32. Richard Ohmann, *English in America* (N.Y.: O.U.P., 1976) pp. 75–6.
33. Ibid., pp. 76, 78.
34. Valency, p. 184.

NOTES TO CHAPTER 2

1. For if it is the second of these which has suffered most among· traditional literary critics it is the last, the author who, as we will see, is most neglected by current forms of structuralism.
2. Roland Barthes, *Elements of Semiology* (London: Cape, 1967) p. 39; and Roland Barthes, 'Literature as Rhetoric', in Elizabeth and Tom Burns (eds) *Sociology of Literature and Drama* (Harmondsworth: Penguin, 1973) p. 193.
3. Barthes, *Elements*, p. 40.
4. Christian Metz, 'Methodological Propositions for the Analysis of Film', *Screen*, 14, (Spring/Summer 1973) 97.
5. Roland Barthes, 'Style and its Image' in S. Chatman (ed.), *Literary Style: A Symposium* (N.Y.: O.U.P., 1971) p. 8.
6. Ibid., p. 6.
7. See Roland Barthes, *Writing Degree Zero* (London: Cape, 1967).
8. Barthes, *Elements*, p. 92.
9. Barthes, 'Literature as Rhetoric', p. 194.
10. Ibid., p. 194.
11. Geoffrey Borny, *The Subjective and Objective Levels of Reality in Chekhov's 'Ivanov' and 'The Cherry Orchard': A Study in Dramatic Technique* (unpublished Fourth Year Drama dissertation, University of New South Wales, 1969).
12. For the relationship of this to Chekhov's positivism, see J. C. Tulloch, *Anton Chekhov: A Case Study in the Sociology of Literature* (Ph.D. thesis, University of Sussex, 1973) ch. 6.
13. Barthes, 'Literature as Rhetoric', p. 195.
14. Ibid., p. 195–6.
15. Winner, p. 26.
16. Chekhov to Grigorovich, Feb. 1888.
17. Cited in an article by Ye. Polferov of 24 July 1904, quoted in R. Hingley (ed.) *The Oxford Chekhov* (London: O.U.P., 1964–   ) vol. 8, appendix ix, p. 310.

18. The Russian world of 'poshlost', a word representing the vulgarity, banality, meanness and parochial materialism of provincial life which is frequently exposed in Chekhov's works.
19. For my analysis of these and other stories, see Tulloch, *Anton Chekhov*, vol. 2.
20. See ch. 8.
21. Barthes, 'Style and its Image', p. 9.
22. Winner, p. 188.
23. Ibid., p. 216.
24. In fact there was a deeper irony here, since Konstantin represented the type of neurasthenic Chekhov had first diagnosed 'correctly' (according to the latest medical theory) in *Ivanov*. This interpretation was a social and evolutionary one, in contrast to the static and purely psychological understanding of fixed personality-types which underlay conventional portrayals of the 'superfluous man'. By identifying himself with the Russian version of Hamlet, the first static 'type' for the morbid neurasthenic, Konstantin, all the time seeking new forms, ironically enough adopted the 'outmoded' interpretation of *himself*, thereby cutting off hope of change.
25. Metz, pp. 90–1.
26. See for instance, W. H. Bruford, *Chekhov and his Russia: a Sociological Study* (London: Kegan Paul, Trench, Truber, 1947).
27. David Magarshack, *The Real Chekhov: an introduction to Chekhov's Last Plays* (London: Allen and Unwin, 1972).
28. Barthes, *Elements*, pp. 91–2.
29. Roland Barthes, *Critical Essays* (Evanston: Northwestern U.P., 1972) pp. 67–8.
30. See Tulloch, *Anton Chekhov*, ch. 6.
31. Roland Barthes, 'Criticism as Language', *Times Literary Supplement*, 18 Sept. 1963.
32. Jonathan Culler, *Structuralist Poetics: Structuralism, Linguistics and the Study of Literature* (London: Routledge and Kegan Paul, 1975) pp. 97, 123.
33. Ibid., pp. 119, 132.
34. See for instance, Culler's analysis of genre, p. 136.
35. Ibid., pp. 260–61.
36. Peter L. Berger, *Invitation to Sociology. A Humanistic Perspective.* (Harmondsworth: Penguin, 1966) pp. 32–51.
37. Culler, p. 28.
38. Ibid., p. 29.
39. Ibid., p. 230.
40. Ibid., pp. 140, 258.
41. Claude Lévi-Strauss, cited in Culler, p. 28.
42. Michel Foucault, cited in Culler, p. 28.
43. Berger, p. 82.
44. Ibid., p. 29.
45. Peter Worsley et al., *Introducing Sociology* (Harmondsworth: Penguin, 1970) p. 31.
46. Culler, p. 30.
47. Peter L. Berger and Thomas Luckmann, *The Social Construction of Reality* (London: Allen Lane, 1967) p. 79.
48. Ibid., pp. 66–7.

49. Berger, pp. 163–4.
50. Berger and Luckmann, pp. 69–70.
51. Ibid., pp. 76–7.
52. Berger, p. 109.
53. Ibid., pp. 148–9.
54. Berger and Luckmann, pp. 103, 143.
55. Berger, pp. 63, 74, 71–2.
56. Ibid., p. 195.
57. Ibid., p. 124.
58. Berger and Luckmann, p. 151.
59. Jean-Paul Sartre, *The Problem of Method*, trans. by H. E. Barnes (London: Methuen, 1963) pp. 57–60.
60. Berger and Luckmann, p. 190.
61. Tulloch, *Anton Chekhov*, ch. 6.
62. Ibid.
63. See J. C. Tulloch, 'Sociology of Knowledge and the Sociology of Literature', *British Journal of Sociology*, 27 (1976) 197–210.
64. Primarily this relates to Goldmann's notion of the aesthetic tension between 'coherence' and 'multiplicity'. I have dealt with this problem in my article 'Sociology of Knowledge and the Sociology of Literature', developing it in the context of Chekhov's duality of roles, and asking there the question of which 'inauthentic' roles Chekhov could afford to reject dogmatically (false doctors and scientists—Ionych, Van Koren etc.), and which ones he rejected in a much more sympathetically ambivalent way (literary figures—Konstantin, Trigorin, etc.).
65. Lucien Goldmann, *The Hidden God. A Study of Tragic Vision in the Pensées of Pascal and the Tragedies of Racine*, trans. from the French by Phillip Thody (London: Routledge and Kegan Paul, 1964); R. Pincott, 'The Sociology of Literature', *Archives Européennes de Sociologie*, 11 (1970) 177–95.
66. L. Goldmann in discussion with R. Barthes, in R. Macksey and E. Donato (eds), *The Structuralist Controversy: the Languages of Criticism and the Sciences of Man* (Baltimore: John Hopkins, 1970) p. 184.
67. Culler, pp. 4, 5.
68. Ibid., pp. 11–13.
69. Ibid., pp. 207–8.
70. Ibid., pp. 99–100.
71. Goldmann, p. 57.
72. Ibid., pp. 348–9.
73. See my analysis of *Peasants* in Tulloch, *Anton Chekhov*, vol. 2.
74. Culler, pp. 11–12.
75. Tulloch, *Anton Chekhov*, ch. 6.

NOTES TO CHAPTER 3

1. See L. Goldmann, *The Human Sciences and Philosophy*. (London: Cape, 1971) ch. 3 and 4.
2. R. Wollheim, 'Sociological Explanations of the Arts: Some Distinctions', in

M. C. Albrecht, J. H. Barnett and M. Griff (eds), *The Sociology of Art and Literature: a Reader* (London: Duckworth and Co., 1970) pp. 574–81.

3. Elsewhere I have shown that his literary identity was not discrete, but was defined *in terms of* these medical values; see Tulloch, *Anton Chekhov*, ch. 6.

4. This is obviously necessary to avoid circular argument. However, an over-rigid application of this rule seems silly where a point about a text can be illustrated. From time to time, where sufficient evidence external to his works has been presented to make a point, texts will be referred to.

5. In this respect my approach will be similar to E. A. Krause's in *The Sociology of Occupations* (Boston: Little, Brown, 1971). To some extent I agree with Krause that the four analytical approaches should not be considered as mutually exclusive 'but rather as complementary, as walking around a statue and viewing it from four standpoints is more satisfying and thorough than approaching it from only one direction' (p. 8). Generally the perspectives focus on different substantive issues at different levels of generality. However, there can be fundamental differences of assumption, as between functionalist and conflict theory for example. To avoid complete eclecticism I have therefore commented on each perspective from within my own conflict perspective. This does not, I think, diminish the usefulness of using the four perspectives.

6. T. Johnson, *Professions and Power*. (London: Macmillan, 1972).

7. T. Kuhn, *The Structure of Scientific Revolutions*, 2nd ed. (Chicago U.P., 1970).

8. R. MacIver, 'The Social Significance of Professional Ethics', in H. M. Vollmer and P. L. Mills (eds), *Professionalization* (Englewood Cliffs, N. J.: Prentice Hall, 1966) pp. 52, 55.

9. As an analysis of the 'service' to underprivileged groups within a system of private medicine would quickly demonstrate.
   Similarly, as Johnson points out, the 'law profession will not embody or apply values which are of equal relevance to all, and the values and organisation of that profession will vary in their consequences for different class or status groups'.

10. D. Apter, *The Politics of Modernization* (Chicago U.P., Phoenix Edition, 1967).

11. The substantive material of this chapter is drawn from a very wide range of sources listed in my Ph.D. thesis, *Anton Chekhov: A Case Study in the Sociology of Literature* (University of Sussex, 1973). Since this chapter can be no more than an overview of the research into Russian professionalisation presented there, detailed references to all these sources seemed out of place unless the source is specifically mentioned. Terence Emmons, *The Russian Landed Gentry and Peasant Emancipation of 1861* (Cambridge U.P., 1968) is a major source for this section.

12. Cited in P. L. Alston, *Education and the State in Tsarist Russia*. (Stanford U.P., 1969) p. 125.

13. Ibid., p. 240.

14. Ibid., p. 99.

15. Ibid., pp. 156, 248.

16. Dr I. N. Al'tschuller, 'O Chekhove', in N. I. Gitovich and I. V. Fedorova (eds), *A. P. Chekhov v vospominaniyakh sovremennikov* 4th ed. (Moscow, 1960). Particularly influential was the circle of Dr Arkhangel'skii at Chikino

Zemstvo hospital near Voskressensk where, every evening as Chekhov's brother recalls, the talk ran to liberalism, Turgenev, Saltykov-Shchedrin, and important advances in science and literature.

17. Letter from Chekhov to Suvorin, 24 Dec. 1890.
18. Letter from Chekhov to Pleschcheyev, 9 Oct. 1888.
19. M. A. Chlenov, 'A. P. Chekhov i meditsina', *Russkie vedmosti,* no. 91 (5 April 1906); P. I. Kurkin, 'Anton Pavlovich Chekhov ka zemsky vrach', *Obshchestvenny vrach,* no. 4. (1911).
20. Letter from Chekhov to Suvorin, 18 Aug. 1891.
21. Letter from Chekhov to Suvorin, 24 Dec. 1890.
22. Chekhov to Suvorin, 16 Aug. 1892.
23. E. Ossipow (Osipov), I. Popow (Popov) and P. Kourkine (Kurkin), *La Médicine du Zemstvo en Russie* (Moscow, 1900).
24. Chekhov to Suvorin, 1 Aug. 1892.
25. Chekhov to N. M. Lintvareva, 22 July 1892.
26. Chekhov to Suvorin, 16 Aug. 1892.
27. Chekhov to Suvorin, 10 Oct. 1892.
28. I. Ye. Repin to T. L. Tolstaya, 20 Jan. 1893, *Pisma I. Ye. Repin* (Moscow, Leningrad, 1946–52).
29. Chekhov to A. B. Bernshtein, 23 Jan. 1903.
30. Ossipow et al., p. 253.
31. *Bol'shaia Meditsinskaia Entsiklopedia* (Moscow, 2nd ed.).
32. Chekhov to A. Evreinova, 7 Nov. 1889.
33. Chekhov to Suvorin, 23 Jan. 1900.
34. Report to Serpukhov Zemstvo, 1892, cited in *Obshchestvenny vrach,* no. 4 (1911); see also letter from Chekhov to Suvorin, 14 Dec. 1896.
35. Maxim Gor'kii, 'Anton Tchekhov: Fragments and Recollections', in *The Notebooks of Anton Tchekhov together with Reminiscences of Tchekhov by Maxim Gorky,* trans. by S. S. Koteliansky and L. Woolf (Richmond: Hogarth Press, 1967) pp. 91–3.
36. Ibid., p. 95.
37. Ibid., p. 92.
38. Ibid., p. 95.
39. D. M. More, 'The Dental Student', *Journal of the American College of Dentists* (Sept. 1957) 165.
40. Indeed, the most essential characteristic of the self-concept of professionalism is its identification with the sense of an autonomous, ordered and probably terminal career. In contrast, under both the eighteenth-century aristocratic forms of patronage and the more contemporary corporate forms, 'professional' identity has depended on exchange value rather than peer group solidarity since the practitioner has been dependent on the satisfaction and good will of his employer. As Johnson has said, 'in oligarchic forms the practitioner seeks "preferment" which in the most successful cases leads to "landed leisure", while the corporate practitioner can look forward to "plum jobs" on boards of directors'. But within the particular historical phenomenon we have defined as 'professionalism' the practitioner's concept of himself largely depends on 'significant others' within his peer group. It is their esteem he seeks, their values he internalises, their norms of conduct with which he evaluates.

Notes

Notes 211

41. T. Shibutani, 'Reference Groups as Perspectives', *American Journal of Sociology*, 60 (1955) 562–9.
42. Alexander Vucinich, *Science in Russian Culture (vol. 2), 1861–1917* (Stanford U.P., 1970) pp. 230–31.
43. Johnson, p. 57.
44. Cited in W. Horsley Gantt, *Russian Medicine* (A Series of Primers on the History of Medicine, ed. E. B. Krumbhaar) (N.Y., 1937) pp. 78–9.
45. A. Vucinich, *Science in Russian Culture (vol. 1), A History to 1860* (Stanford U.P., 1963) p. 342.
46. *The Lancet*, 2 (1897) 343.
47. Ossipow et al., p. 173.
48. Ibid.
49. Ibid., p. 94.
50. Ibid.
51. Chekhov to Suvorin, 21 Oct. 1895.
52. A. D'yakonov to Chekhov, *Polnoe sobranie sochinenii i pisem. A. P. Chekhova* (Moscow, 1944–51) vol. 20, p. 455.
53. At the other end of the scale from international congresses was the small society of doctors which graduated at Moscow University in 1884 to which he sent annual dues.
54. M. Chlenov, 'A. P. Chekhov i meditsina'.
55. Cited in S. S. Koteliansky and P. Tomlinson (eds), *The Life and Letters of Anton Tchekhov* (London: Cassell, 1925) p. 279, note.
56. Cited in Chlenov.
57. Chekhov to Kurkin, 13 Jan. 1902.
58. Chlenov, 'Chekhov i meditsina'.
59. Chekhov to M. A. Chlenov, 19 Jan. 1901.
60. Chekhov to Kurkin, 23 Dec. 1899, and to Shakhovskii, 15 Mar. 1894.
61. Chekhov to A. M. Evreinova, 7 Nov. 1899.
62. G. Rossolimo, 'The Patient and the Doctor', *Report to the Moscow Neuropathological Society*, cited in Chlenov; N. P. Nikitin, 'News about Psychology, Criminal Anthropology and Hypnotism,' no. 1(1905), cited in I. M. Geizer, *Chekhov i Meditsina* (Moscow, 1954) p. 86.
63. See *A Country Doctor, Surgery, An Unpleasantness, Ward Number Six*.
64. Chekhov to M. P. Chekhova, 16 May 1890, and to Suvorin, 16 Aug. 1892.
65. Ossipow et al., p. 75.
66. Chekhov to Iordanov, 31 Aug. 1903.
67. Chekhov to Suvorin, 9 Dec. 1890 (This is *not* in the Complete Works, 1944–51 edition, but was re-installed in the 1963–4 edition).
68. Chekhov to L. Sulerzhitskii, 5 Nov. 1902.
69. Chekhov to Y. Yegorov, 11 Dec. 1891.
70. Chekhov to V. V. Rozanov, 2 Apr. 1885.
71. M. R. Kapoustine, 'Fundamental Questions of Zemstvo Medicine', cited in Ossipow et al., p. 88.
72. Ossipow et al., p. 178.
73. Chekhov to I. Orlov, 22 Feb. 1899.
74. Chekhov to Aleksandr Chekhov, 19 May 1883, and to Ol'ga Knipper, 4 Sep. 1901.

75. E. Greenwood, 'Attributes of a Profession', in Vollmer and Mills, p. 12.
76. See Johnson, *Professions and Power*.
77. Kuhn, p. 19.
78. C. Bernard, *An Introduction to the Study of Experimental Medicine*, trans. by G. H. Greene (N.Y.: Dover Publications, 1957) pp. 208–9.
79. C. A. Timiriazeff (K. Timiryazev), *The Life of the Plant*, trans. by Anna Chermeteff (London: Longman, 1912) p. 8.
80. A. Vucinich, *Science in Russian Culture*, vols. 1 and 2.
81. Cited in Vucinich, vol. 1, p. 237.
82. Cited in Vucinich, vol. 1, p. 380.
83. Cited in Vucinich, vol. 1, p. 381.
84. Vucinich, vol. 2, p. 74.
85. Ibid., p. xi.
86. Vucinich, vol. 1, pp. 237–8.
87. Cited in Vucinich, vol. 1, p. 238.
88. Vucinich, vol. 2, p. xii.
89. M. E. Saltykov-Shchedrin, cited in Vucinich, vol. 2, p. 15.
90. Vucinich, vol. 2, p. 126.
91. Ibid., p. 127.
92. Ibid., p. 307.
93. Antonovich, cited in Vucinich, vol. 2, p. 20.
94. Vucinich, vol. 2, p. xiv.
95. I. M. Sechenov, *Selected Works* (Moscow-Leningrad, 1935) p. 32.
96. Chekhov to Suvorin, 15 May 1889.
97. Chekhov to Suvorin, 7 May 1889.
98. Ibid.
99. Sechenov, p. 185.
100. Chekhov to Suvorin, 7 May 1889.
101. Chekhov to Suvorin, 15 May 1889.
102. Chekhov to S. P. Dyagilev, 30 Dec. 1902.
103. Sechenov, p. 152.
104. Chekhov to Suvorin, 7 May 1889.
105. Chekhov to Kurkin, 23 Dec. 1899.
106. Chekhov to Suvorin, 9 Mar. 1890.
107. Bernard, p. 52.
108. See my analysis of *Dreary Story* in 'Conventions of Dying: Structural Contrasts in Chekhov and Bergman', in J. Tulloch (ed.) *Conflict and Control in the Cinema* (Macmillan: Melbourne, 1977) pp. 736–55.
109. A. P. Chekhov, 'N. M. Przheval skii', in *Polnoe sobranie sochinenii i pisem A. P. Chekhova*.
110. For example the student hero of *Nervous Breakdown*. Interestingly, the fate of Ivanov is to shift from being a man of faith to a cynic, from the sixties to the eighties.
111. S. S. Koteliansky and L. Woolf (eds), *Fragments of Recollections in the Notebooks of Anton Tchekhov* (Hogarth Press, 1967) p. 62.
112. Sechenov, p. 198.
113. Bernard, pp. 205, 209, 26, 27; Chekhov to A. N. Pleshcheyev, 6 Mar. 1888; Chekhov to Suvorin, 18 Oct. 1888; Chekhov to Suvorin, 23 Dec. 1899.
114. A. P. Chekhov, 'Conjurors', Oct. 1891.

115. Chekhov to Suvorin, Aug. 1891.
116. M. A. Chlenov, 'A. P. Chekhov i kultura', *Russkie vedomosti*, no. 169, (2 July 1906), reprinted in Gitovich and Fedorova.
117. Chekhov to Suvorin, 27 Dec. 1889; Chekhov to Suvorin, 27 Mar. 1894; Chekhov to I. Orlov, 22 Feb. 1899; Chekhov to Dyagilev, 30 Dec. 1902.
118. Krause, p. 105.
119. For example, doctors' assertions of the universal sanctity of the private physician/patient relationship.
120. See Apter, *The Politics of Modernization*.
121. G. E. Kline, 'Darwinism and the Russian Orthodox Church', in E. J. Simmons, *Continuity and Change in Russian and Soviet Thought* (N.Y.: Russell and Russell, 1967) pp. 307-8.
122. Cited in Kline, p. 308.
123. See A. Gerschenkron, *Economic Backwardness in Historical Perspective* (N.Y.: Praeger, 1965); also V. Bill, *The Forgotten Class: The Russian Bourgeoisie from its Earliest Beginnings to 1900* (N.Y.: Praeger, 1959).
124. Vucinich, vol. 2, p. 274.
125. Elie Metchnikoff (I. I. Mechnikov), *The Prolongation of Life*, trans. by P. Chalmers Mitchell (London: Heinemann, 1910) p. 323.
126. O. Metchnikoff, *Life of Elie Metchnikoff, 1845-1916*. (Boston: Houghton-Mifflin, 1921) p. 164.
127. For an overview of this subject see J. Ben-David, 'Professions in the Class Systems of Present-Day Societies', *Current Sociology*, xii, no. 3, (1963-4).
128. Ossipow et al., p. 112.
129. Ibid., p. 139.
130. For data on the work and teaching of Zakhar'in, Ostroumov, Erisman etc., see *Bol'shaia Meditsinskaia Entsiklopedia* (Moscow, 2nd ed.); also *Review of Eastern Medical Sciences* and *Review of Soviet Medical Sciences*. Also for brief synopses and references in English, see *Great Soviet Encyclopedia* (N.Y.: Macmillan, 1973-8).
131. Chekhov to E. M. Shavrova, 28 Feb. 1893.
132. Ibid.
133. M. P. Chekhov, *Vokrug Chekhova* (Moscow, 1964) p. 237.
134. Layevskii is carefully ascribed the central symptoms of degeneracy isolated by Lombroso and Nordau.
135. Chekhov to Suvorin, 27 Dec. 1889.
136. For example, in *Black Monk, Nervous Breakdown, Ward Number Six, The Seagull*.
137. Chekhov to Bilibin, March 1886.
138. Chekhov to Aleksandr Chekhov, April 1883.
139. See for instance Chekhov's letters to Ol'ga Knipper, 1 Sept., 1901 and 2 Feb., 1902, and to Chlenov, 13 Sept., 1903.
140. Chekhov to Suvorin, 28 May 1892.
141. Chekhov to Orlov, 22 Feb. 1899.
142. Chekhov to Tikhonov, cited in E. J. Simmons, *Chekhov, A Biography* (London: Cape, 1963) pp. 570-1.
143. Sechenov, p. 286.
144. E. Metchnikoff, p. 231.
145. Geizer, p. 92.

214   *Chekhov: A Structuralist Study*

146. Cited by G. I. Rossolimo, 'Vospominaniya o Chekhove', in Gitovich and Fedorova, pp. 661–72.

NOTES TO CHAPTER 4

1. Kenneth Burke, *The Philosophy of Literary Forms: Studies in Symbolic Action* (Baton Rouge: Louisiana State University Press, 1941) p. 304.
2. For a fuller analysis of this point, and of the relationship between Chekhov's primary socialisation and that of his literary peers, see J. Tulloch, *Anton Chekhov*, ch. 6.
3. M. Bradbury, 'Sociology and Literary Studies, II: Romance and Reality in Maggie', *Journal of American Studies*, iii, (1969), 114.
4. L. Goldmann, *The Hidden God*; R. Pincott, 'The Sociology of Literature', *Archives Européens de Sociologie*, xi (1970), pp. 177–95; Z. Barbu, 'The Sociology of Drama', *New Society* (2 Feb. 1967) pp. 161–3.
5. Socially, primarily by the pressure of the state on professional autonomy; psychologically because of the continuation within his *literary* reference group of the ascriptive values of his childhood which he had superseded as a doctor, see J. Tulloch, *Anton Chekhov*, ch. 6.
6. George Steiner, *Tolstoy or Dostoevsky* (Harmondsworth: Penguin, 1967); Sir Charles Bowra, *From Virgil to Milton* (London: Macmillan, 1945); *Heroic Poetry* (London: Macmillan, 1952).
7. Georg Lukacs, *The Theory of the Novel*, trans. by Anna Bostock. (London: Merlin, 1971) p. 47; see also Goldmann, *The Hidden God*, p. 42, footnote.
8. Goldmann, *The Hidden God*, pp. 41–4.
9. Steiner, p. 76; Bowra, *From Virgil to Milton*, p. 12.
10. Steiner, p. 77.
11. Ibid., pp. 76–7.
12. Ibid., p. 80.
13. G. Lukacs, *Studies in European Realism*. (N. Y.: Grosset and Dunlap, 1964) p. 191.
14. Ibid., p. 191.
15. Marx, in an important sense, synthesised these opposite notions through his *materialist* nostalgia for the 'childlike' epic of the Greeks (a low level, limited harmony of man and the world) and his prediction of a socialist society that would 'reproduce' the truth of the Greeks at an infinitely higher level.
16. Goldmann, *The Hidden God*, pp. 58–9.
17. Ibid., p. 67.
18. Linda Nochlin, *Realism*, (Harmondsworth: Penguin, 1971) p. 36.
19. Anton Tchekhov, *Notebooks*, p. 12.
20. Chekhov to Suvorin, 27 Mar. 1894.
21. Chekhov to N. A. Leikin, 2 Sept. 1887.
22. Chekhov to Shcheglov, 20 Jan. 1899.
23. Chekhov to Shcheglov, 2 Feb. 1900.
24. Chekhov to Suvorin, 3 Dec. 1892.
25. Chekhov to Suvorin, 25 Nov. 1892.
26. Chekhov to Suvorin, 18 Oct. 1888.
27. Chekhov to Shavrova, 23 Feb. 1893.

28. Chekhov to Suvorin, May 1889.
29. René Wellek, 'The Concept of Realism in Literary Scholarship', in *Concepts of Criticism*, (Yale U.P., 1969) p. 253.
30. For a valuable analysis of this see G. Borny, *The Subjective and Objective Levels of Reality in Chekhov's 'Ivanov' and 'The Cherry Orchard': A Study in Dramatic Technique*.
31. Chekhov to Lydia Avilova, 29 Apr. 1892, 19 Mar. 1892.
32. Chekhov to Suvorin, 27 Oct. 1888.
33. Chekhov to Avilova, 15 Feb. 1895.
34. Chekhov to Suvorin, 24 Feb. 1893.
35. Chekhov to Suvorin, 1 Apr. 1890.
36. Chekhov to A. Chekhov, 10 May 1886.
37. Chekhov to Ol'ga Knipper, 2 Jan. 1900.
38. Chekhov to V. E. Meierkhol'd, in the *Yearbook of the Imperial Theatre*, no. 5 (1909) in L. S. Friedland (ed.) *Anton Chekhov: Letters*, (N.Y.: Dover, 1966) p. 183.
39. Cited in Martin Esslin, *Brecht, a choice of evils* (London: Eyre and Spottiswoode, 1963) p. 127.
40. E. B. Brecht, *Our Theatre: The Development of an Aesthetic*, trans. and notes by John Willett (London: Methuen, 1964) p. 71.
41. Cited in D. Magarshack, *Chekhov the Dramatist*, p. 14.
42. Or *tries* to, because the notion of appealing to the spectator's critical awareness and directing him to action does depend on some degree of understanding between the artist and his audience. In *The Seagull* for example, Chekhov used a typically Brechtian 'alienating' device to create discontinuity and upset expectation. This was Konstantin's little play-within-a-play—similar in form to Brecht's use of film in his plays. The idea was to encapsulate a *fatalist* Darwinist content in an *idealist* Symbolist form, thereby relating and subverting both (see J. Tulloch, *Anton Chekhov*, ch. II). However, the audience had very different expectations of what it was paying to see, and the first performance was a disaster.
43. Goldmann, *The Hidden God*, p. 61.
44. Georg Lukacs, *The Historical Novel*, trans. by Hannah and Stanley Mitchell (Harmondsworth: Penguin, 1969) p. 171.
45. See for instance my analysis of *The Seagull*, J. Tulloch, *Anton Chekhov*, ch. II.
46. Steiner, pp. 91-2.

NOTES TO CHAPTER 5

1. John Carroll, *Break-Out from the Crystal Palace: The Anarcho-Psychological Critique: Stirner, Nietzsche, Dostoevsky* (London: Routledge and Kegan Paul, 1974) p. 97.
2. Ibid., p. 60.
3. J. Tulloch, *Anton Chekhov*, ch. 6.
4. R. Dubos, *Man, Medicine and Environment* (Harmondsworth: Penguin, 1970) pp. 84-8.
5. Carroll, p. 151.

6. Ibid., p. 146.
7. The distinction *between* these alternatives, as between say inauthentic artists and doctors, and what these distinctions signify, is a more complex problem; see J. C. Tulloch, 'Sociology of Knowledge and the Sociology of Literature'.
8. For an analysis of *Dreary Story*, see J. Tulloch 'Conventions of Dying: Structural Contrasts in Chekhov and Bergman'.
9. See Max Nordau, *Degeneration*. (London: Heinemann, 1895) p. 537.
10. Ibid., p. 541.
11. M. Nordau, *Paradoxes* (London: Heinemann, 1896) p. 176.
12. Ibid., p. 237.
13. Ibid., p. 329.
14. Nordau, *Degeneration*, p. 557.
15. Ibid., p. 557.
16. Nordau, *Paradoxes*, p. 331.
17. Chekhov to Suvorin, 27 Mar. 1894.
18. See Tulloch, *Anton Chekhov*, ch. 6.
19. Chekhov to Mikhail Chekhov, Apr. 1891.
20. For a development of this point, see Tulloch, *Anton Chekhov*, ch. 6, and Tulloch, 'Sociology of Knowledge and the Sociology of Literature.'
21. Karl Kramer, *The Chameleon and the Dream: The Image of Reality in Cexov's Stories* (The Hague: Mouton, 1970) p. 124.
22. As for 'intensity of feeling', perhaps it is wise to recall Chekhov's own struggle with 'childhood fantasies and adult dreams' (and his connection with the despair and suicide of writers like Garshin whose saving 'red flower' had itself been a fantasy) before considering Layevskii's despair. (see Tulloch, *Anton Chekhov*, ch. 6.)

NOTES TO CHAPTER 6

1. Steiner, p. 76.
2. Leo Lowenthal, *Literature and the Image of Man, Studies of the European Drama, and Novel (1600–1900)* (Boston: Beacon Press, 1957) p. 191.
3. Cited in an article by Ye. Polferov of 24 July 1904, in Hingley, *The Oxford Chekhov*, vol. 8, appendix ix, p. 310.
4. Cited in O. Metchnikoff, pp. 214–16.
5. A. I. Kuprin, 'Pamyati Chekhova', in N. I. Gitovich and I. V. Fedorova (eds), *A. P. Chekhov v vospominaniyakh sovremenikov* 4th ed. (Moscow, 1960) p. 52.
6. Chekhov to Suvorin, 18 Oct. 1888.
7. Timiryazev, *The Life of the Plant*, p. 5.
8. I. I. Metchnikoff, *The Prolongation of Life*, e.g. pp. 323, 333.
9. Cited in O. Metchnikoff, p. 186. Above all, science would cultivate our minds: 'Human nature, which like the constitution of the organism, is subject to evolution, must be modified according to a definite ideal. Just as a gardener or stock raiser is not content with the existing nature of plants and animals he is occupied with, but modifies them to suit his purposes, so also the scientific philosopher must not think of existing human nature as immutable but must try to modify it for the advantage of mankind'; I. I. Metchnikoff, p. 323.

10. Chekhov to Grigorovich.
11. In John Lucas (ed.), *Literature and Politics in the Nineteenth Century* (London: Methuen, 1971) p. 259.

NOTES TO CHAPTER 7

1. Chekhov to Aleksandr Chekhov, April 1883.
2. If that is the general aim of the thesis, the more particular goal is to put the 'woman question' on scientific grounds, thus shaming feminists, female emancipators and other 'ideologists'.
3. In both the contrast is made between the more educated Russian woman who is good at anything but independent creative work, and the ideal woman who can think logically and creatively: 'She is a good doctor, a good lawyer, but creatively she's a non-starter' ('History of Sexual Authority'). 'It's not all that hard to find a skilled nurse or female pianist. But you find me a woman who's fair minded, not cruel, and can argue logically' (*Ariadne*—first version, the *Russkaya mysl* text, cited in Hingley (ed.) The Oxford Chekhov, vol. 8, p. 285).
4. Herbert Spencer, *Education: Intellectual, Moral and Physical* (Edinburgh: Williams, 1879).
5. Ibid., p. 144.
6. Ibid., p. 40.
7. Ibid., p. 4.
8. Ibid., p. 4.
9. Chekhov to Orlov, 22 Feb. 1899.
10. See Tchekhov, *Notebooks, op. cit.*, p. 15.
11. Spencer, p. 149.
12. Here art might stand in for science. Both Spencer and Chekhov believed that true art was based on an understanding of scientific principles underlying life, and that the artist must therefore 'know what these laws are'. (Spencer, p. 32) Fundamental to the social and educational belief of each man is the belief that the 'opinion that science and art are opposed is a delusion' (Spencer, p. 36), and that 'both have the same aims, the same nature' (Chekhov to Grigorovich 1887).

   By comparing Spencer's and Chekhov's notions of the importance of evolutionary theory and the scientific method to education and art we are not concerned with 'influences' in the simplistic sense the term is often used in literary criticism. We are, of course, concerned with influence through socialisation, but again, not too directly. One needs always to take account of the social position and other values of the *recipient*, since any influence can be received and structured in a number of ways. For instance, Darwinism was assimilated by Paul Bourget, Max Nordau and Chekhov (all writers closely linked with scientific medicine) in very different ways, according to the class, racial, ideological and occupational constituents of their respective social positions. Spencer's extension of evolutionism to men, his belief in a sociology and an education based on the medical sciences, and his rejection of ascription and status for merit, were all taken up by Chekhov, yet were themselves rooted in a specific social infrastructure quite different from Chekhov's. Spencer believed firmly in both the moral purity of his social group and its *inevitable* centrality in the perfecting of society at large. Hence he could cheerfully oppose schemes for nation-wide educational legislation in a way Chekhov would never have done. Chekhov's position as a partially integrated, partially alienated professional doctor was a very different one. Given the apparent immobility of a detested social system he could not place his hopes in the inevitability of natural evolution. Consequently he was completely dedicated to professional monopoly and social engineering and rejected Spencer's laissez-faire ideology. In his view, but not in Spencer's, development could be permanently hindered by actual social evolution, and there is a corresponding emphasis on man's 'higher' aims—art, science, education etc.—frequently juxtaposed with his remarks about natural evolution. There was in fact no 'natural' development of women within society, because any educational pattern was enclosed in an ideological system.

13. René Girard, *Deceit, desire and the novel: self and other in literary structure*, trans. by Y. Freccero (Baltimore: John Hopkins Press, 1965) p. 65.
14. Ibid., p. 65.
15. Ibid., p. 19.
16. Ibid., p. 89.
17. Ibid., p. 89.
18. Carroll, p. 29.
19. Tolstoi's criticism of *The Darling*, from 'Readings for Every Day of the Year', in C. Garnett (trans.) *Tales of Tchekhov*, vol. 1, (London: Chatto and Windus, 1916) pp. 22–7.

NOTES TO CHAPTER 8

1. Valency, p. 243.
2. Styan, pp. 172, 188, etc.
3. Raymond L. Garthoff, *Soviet Military Policy: An Historical Analysis* (London: Faber, 1966) p. 30.
4. Stanislavskii, quoted in 'Chekhov i teatr', cited in R. Hingley, *The Oxford Chekhov*, vol. 3, pp. 315–6.
5. See Tchekhov, *Notebooks, op. cit.*
6. Styan, p. 219.
7. Ibid., p. 174.
8. Ibid., p. 170.
9. Ibid., p. 189.
10. As Styan says, ' . . . moving into a smaller room gives a visual impression of the dispossession that is under way. Life is closing in on them.'
11. Styan, p. 213.
12. Mierejevsky 'Mental and Nervous Diseases in Russia', p. 136.
13. V. V. Luzhskii from his recollections cited in 'Chekhov i teatr' p. 353, cited by Hingley, *The Oxford Chekhov*, vol. 3, p. 316.

NOTES TO CHAPTER 9

1. Styan makes the point for the circular motion of time very well: 'the return to the setting of the first act, the cyclical balance of departure with arrival, and of autumn with spring, must make this a scene of echoes'—but he typically neglects the agent of change.

2. Chekhov's familiar juxtaposition of the enclosed social world and a world of natural potential.

3. While the naturalistic sounds which Stanislavskii prepared for the first production crudely destroyed the balance between the worlds of nostalgia and change.

4. Styan's argument relating the failure of this 'courtship' to Lopakhin's lingering feelings of social inferiority may have some weight, though Varya's own humble origins speak against it. More fundamentally, Varya's typical situation, for which the whole pattern of her life prepared her as certainly as Ranevskaya's prepared her for Paris, was ritualised service; hence she goes off to perform it elsewhere. It is unlikely for this nun-like girl to have married the active Lopakhin. If she had the open ending would have been lost—just as it would in *Uncle Vanya* if Astrov had been seduced by Yelena, or, alternately, married Sonya—and the structure of the drama altered.

5. Styan makes the point well: 'when with outrageous baby noises on the sofa in the chilling nursery, Chekhov is both setting the play back on its course of comic objectivity and demanding of his audience a newly creative frame of mind'.

6. Chekhov to A. F. Koni, 26 Jan. 1891.

7. Chekhov to Ol'ga Knipper, 28 Oct. 1903.

8. Chekhov to K. S. Stanislavskii, 30 Oct. 1903.

9. Magarshack, *Chekhov the Dramatist*, p. 275.

10. Chekhov to Nemirovich-Danchenko, 2 Nov. 1903. Stanislavskii's decision to play Gayev suggests where *he* thought the centre of the play lay, and also, of course, indicates the value system which influenced his production of the play as a tragedy.

11. The actor L. M. Leonidov, cited in *Chekhov i teatr*, p. 351.

12. Thus when Trofimov tells Lopakhin in the final Act to avoid sweeping gestures and generalisations it is ironically comic in the same way as the idle Serebryakov telling Uncle Vanya that the main thing in life is work.

13. Valency and Styan are quite wrong here, and illustrate the dangers of extracting meaning from textual analysis alone. For Valency, Gayev's speech says 'all that can be said of the mystery of life, and . . . is the essential theme of the play . . . It is indicative of the nature of humanity that the young and the old are seldom on speaking terms'; Styan avoids this level of banality, but he too is impressed with absurdity. For him Gayev's speech contains the 'heart of Chekhov's truth . . . The omnipotent divinity of nature has been made a jest by its human creation, and Chekhov laughs at his most profound thoughts.' (Valency, p. 286; Styan, pp. 286–7).

14. Vucinich, vol. 2, p. 430.

15. 'While we intellectuals are rummaging among old rags and, according to the old Russian custom, biting one another, there is boiling up around us a life that

we neither know nor notice. Great events will take us unawares, like sleeping fairies, and you will see that Sidorov, the merchant, and the teacher of the district school at Yeletz will see and know more than we do, will push us far into the background, because they have accomplished more than all of us put together', *Notebooks*.

16. Magarshack, *Chekhov the Dramatist*, pp. 274–5.
17. To take this further, see Tulloch, *Anton Chekhov*, ch. 6, and Tulloch 'Sociology of Knowledge and the Sociology of Literature.'

Index

221